Roughnecks, Drillers, and Tool Pushers
Thirty-three Years in the Oil Fields

Personal Narratives of the West Series

ROUGHNECKS, DRILLERS, AND TOOL PUSHERS

THIRTY-THREE YEARS IN THE OIL FIELDS

By Gerald Lynch

Introduction by Bobby Weaver

 UNIVERSITY OF TEXAS PRESS   AUSTIN

First paperback printing, 1991

Requests for permission to reproduce material from this work
should be sent to:
   Permissions
   University of Texas Press
   Box 7819
   Austin, Texas 78713-7819

Library of Congress Cataloging-in-Publication Data

Lynch, Gerald, 1908–
   Roughnecks, drillers, and tool pushers.

   (Personal narratives of the West series)
   Includes index.
   1. Lynch, Gerald, 1908–   2. Petroleum workers—United
States—Biography.   3. Petroleum industry and trade—United
States—History—Sources.   I. Title.   II. Series.
HD8039.P42L95   1987   331.7′6223382′0924   [B]
87-13857
ISBN 0-292-71553-6
ISBN 0-292-77052-9 pbk.

∞ The paper used in this publication meets the minimum re-
quirements of American National Standard for Information Sci-
ences—Permanence of Paper for Printed Library Materials, ANSI
Z39.48–1984.

In memory of my wife, June Lynch

Contents

Illustrations

Maps

Figures

Introduction *by Bobby Weaver*

GERALD LYNCH has written a book describing his life as an oil-field worker. He began working on drilling rigs as a teenager at Corsicana in 1925. He followed that trade from boom to boom and progressed from floor hand to boiler man to derrickman to driller and finally to tool pusher. The thirty-three years he worked at his occupation provided a wealth of experience and observation that brings an air of reality to one of the most romanticized and publicized industries in the world.

I am honored to do the introduction for this book. The "oil-field trash" described in this volume are my people. One of the most vivid memories of my childhood is following my father into the Trolly Inn Diner at Second and Dixie in Odessa, Texas, before daylight one cold December morning. The place was crowded with men wearing rough work clothes, clamoring for breakfast and ordering "short lunches" to take on the job. I was a wonder-struck twelve-year-old visiting Dad, who had gone to the oil patch from our little farming community in Central Texas. The thing that most caught my imagination that morning, my first in the oil field, was the strong, acrid odor that permeated the air in the little diner. I soon discovered that the smell came from crude oil on the men's work boots and clothing. The people and the activity that accompany that peculiar smell have continued to be a major part of my life since that day over forty years ago.

I lived in Odessa for twenty years. I became one of those oil-field hands and met scores of men who had made every boom from Smackover to Snyder. Their stories fascinated me, and I listened to them for hours at a time during those long years we worked together. Then one day, when I was thirty-two years old, I decided to go to college. I never figured out why; it just seemed to be the thing to do. After I got into college it became such a habit that I kept at it until they gave me a Ph.D. to get me out of the place.

In graduate school it began to dawn on me that most folk know very little about those oil-field hands and the work they do. During a 1975 history seminar the question was put to me as to why oil-field workers have such a rough reputation. I had never really thought about it before because they didn't seem particularly tough to me. But I was one of them, and from time to time outsiders have a tendency to be treated pretty badly by the "oil-field trash" fraternity. My answer, after I thought about it for a while, was that most of the oil-field hands were originally farm and ranch boys who had spent most of their lives at hard work for little pay. Back on the farm they got to go to town on Saturday night with a couple of dollars in their pockets and kick up their heels. When they left the farm for the oil patch the work wasn't a bit harder and they had plenty of money in their pockets. Thus every night became Saturday night. Nevertheless, those wild young men are the same people who became the backbone of the oil industry in their later and more settled years.

Since those days I have spent considerable time engaged in historical research concerning the oil and gas industry. Despite a life spent in close association with the oil-field hands, I have never been able to write adequately about the life style that I knew so well. Nor, until I was given Mr. Gerald Lynch's manuscript, had I ever read anything that captured the flavor of the working man's oil patch. His story comes straight off the rig floor and describes a way of life peculiar to the oil and gas industry.

The fact that usually escapes most people is that the Texas oil and gas industry is young. When Gerald Lynch began his oil-field career it was very, very young. Although a small oil field developed near Corsicana as early as 1894 and the state's first oil refinery was built in the vicinity, no significant production existed in the state prior to the turn of the century. Then on January 10, 1901, all that changed. On that date the Lucas gusher blew in at Spindletop near Beaumont on the Gulf Coast and twentieth-century Texas blew in with it.

Within three or four years most of the salt dome formations lying along the Gulf Coast were being successfully drilled. Booms developed at places like Sour Lake, Batson, and Humble. The unprecedented oil production of those new fields created a tremendous oil glut that drove prices down. At the same time, however, great personal wealth generated by the finds created instant fortunes for many, and an aura of romance and adventure surrounded the business as the theme of the Texas oil millionaire captured the imagination of the public.

An "oil fever" enveloped Texas when men with that "I'm going to be an oil millionaire" gleam in their eyes fanned out across the state. Between 1902 and 1907 they found another large field at Petrolia in Clay

County. By mid-1911 a boom developed at Electra, west of Wichita Falls, but nothing to match the massive Gulf Coast finds materialized. Then, on July 29, 1912, the discovery well was drilled at Burkburnett along the Red River on the northern border of Texas. That boom did indeed match the frenzied activity of the original discoveries.

The Burkburnett phenomenon was repeated in 1917 at the little West Central Texas towns of Ranger and Desdemona. Within a year of those discoveries, and in the same general area, a spectacular boom developed at Breckenridge. Those finds seemed to confirm in the minds of the general public that Texas floated on a sea of oil that simply awaited someone to come along and tap the wealth.

The 1920s witnessed an increase in the tempo of Texas petroleum activity. The decade began with major finds near Mexia. The Mexia boom developed along an interesting geologic phenomenon known as the Mexia fault line. This subsurface structure ran for a great distance across the Texas landscape, and the wells were drilled for many miles along its length. The resulting oil field was called the "Golden Lane" because its less than one-half-mile width was covered with closely packed wells, many of which produced as much as twenty thousand barrels per day. In 1922, much farther south along the same fault line, a large field was developed at Luling. The following year production was found near Powell on the northern end of the fault line. In this general area, in 1925, Gerald Lynch began working in the oil patch among a group of men who had been involved in the industry practically since it had begun.

Meanwhile, the western portions of Texas were also experiencing a considerable amount of oil development. Between 1918 and 1926, discoveries in the Panhandle opened the largest gas field in the world. As the Panhandle oil and gas reserves were coming to light, finds surfaced in other parts of West Texas. Beginning in 1920 with a small well near Colorado City, the vast reserves of the Permian Basin, which covered 76,000 square miles and eventually produced ten major fields, gradually came to light. Numerous towns, including Big Lake, Odessa, Midland, and Hobbs, New Mexico, were transformed by the influx of oil-field workers who overloaded the meager means of the towns to cope with the rapid growth that oil wealth brought. It was in this massive oil-producing region that Lynch spent the last years of his oil-drilling career.

By 1930 it seemed that Texas had exhausted its ability to astound the world with spectacular oil and gas discoveries. But that was not the case. Late that year the No. 3 Daisy Bradford came in near Overton in East Texas. That discovery ushered in the greatest oil boom Texas had experienced. Thousands of men rushed to the discovery, Gerald Lynch among them, and they all witnessed what was, perhaps, the last great uncontrolled oil boom to dominate the Texas industry. It was because of the massive production and resulting price fall caused by the great East Texas boom that serious oil and gas conservation efforts began in the state.

The discovery and development of the East Texas field marked the end of the gigantic early Texas oil booms. Although many fields were brought in afterward, none had the unbridled speculative characteristics of the times between 1901 and World War II. The period of Gerald Lynch's active career, which lasted from 1925 until 1958, spanned the time from the last of the great booms until well into the period of stabilization following World War II. Thus, his observations on changing times in the industry have considerable relevance.

The literature spawned by the Texas oil and gas industry has reached into the hundreds of volumes. Perhaps the most comprehensive study of the subject is Carl Coke Rister, *Oil! Titan of the Southwest* (Norman: University of Oklahoma Press, 1949). That scholarly volume traces the history of oil and gas in Texas and surrounding states of the southwestern United States. Its method is the traditional "bare bones" approach of first discoveries, significant developments, and other basically economic aspects of the industry. A nice supplement to the pioneering Rister work is Walter Rundell, Jr., *Early Texas Oil* (College Station: Texas A&M University Press, 1977) which, although it is primarily a pictorial study, presents a fairly comprehensive history of the industry as well as giving some of the flavor of the life style.

Naturally, such a significant industry has produced a whole raft of company histories and biographies of the great men who made those companies important. These include such monumental works as Henrietta M. Larson and Kenneth W. Porter, *History of Humble Oil and Refining Company* (New York: Harper and Brothers, 1959), and Kendall Beaton, *Enterprise in Oil: A History of Shell in the United States* (New York: Appleton-Century-Crofts, 1957). Although these types of presentations provide valuable insight into the history of the industry, they give little information concerning the life style and work done by the oil-field hands.

The type of literary work that can best present the point of view of the oil-field workers has to emanate from the hands themselves. Despite the colorful nature of the business, very few reliable firsthand workers' accounts have been written. Most of those that exist are sensationalist publications with titles revolving around the theme "I made this, that, or the other boom and life was tough." These usually involve individuals who were in a boom-town environment for a relatively short time and usually were not even involved in actual oil-field work. Typical of this genre of book are those written by journalist Boyce

House. His publications include *Were You in Ranger?* (Dallas: Tardy Publishing Company, 1935); *Oil Boom* (Caldwell, Idaho: Caxton Printers, 1941); and *Roaring Ranger: The World's Biggest Boom* (San Antonio: Naylor Company, 1951). These books always present oil booms as places where the main occupations seem to be murder, vice, and assorted types of mayhem. Considering the large numbers of men that I personally knew who lived through those adventurous times, it has always been somewhat of a mystery to me how so many survived if indeed the conditions were as dangerous as so much of the literature makes it seem.

An outstanding contribution to the understanding of who those oil-field hands are and what they have done lies with the work of folklorist Mody Boatright. Selected interviews with oil-field workers were published by him and William A. Owens in *Tales From the Derrick Floor: A People's History of the Oil Industry* (Lincoln: University of Nebraska Press, 1982). This reprint of their original 1972 book presents vignettes of life in the oil patch, as told by the participants, from the time of the Spindletop discovery through the period of all the great early booms. Despite its authenticity and appeal, the book does not present a well-ordered chronological story as a biography can do so well.

It is difficult, if not impossible, to find a biographical work from the pen of an oil-field worker. The only publications approaching this type of presentation are a couple produced in the 1920s and 1930s which only detail experiences over a relatively short time span. Several autobiographical works exist by individuals engaged in white-collar oil-field occupations. Clarence Pope, *An Oil Scout in the Permian Basin* (El Paso: Permian Press, 1972), is typical of these, but they were not written by one of the hands. The reminiscences of Gerald Lynch are the first I have seen that document what it was to live and work in the oil patch from the early booms through the later, more settled times.

Lynch makes a number of points in his presentation. For example, he makes a good case for the place of origin of most of the oil-field workers. Using numerous incidents from his long experience in the business, he clearly demonstrates that, for the most part, the oil-field hands in Texas are products of changing times in the state. They are overwhelmingly economically displaced agricultural or small-town workers who gravitate to the expanding petroleum industry as their traditional source of economic livelihood begins to dry up.

This theme of the place of origin of the workers is not given in a lecture sort of presentation. It, like so many other subjects covered in the narration, builds up gradually as Lynch chronicles his life style over the decades he was in the business. Beginning with the early days, one learns what it was like to live in a "bowl and pitcher" hotel or in a boarding house in a boom town and work twelve-hour tours on a rig. Numerous episodes illustrate how the new hands came to the job and what eventually happened to most of them. Later, after Lynch married and moved to the Permian Basin, the life style changed somewhat when trailer houses replaced hotels and boarding houses as places for the mobile oil-field population to live. But the young hands, straight off the farm, continued to arrive to work on the rigs. Some of them stayed and became permanent members of the "oil-field trash" fraternity and some of them traveled on, but they all had some kind of story to relate and Lynch manages to tell a number of those tales.

Naturally, a man who is telling his life story in an industry is describing a social phenomenon. The things he saw and the things he experienced combine to present a way of life. He was not an outsider there for a short time to report on an exotic experience. He was the exotic experience and it didn't seem so exotic to him. It was a world of hard work, hard play, and relatively good pay for a man of his background. There is a lot of skill in the work he did, and that work is the source of his pride. The pride comes from the fact that few people can do what the oil-field hands do. They feel they are a cut above ordinary folk as they wander across the face of the world, proving it over and over again each time they bring in a new well.

Perhaps one of the most important aspects of Lynch's book is his explanation of the technical aspects of drilling oil wells. He has the ability to describe extremely technical procedures in an understandable manner. Not only that, he describes the activities of a day long gone by, and then, as his story progresses, he gives explanations of solving similar problems using more modern equipment. Those observations on the changing technology of the oil field over a long period of time, and particularly how that technology was applied by the hands, provide exceptionally important information. Of course the evolution of oil-field technology has been chronicled by several writers. The classic work of J. E. Brantley, *History of Oil Well Drilling* (Houston: Gulf Publishing Co., 1971), is the premier example. However, it is a rare case when we have the opportunity to understand the application of that technology from the point of view of the worker.

I am obviously prejudiced in favor of "oil-field trash." Oil-field workers admittedly have a bad reputation. The young hands drink and carouse and run off with the local girls and are generally looked upon as less than desirable company. But they go places and do things that ordinary folk would never attempt. They provide the world with the energy that keeps it productive. They are not the millionaires that sit around the petroleum clubs. They are the people Gerald Lynch tells about so well.

Roughnecks, Drillers, and Tool Pushers
Thirty-three Years in the Oil Fields

Prologue

Have you ever wondered how the pretty blue flame on your cookstove burner came to you? Or how the fifteen gallons of gasoline that you just bought got into the service station pump? Would you like to know? I doubt it, but I'll tell you anyhow.

They both got there through the combined efforts of a diverse group of men, most of whom are as alien to the average citizen as men from Mars. Included are geologists, landmen, pipe liners, refiners, production specialists, drillers, roughnecks, truck drivers, oiler boatmen, and salesmen of all kinds, all of the many types known generally as "oilfield trash."

This story is about just one segment of the oil fields, drilling. It is mostly about the people who moved with the rigs, lived in the little overcrowded boom towns, ate in cheap boarding houses, drove many miles to work, got killed, crippled, and generally, lived a hectic, different life. I'm not talking about your average citizen. Those guys were and are anything BUT "average."

The first oil wells in Texas were drilled in Corsicana in 1894. They were shallow wells, 800 feet deep, drilled with "cable tools." This was a drilling method using a high "stardrill" type bit, suspended by a cable on rope. The first oil well in the United States was drilled by this method.

The rotary rig was born in Corsicana, and its followers are the people that I knew, worked, lived, and fought with; the roughnecks, drillers, and—later—the "tool pushers." They were the men who made the "wheels go round."

They came off the cotton farms, out of the little towns and villages, and away from the sawmills and cottonseed-oil mills. They came from Texas, Oklahoma, Louisiana, and Arkansas. A few were from other states. From the beginning, they favored their own kind, since they spoke the same language and came from the same backgrounds. They developed a feeling of kinship with each other, and years went by before "outsiders" broke into the fraternity.

Mostly they were tough, adventurous, and bold men: men that were never content to just farm, clerk in a store, or be regimented in any way. They were happy only when they felt free to "get full of quit." Then they would "drag up" and go elsewhere to look for work—a job probably no better, maybe not even as good, as the one they had just quit. But asserting their independence in this manner was their way of staying free.

Following the rigs was a peculiar way of life. The married men left their wives and kids in their hometowns, lived in raw-lumber clapboard hotels, and ate in boarding houses, little cafes, and diners. Most of their salary was sent home to their wives, and since those dreary little towns had few, if any, recreation places, they spent the little money they had left on whores, whiskey, pool, and dominoes. Every little town in Texas had a domino hall or two, and pool halls, too, so gambling was rampant. The hookers, pimps, and bootleggers followed the booms, got drunk the next payday, then told anyone who would listen how close they came to getting rich.

None of us really knew a great deal about the techniques of drilling. We were still learning a new trade, doing something never done before, deep drilling. We didn't know much, but we did know more than anyone else, and it made us think we were smart. We learned by doing, although we made many mistakes. From this process gradually evolved an industry new to the world, drilling for oil.

We lived a tough, rough life, and we forever changed the world.

All of this made the internal combustion motor possible, and ushered in the Golden Age of Oil. The Old Boys who pioneered the oil fields are the same ones who exported their expertise to other countries. Think how *your* life would be without gasoline or natural gas.

These were and are my people. I loved and hated them, and am proud to be "oil-field trash." I spent fifty-eight years working and living among those clods, and am glad that I did. They were, and still are, a hell of a bunch.

We had our own language. Some of it is very odd, but the old-time names have endured. We mispronounced many words and have clung to our mistakes. So I will try to explain some of the terms as we go along. I really think you will find them, and how they were derived, interesting. And above all, keep this firmly in mind: the drilling business was and still is a crazy business. It is the *only* business in the world in which you can work a lifetime and *never* see what you are doing. For when a new bit goes into the well bore, as it goes down through the rotary table, it goes out of sight. You never see it until it has done its chores and you pull it out of the hole, so you are actually "flying blind," using experience, a sense of feel, and, even today, some guesswork.

So you see, it really is crazy.

Note: All the people and events described in this book are real, but some of the names have been changed.

Chapter One

Breaking In

I came into the oil patch in June of 1925. I had just graduated from high school and was just "raring" to earn some money. I had never *had* any money and was very tired of being broke, which had been a chronic thing with me. For the past two years, all the money I had was earned after school and on Saturdays, clerking and working stock in dry-goods and department stores. For those jobs, I was paid the sum of 30 cents an hour.

In 1925 I was seventeen years old, 5 feet 8 inches tall, tow headed, and weighed 128 pounds. The Corsicana oil fields were thirty-one years old that year, just fourteen years older than I was. We have grown old together. Corsicana was just coming out of a big boom, the Corsicana-Powell boom. The rig count had fallen from around one hundred active rigs to about thirty. It was still a pretty good little boom. I got started just in time and was lucky.

My uncle, Jimmie Colvin, my mother's younger brother, gave me my first roughnecking job. I had grown up around rigs and pretty well knew how to handle the job. But in order to keep down any talk of favoritism, Unk made it rough on me. It was the best thing that ever happened to me; I "earned my money" from my very first day.

Uncle Jim was drilling "daylights" on a small rig. It was running about 7 miles northeast of Corsicana, and the company was the John Champion Drilling Company. The equipment was primitive, even for those days. We worked twelve-hour shifts, from 6:00 A.M. till 6:00 P.M., 6:00 P.M. to 6:00 A.M., commonly called "days and nights." It was a long-established, customary thing, and caused no comment, since twelve hours was the usual workday.

Mr. John Champion, an old-time drilling contractor, was ready to retire. He worked that old rig for just a few old clients. For him, it was more of a pastime, as he really did not need the money. He picked his clients and was choosy about for whom he drilled, for his old rig was a venerable relic, just about ready for the "bone yard." Mr. John had known my Uncle Jim for years and asked him to drill three wells to a depth of 1,800 feet in what was known as the Old Field, northeast of Corsicana. Jimmie took the job, even though in many ways it was a mean job. The old rig was antiquated, hard to run, and hard to work on, but Unk liked John Champion and agreed to drill the three wells. They were the last wells that old rig ever drilled. That fall we stacked it, forever!

Mr. Champion was an immensely fat man. He was in his sixties, and apparently in excellent health. He loved a joke, laughed a lot, and was very, very light on his feet. One of his favorite tricks was to get someone to hold a light bulb up about 6 feet above ground, then jump and kick the bulb out of their hand, laugh delightedly, and say, "I'll bet you can't tie that kick."

At seventeen I was in awe of him, but thought both he and his old rig were marvelous. I was making six whole dollars every day, much more than any of my high school friends. I had been looking at secondhand cars, and was quite sure that the oil fields were the wave of the future, at least for me. It didn't take much money to go to my head.

All of us felt that we were at least a "cut above" the average man in a mostly rural society. We had an opportunity to become drillers; make twelve whole dollars a day; wear knee-high "witch Elk" boots, a Stetson hat, and be "looked up to." This was a shining goal. The old-time drillers fancied themselves to be exceptional fellows, and sometimes they really were that. They had come up from roughnecks to being drillers. They were "self-admitted" experts in a new business, rotary drilling; they felt themselves to be the cream of the crop, and would gladly tell you so, even without being asked.

Actually, we did not know nearly as much as we *thought* we did, but since *no one* knew much about rotary drilling, our ignorance did not show too much. We did know more about it than anyone else, so, in our opinion, it made us smart. We loved it and kept at it through good times and bad. I know that I did, and perhaps that makes me as crazy as the drilling business. I had plenty of opportunities to get out, but did not take them, and as a consequence, I have lived a very tough life. Being oil-field trash ain't a bed of roses.

John Champion's old rig did not have a "kelly joint." We used a thick-walled, round pipe called a "grip ring," and circulated through a "circulating head." The circulating head was the primitive forerunner of the modern swivel, but it did enable us to turn the drill pipe and circulate fluid through it at the same time. We circulated the fluid down the inside of the pipe and it returned to the surface outside the drill pipe, between the drill pipe and the wall of the bore hole. The space between the pipe and hole wall was known as the "annulus." It will be used many times later in this story, so remember it. The cuttings formed by the bit returned to the surface up the annulus, and were deposited in the slush pits by way of an earthen ditch from the well bore to the pits. The pits were usually 50 feet long, 10 feet wide, and 4 feet deep, and ran lengthwise down the side of the derrick on the left-hand side of the driller's station.

Since I was the "boll weevil" in the crew, I got a firsthand, intimate acquaintance with the grip ring and grief joint. But a description of the kelly joint, grief joint, and grip ring must come later when I tell you how the kelly got its name.

The crew that broke me in consisted of four men. My Uncle Jim was the driller. "Conductor" Rogers, the fireman, was a small, quiet man, an excellent fireman who coaxed those two elderly boilers to surpass themselves. Then there was Sam Sikes; 6 feet 3 inches tall, a strong, gentle man. Sam was about thirty years old at that time. He had drilled and knew lots about the drilling business. He was skilled, patient with me, and I thought him a great teacher. He also had the biggest hands I had ever seen, and was extremely strong. The last man on the crew was "Dee" Gregory—big, gruff, single, and a hell of a fine roughneck. He had one weakness: he loved to drink and "came drunk" almost every payday and would be off a day. But he didn't care. He did not want the responsibility of a drilling job, but he helped me and I thought him fine. He taught me lots about being a real hand.

I was lucky. Those old boys set out to make a top hand out of a skinny, seventeen-year-old kid, and succeeded.

To my dying day, I will remember that they never hazed, ribbed, or harassed me. They answered my questions honestly, and tried in every way to take care of "the kid." Many years later when he was gray and grizzled, I met Sam on the street. We greeted each other joyfully, and Sam said to me, "Kid, you turned out real good, but I always knowed you would, you were so damned eager."

They were great old boys. Sam had a little farm north of town, and between jobs he farmed a little. He wouldn't take a job away from Corsicana. But Dee, who was single, and I made two booms at the same time and worked together on several jobs.

We drilled those little 1,800-foot-deep wells north of town for Mr. John. I learned a great many things and began to think of myself as a "roughneck"—not a "weevil." It was kind of like growing up, but not as lengthy.

All of our derricks in those days were made of wood—mostly unfinished sawmill "roughs." The foundation sills were generally 8-by-10-inch fir timbers; the floor of the derrick was made of 3-by-12-inch raw

Map 1. Places mentioned in this book. Areas inside dotted lines are shown in detail in Maps 2 and 3.

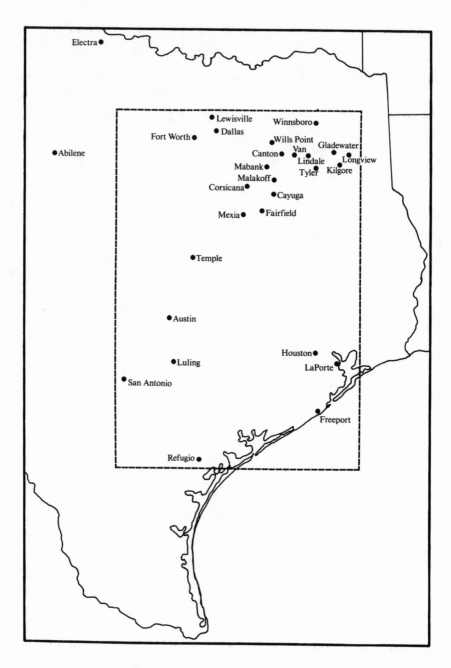

Map 2.   East Texas, Central Texas, and Gulf Coast.

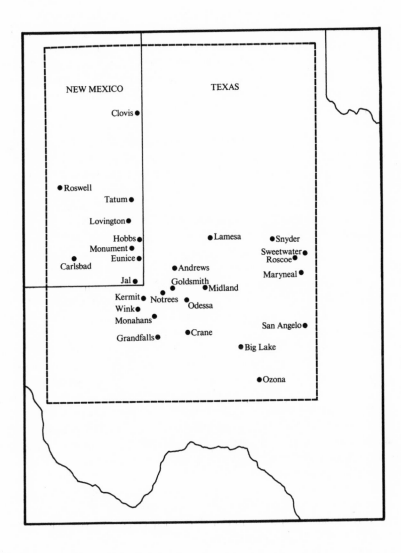

Map 3.   West Texas and Southeastern New Mexico.

lumber boards. The legs were spiked together as the derrick was built. They were 2-by-8-inch finished boards of different lengths, nailed together with thirty-penny nails. As the derrick went up, the legs were pulled up by pulley and "gin pole" and nailed together a piece at a time. Considering the amount of effort involved, derricks went up rather rapidly. The derrick "patterns" were premeasured and sawed in the rig-building contractor's yard in town, hauled to the well site, and erected there, a piece at a time.

There was little standardization in the oil fields in those days. Things were evolving. Change happened all the time as new ideas were tried, discussed, cussed, resisted, or adopted. Everyone had ideas, and everything stayed in a constant state of flux. It was a heady, intoxicating time. We loved it! And damn near everybody got into the act.

Our derricks at that time came in three sizes and heights. They were 84, 96, and 108 feet high, known familiarly as doubles, thribbles, and fourbles. The names came from the heights of a "stand" of pipe when going in or coming out of a hole. Doubles were two joints of pipe left screwed together, broken off, and stood in the derrick. The pipe came in approximately 20- to 22-foot lengths. So the derrickman's domain was the double board, roughly 35–36 feet above the derrick floor. Three joints needed a thribble derrick and four joints a fourble. The excess room above was known as "head room" and was needed in order to be able to maneuver the traveling block on "trips" to change bits. (Incidentally, a "trip" is whenever you pull pipe out of the hole or run it in the hole. The term is still in general use today.) Drillers prided themselves on their speed, so they "ran at" the derrickman when going in the hole, and if he "missed" a stand, they had to stop the traveling block before it crashed into the crown block. If it did run into the crown, it was a major disaster, so we usually made trips in a state of semi-controlled madness.

As the legs rose upward on the derricks, the girts and sway braces were added in sequence. The girts were 2-by-12-inch boards cut to maintain the taper of the derrick. The sway braces were 2-by-6-inch boards, nailed in place to form a big ×.

The old wooden derricks were erected by a very special breed of men. They were called "rig builders." They were highly paid men, drawing $18–24 per day, and were exceedingly strong, ambidextrous, tough, and skillful. They had to be because the work that they did was beyond the capacity of the average able-bodied man. They could hold up and steady a 3-by-12-inch board in a corner of a derrick they were building, then nail it in place with sixty-penny spikes. They used instead of a hammer a long-handled hatchet with a round serrated head opposed to the blade. They would usually sink a sixty-penny spike in three blows, and had to be able to nail left-handed in order to keep up, as the work was fast and furious. Those tough old boys prided themselves on being stronger, tougher, faster, and meaner than anybody, and were just that. The total elapsed time it usually took to build a derrick from starting legs to crown was three days, working off scaffold boards and pounding thousands of nails. They were much men, and even though they pre-sawed the "derrick patterns" in town, everything had to be "laid out" to pattern on the job. The old-time rig builders are all gone, but they were kings in their day. They had the grace and balance of tightwire artists, and more guts than they needed. One of them would "go in the hole," i.e., fall to his death, occasionally. His friends would grieve, wonder what happened, go to his funeral, then go out the next day and build another derrick.

Our derrick for Mr. John was a "thribble" 84 feet tall and 24 feet square at its base. The derrickman's domain was the thribble board, two oak boards, 4 inches thick by 14 inches wide, that lay across the seventh girt, 56 feet above the derrick floor on the side opposite the driller's station. We "racked pipe" in front of the drum when making trips to change bits. The derrickman's duty was to unlatch the elevators when coming out of the hole, then rack the stands of drill pipe against a "finger board" to get it out of the way. Then, when going in the hole, he brought the drill pipe out of the rack and latched the elevators "on the fly." No derrickman worth his salt wanted his driller to slow down for him. He prided himself on his ability to catch 'em as they went by, with his only safeguard a wide leather belt with a large metal ring in the back with a rope through the ring, tied to the x-brace behind him. It was his only lifeline.

We have built our derrick, finally, and can go on with our drilling, 1925 style. Our rig was an antique even then, and should have been retired. Still, it was a good example of the kind of drilling rig that had been in general use a short time before. They were rapidly going out of style since they were very inefficient, clumsy, and slow. But those old babies had drilled many shallow wells around Corsicana in years gone past!

The rig was steam powered, with two 90-horsepower, locomotive-type boilers. We drilled with 180 pounds per square inch steam pressure. The abbreviation is PSI and will be used from now on in this story to denote pressure of any kind.

Our draw works was a two-speed, jaw-clutch, jack-post rig, built by the Union Tool Works in Pennsylvania. Union Tool Company was later absorbed by the National Supply Company and became the manufacturing arm of that giant company.

Titusville Iron Works of Titusville, Pennsylvania, built the single-cylinder steam engine we used for power. It had a flywheel and was

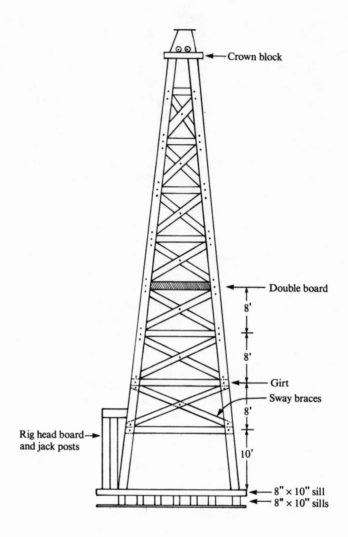

Figure 1. Wooden double derrick. Based on a drawing by Bobby Weaver.

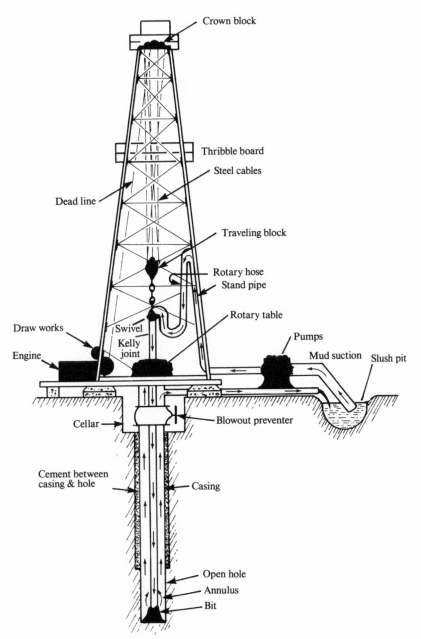

Figure 2. Rotary rig with steel derrick. Partially based on a drawing in *Spudding In: Recollections of Pioneer Days in the California Oil Fields,* by William Rintoul (San Francisco: California Historical Society, 1976), p. 117.

prone to hang up and stop "on center," especially when you reversed it, which you often did, to engage a clutch. Then you had to tip it off, usually by stepping down on a spoke in the flywheel. This was a very dangerous thing to do, as it usually came off center very abruptly, and sometimes trapped a man's foot or leg, pulled him down, and killed him. The flywheel's grisly nickname was the "widow maker." I speak with sure knowledge of their ability, as a driller I was working for got killed just that way and it put a real fear into me. I was very careful when I had to kick one off center. Those engines have a great amount of power, but we were not drilling very deep. As the wells got deeper, the old "single-barreled" motors fell by the wayside. The new twin-barreled 10-by-10-inch or 12-by-12-inch motors came into vogue and endured for many years. They were strong, fast, and almost trouble-free. I still remember them pleasantly after all these years. They were a pleasure to drill with and had no smoke or fumes to pollute the air.

We had no "slips," and here I go with another description. "Slips" is a misnomer. The things are really wedges designed to hold pipe and keep it in place while going in and coming out of the hole. Before slips came into use, two sets of elevators were used while tripping pipe.

Elevators are devices that are used to lift and lower drill pipe. They have "bails" which hang or suspend them from the big "hook" that hangs below the traveling block. More later about traveling blocks. Elevators latch around the drill pipe. The pipe in those days was "collared"; the elevators fitted the pipe and the collar, which was, of course, larger in diameter than the pipe itself, enabling you to pull and lower pipe safely. Without slips, you used two sets of elevators, leaving the pipe resting on one while going up after or pulling a stand, then shifting the "hook" from set to set. It was slow, tedious, and the greatest breaker and crusher of fingers ever used. This process was known as "juggling elevators."

Back to "slips": The first slips were smooth and curved on the back side, to fit the taper and curve in the rotary table. The inside of the slips had teeth, cut to fit the outside of whatever size pipe you were drilling with, or, in the case of casing, the size pipe you were running. They were two or three in number and had a wire handle. They could, and would, fall through the rotary and cause a nasty fishing job, so usually we tied a strong cord to them to enable us to have a better hold on them. When placed around pipe in the rotary, then slacked off on, the teeth would "bite" into the pipe and the taper of the bowl would hold the grip tightly. The pipe stayed put, and would stay in place while "breaking out" or "making up." They beat the living hell out of juggling elevators. Slips have changed down through the years, but the latest models have most of the elements of the very first ones, and the name is very misleading, because if the "slips" slip, they are not doing their job.

Our pump was a steam-powered two-cylinder one. The water or fluid end was also two cylindered. It was not large and was not very efficient, but did move fluid and did have enough velocity to bring cuttings up out of the hole.

Okay, we have built our derrick, rigged up our rig, and are ready to start drilling the surface hole. Remember, this is 1925. Our bit is a "fishtail," a two-bladed bit with a drilled water course on each side. Bits have evolved down through the years from fishtails to drags, to tricone and flat-bottom rock bits, to the journal bearing bits of today. But this was a $12\frac{1}{2}$-inch-wide fishtail, and we are going to drill 200 feet of hole and cement that much $10\frac{3}{4}$-inch casing to protect shallow water sands from contamination. We make the bit up on the bottom of the "kelly joint," a square or hexagon-shaped length of very heavy pipe. The "kelly" is mounted under a "swivel" which permits the pipe to turn without strain. This swivel, in turn, connects to a rotary hose, which is connected to a "stand pipe" in the corner of the derrick, and a line runs from the bottom of the stand pipe to the pumps. The pump sucks up fluid from the slush pit. This fluid is pushed through the stand pipe and hose and then pumped down the inside of the drill pipe and out through the water courses in the bit; then it returns up the hole outside the pipe, bringing with it the "cuttings" made by the bit. These settle out in the slush pit and are eliminated later. This whole assembly is supported by a pulley arrangement, from the top of the derrick, where fixed pulleys form the crown block, to the traveling block, which moves up and down the derrick as the drill pipe is raised or lowered, and the blocks are strung with cables or, in oil-field lingo, "wire rope." The "fast line" reels in on the drum shaft and is controlled by gears when hoisting pipe, and by the "brake" when actually drilling. Since a drill string is heavy, the brake is all important, as by "feeding off" or "holding up" on the brake, you control the amount of weight on the bit and, hence, the rate of penetration. This kept the driller standing at the brake practically all of the time, and in order to be free of the constant "slacking off," he usually had a favorite roughneck who "spelled" him. This training was invaluable to a roughneck who wanted to become a driller. It was a prized thing to be made a "brake weight," even though the other hands were jealous, and made caustic comments about "brown-nosers" and "ass-kissers."

Since it took considerable skill and a sense of "feel" to "drill" without bogging'er down or "twisting off" or just fanning, such training was a necessity. We had in those long-ago days no way to know how much weight we had on the bit. Weight indicators hadn't been invented, so we literally drilled by the "seat of our pants." Some guys had the feel; some did not; but we all learned by doing; the "did nots" stayed roughnecks all their lives, and probably felt that they had been discriminated against.

We have drilled and run 10 3/4-inch casing, then cemented it in place, and have reduced our bit size to 8 3/4 inches in diameter, and are headed for the pay zone at a depth of 1,800 feet—not too shallow in 1925, when 4,000 feet deep was *deep*. The formations are mostly sticky shales, marls, and shells. Some of those million-year-old shells were 3 feet thick and 6 to 8 feet wide. They were tough to drill and dulled bits rapidly. And sometimes when you "broke through" one, the bit would hang, and unless the driller was alert and shut off the throttle, he would "twist off," and that meant a fishing job, still one of the pet hates of drillers.

The shales we have drilled through have "made mud" out of dissolved solids. This mud has "walled" the well bore and prevented sloughing and caving in, so we finish up, run 5 1/2-inch casing, and cement it in place. After the cement set, and in those days we waited seventy-two hours, we "drilled out" and completed the well.

So now you know how we started out, and since we started from "scratch" so to speak, we were in a business never done before— "drilling for oil"—and it took a bit of doing.

We drilled three 1,800-feet deep wells north of town for Mr. John, and I learned a lot, and since it was the only *really old* drilling rig that I ever got to work on, I look back and am glad that I had the experience. There are very few men alive today who have even seen a rig like that, much less worked on one. I feel lucky to have been able to do it, although I must admit that I didn't feel a bit lucky at the time I was doing the work.

Chapter Two

From Weevil to Top Hand

We finished drilling those wells for Mr. John Champion, then stacked his little old rig, forever! It had been a real experience.

My Uncle Jim had been approached by Fred Shields, who had just gone to work "pushing tools" for a new oil-field millionaire named Garland Kent. Mr. Kent had just bought a "Russian model" Johnson drilling rig. The Johnson rig was made in Corsicana and was named after Mr. Horace Johnson, one of the owners of the American Well and Prospecting Company. It was an excellent rig, a popular make, and a brag thing for Corsicana. Bethlehem Steel finally bought the plant and manufactured rigs there for many years. They finally shut down and turned the rig manufacturing over to Continental-Emsco Company.

Jimmie took the job with Garland Kent. It was a daylight job, from 6:00 A.M. to 6:00 P.M., and the location was in Chambers Creek Bottom about 7 miles east of town, just off the Corsicana-Powell "pike road," on the west side of Chambers Creek. The wells were 3,000 feet deep and the pay zone was the Woodbine sand. The rig was new and modern, and Fred Shields had been given a free hand by Mr. Kent. It all added up to an extraordinary job, and it turned out to be just that.

The night driller was a man named Bell White. He was a short, blond man, with a high-pitched voice, and was the most deceptive-looking man I ever saw in my life. He looked like a cherub, but was as genuinely tough as Attila the Hun. He was utterly fearless, and was already known to have killed two men who made war talk at him. We called him "Bennie," and all liked him immensely. He was easygoing, mild in manner, and a hell of a good driller. The only thing different about him was, if you pushed him hard, he pushed back, and was willing to back it "all the way," so few men did push him. I knew him many years and was proud to call him friend.

It was early October of 1925 and I had been roughnecking three months. I had made a down payment on my first car, a 1924 Model T. It cost $180; I paid $100 down with four monthly payments of $25 each. The color was basic black, just like all Fords then, but to me it was a beautiful car. I was awfully tired of walking. The car also enabled me to move back out to Mother's to live. I paid her and my stepfather, Mr. Andy, $30 per month room and board. They needed the "cash money" and I needed a decent place to live that was cheaper than a room in a "bowl and pitcher hotel" in town, besides having had to eat in a boarding house.

Mother did not approve of my working in the oil fields. She felt that if I lived at home, she could somehow fend off the "evil companions" she was sure I associated with when I was out of her sight. She had little to worry about, since twelve hours on the job, one and a half hours' travel time, eating, bathing, and all the little daily things left very little time for hell raising. Roughnecking was a dirty job; drilling mud, the compound used to grease pipe with, cleaning out the shale, and ditch all combined to make necessary a daily bath. Back in those days, a daily bath was almost unheard-of, a Saturday-night bath being the rule of thumb. All this bathing put a burden on Mother, but she had just moved into a house with a real bathtub to replace the old familiar No. 3 tin washtub, so she bore it cheerfully.

Sam and Dee had decided to make a derrickman out of me, so when we began to rig up our new rig, they told Jimmie that I was ready for the derrick job. He was dubious because I was so small. Dee had been working derricks, and he outweighed me almost exactly 100 pounds, but I was all for it, so Jimmie said he would let me try the derrick job. If I couldn't hack it, he would put Dee back in the derrick. It never happened because I was a natural. Working derricks came easily to me. Two weeks after starting, I could hold my own anywhere as a derrickman. I was wiry, quick, exceptionally strong, and possessed a sense of timing that was excellent, so Sam and Dee were proud of me. Uncle Jim finally admitted that I was a good "attic hand." My life changed then; at last I was accepted; a man among men. This was strong medicine for a seventeen-year-old.

It took us eight days to rig up that first time. We used mule teams, chain falls, main strength, and awkwardness. Since it was a "first" rig-up, we had to measure everything out, using the center line of the rig as a focal point. We were very careful in our measuring. To rig up "off center" was a huge no-no. Those old-time drillers, many of whom were illiterate, could figure you out of your socks. I made out reports for many drillers that I roughnecked for. They were canny old boys. They couldn't read too well, but they could certainly drill and were proud of their ability. Our derrick on this Kent job was a tall one, 108 feet, made of wood, a fourble derrick.

We finally got rigged up and spudded in the well. We drilled 300 feet of 12^1/$_2$-inch-diameter hole, and ran and cemented 300 feet of 10^3/$_4$-inch casing. It was here that I saw my first Halliburton Oil Well Cementing Company job. They had not cemented the casings on the Champion Drilling Company jobs.

It was a new technique, worked fine, and impressed me. I have been a Halliburton fan since that first job. They have done many wonderful things since that day, but never have been quite as impressive as that first cement job.

We used two wooden plugs to separate the cement from the drilling fluid, putting one into the casing; then mixing the cement with Halliburton's pumps and mixing device; then, with the cement mixed and pumped inside the casing, installing the other plug on top of the cement slurry. The bottom of the casing was a half-foot off bottom, and when you pumped the cement and plugs down with the rig pump, the 16-inch-long plug would stall the steam pump when it hit bottom. The driller would raise the pipe until the pump started up. When the second plug hit bottom, it stalled the pump, the cement was outside, and the job was complete. We usually waited seventy-two hours before "drilling out" so that the cement would set up. And now you know how we did it in 1925. It was crude and rough, but effective. We use plugs today, though they aren't solid wood. Halliburton's techniques have modernized and become very sophisticated, but basically, we still get the cement in place and hold it there just like in the "bad old days."

We were not alone in our field east of Corsicana. Garland Kent had about 1,200 acres under lease. Just west of his lease line some other independent company owned some leases, and Kessinger Drilling Company was drilling for them. Magnolia Petroleum Company, now Mobil, had a small lease north of us about one-half mile. I forget the contractor's name, but the drillers, John Wilson and "Grandpa" Williamson, became old friends of mine. I roughnecked for both of them later at Nigger Creek and at Mildred, south of Corsicana.

The Kessingers were a locally owned company. Mr. Charlie Kessinger had started out in the very early days in Corsicana. He had acquired his rig slowly and steadily over a period of years while he drilled, pushed tools, and raised a family of five boys and one girl. He was a chunky, strong man about 5 feet 9 inches tall. He weighed close to 190 pounds, and it was all muscle. He was a salty old boy. Four of his sons were grown. The oldest boy, Charles, Jr., nicknamed "Brother," was daylight driller on his dad's rig. The next oldest boy, Ed, drilled nights. Staley and Walter Paul roughnecked, Staley for "Brother," Walter Paul for Ed. It was a "kinfolks" outfit, but a good one. Those boys were all about the size of their father, all strong as bulls, all real workers, and the whole gang lived and breathed "Kessinger Drilling Company." They were a tough, proud bunch and really kept that old rig in top shape. They were tough competition, but we visited back and forth between rigs a lot and got acquainted. This was true of me. I was a new hand; Sam and Dee and the rest of the men had known each other for years. They had all worked together on jobs in years past.

It was the fall of the year, early November. There had not yet been a killing frost, and the leaves were still on the pecan trees. We were not far from Chambers Creek and there were many native pecan trees growing in the bottomlands. The weather around Corsicana is gorgeous in the fall, and we used to wander down to the creek and pick up pecans when we weren't very busy. It was a pleasant change of pace for all the roughnecks.

One pecan tree, about 35 feet tall, was growing outside the levee about a quarter-mile east of our rig. One of the Kessinger hands went down to that tree one afternoon, and in just a short while we saw him hotfooting it to the Kessinger rig. Then he and Mr. Charlie Kessinger hurried back to the tree and the old man was carrying a .22-caliber rifle. Dee and I intercepted them, and they told us the roughneck had spotted a squirrel in that little tree and they were going to shoot him. We followed them and stood back and watched Mr. Charlie Kessinger shoot up a box of fifty shells and never touch that squirrel. He and the squirrel played "dart ass" around that tree for forty minutes. The squirrel probably died from old age later, but Charlie Kessinger earned a nickname he wore the rest of his life. From that day on he was known throughout the oil fields as "Crackshot" Kessinger, and his drilling company became Crackshot's Drilling Rig. You gain fame in odd ways sometimes.

We were having real problems drilling in that area. The formations were mostly shale and shells. Today it is called "snowbank drilling," but then, with fishtail bits and inadequate pumps, sticky shale became "gumbo" and drilling was slow. Trips to change bits were frequent, "balling up" was common, and after "spudding" a ball off a bit, you sometimes spent two hours drilling up the ball.

It was a schooling period for me, and I was a lucky kid. I was learning the drilling business from men who had come into the patch twelve to fifteen years earlier and were among the more knowledgeable in drilling at that time. Some of the things that they devoutly believed were later proven wrong, but both my Uncle Jim and Bell White, Sr., had about eight or nine years drilling experience. They were both good drillers and were just lazy enough to school their hands to do all the work, except actually run the rig. So, even though some of the things that I learned were wrong, most of my learning stuck. I'm still glad that

I got the start in the business that I did from those men, both drillers and roughnecks. Those old boys were very patient with a green, eager boy. It must have been flattering to some of them, because I hung onto their every word. I didn't realize it at the time, but everybody loves to be admired. Sam, Dee, and Conductor did, and spent lots of time acquainting me with the peculiar ways of the oil fields.

It was a different world with an entirely different language. Many names and sayings stemmed from the farm and small-town background of these men. We coined our own vocabulary, and even today some of the terms are "Greek" to the average person.

The fishtail bits we used had to be sharpened and "tempered" after each use, which meant that they were taken to a blacksmith or machine shop, usually a combination of the two. "Dulls" had always been hauled to the shop by the tool pusher, but as the rig count fell, some of the larger shops began to solicit business and would send trucks around to pick up and deliver bits. Of course, the tool pushers loved it and each one had a favorite shop that shaped, sharpened, and tempered the bits just as the tool pusher liked it done, or they were generous with whiskey. The whiskey was bootleg, of course, but popular nonetheless, and "payola" was already rampant in the business.

We were averaging drilling and completing a well every fifty to sixty days. At 3,000 feet it was considered good time, and we were on a company-owned rig. Contractors hurried more, worried more, and were tougher to work for, so we considered ourselves lucky. We finished our fourth well in June of 1926. I turned eighteen years old and was no longer a "weevil." In fact, I was a pretty good hand. I had been working derricks nine months and was "keeping up," so I felt very able to hold my own on any job.

The winter had been a mild one, but it had rained a good bit. We were in a creek bottom in the heart of the "Blackland Belt" of East Central Texas. The land was flat, but that black, waxy soil was something to contend with. It was boggy, deep, and, at certain times, unbelievably sticky. I have seen mud accumulate on truck and wagon wheels until they simply would not turn and had to be cleaned with shovels, axes, hatchets, or anything handy that was sharp. It would also build up under the soles of your boots until you felt that you were walking on stilts.

We "skidded" the derrick on each move that winter. The rig builders moved the derrick while we tore down the boilers and took up the steam lines, as well as water and mud lines. Most of our water storage pits were dug and were open pits. The soil held water like a jug. The rig builders jacked the derrick up, laid a track of 3-by-12-inch boards, and used wooden rollers and a winch truck if possible, or, if it was too muddy, teams of big draft mules. The noise was loud: rig builders shouting, mule skinners cussing at the top of their voices, and all in all, what seemed to be a scene of mass confusion. It wasn't that at all. Those men knew their business. They just liked to holler, and those damned rig builders would pry up those matting boards, which were 30 feet long, and run lay them down again. They would also grab "rollers" behind the derrick and "run" in the mud to replace them in front of the derrick. For once you got a derrick moving, it paid to *keep* it moving, because if you stopped and it settled, you would have hell getting it moving again. So, everyone connected with a rig skid ran, yelled, heaved, and cussed, and it made for a wild day.

We were on 80-acre spacing and the rig moves were only a quarter-mile. It was a good thing, too, since a longer move would have taken two days, and even rig builders and mule skinners, who were the toughest men I ever saw, could not have stood two days like that in the winter. In summer when the ground was dry, I have seen a rig skidded and set down in five hours. The oil fields have always had to contend with adverse weather. A round-the-clock, seven-day-week operation could not be stopped because the weather turned bad. You just endured it and went on with your "rat killing."

I got an unexpected lift that summer. I just happened to hear Sam and Dee arguing with a roughneck off one of the other rigs. He had made some offhand remark about me; nothing really bad, just something like "Oh, he's not a bad kid, but is kind of a smart aleck." To his great surprise, he was informed that I really and truly was smart; that I had graduated from high school, something none of them had done; that I read books for pleasure, knew more already than HE would ever know, and that they, Dee and Sam, didn't want to hear any more bad-mouthing of me. It surprised the hell out of the visitor. It also surprised hell out of me. I knew that Sam Sikes had struggled through the fifth grade in a two-room country school, Dee had finished the sixth grade, and my Uncle Jim, the driller, also had a fifth-grade country-school education. So my modest little high school diploma set me apart. I might be a green hand, but I was a learned green hand. I had never before realized just how much value those old boys placed on education. When they were growing up, the sixth grade was about tops because boys of twelve or thirteen years of age were needed on the farm. They could plow, hay, hoe, plant, and do a man's work, so their fathers yanked them out of school and put them to plowing.

It made me proud that the guys were proud of me. It was the first time that I remember that someone besides my mother had ever bragged on me.

Too, I was beginning to learn that some of the oddly pronounced words that we used every day were pronounced that way because the old-timers who first saw them in print pronounced them phonetically at about the fifth-grade level. For instance, the word "tour." We worked a tour of duty in those days—twelve hours—either from 6:00 A.M. to 6:00 P.M., or from midnight until noon. The word first appeared on a drilling report, and the consensus of opinion is that an old-time driller saw it for the first time, didn't have any idea of how to pronounce it, then had an inspiration. He knew how to pronounce "sour" and this word was spelled exactly the same except that the *s* was a *t*, so he pronounced it that way. It is never pronounced "tower," nor "tour" as in trip, but for sixty years to my knowledge has been called *tour,* pronounced to rhyme with *sour.* A fifth-grade education might inhibit your reading ability, but it didn't dull your brain. When you didn't know, you improvised.

Another badly mispronounced word was, and is, the word "sheave," the technical name for the big, heavy-duty pulleys in the crown and traveling blocks. Someone in the long-ago days pronounced them "shivs," just like a gangster's knife. It is wrong, but stuck, and is today, even with all the educated hands around, still "shivs." We stick to our mistakes just like everyone else.

And I must not leave this word business without a mention of the most-used phrase in the oil-patch vocabulary. It is universal, versatile, has many meanings, can gain you a lifelong friend, or a lifelong enemy, and is used as much today as when I started to work. This wonderful phrase is "son of a bitch." The oil fields are full of sons of bitches. All kinds: dumb ones, smart ones, mean ones, good ones, indifferent ones, and a few real bastards. Men called each other that freely, and it all depended on how it was said. It could bring out a laugh, or bring on a fight. A friend could say to another, "You're a pretty good son of a bitch" and just get a grin, or, as I heard one roughneck tell another once, "He called me a low-life son of a bitch! Can you imagine? What did I do? Well, I swatted him in his big mouth with my wadded-up hand and let that be a learning to him." Believe me, it hasn't changed that much. You can still use it in the old-time way if you are careful.

Corsicana in those days had a licensed "red-light" district. The only other town to have the same thing in Texas was the port city of Galveston. No one knew why, and no one cared. The "district" in Corsicana consisted of six big old two-story houses, about five blocks east of downtown, across the railroad tracks. Four cotton gins mingled with them, scattered over two city blocks, running north and south parallel to the railway. These houses were supervised by "madams" who were licensed by the city. The "sporting girls," as they were called, were examined by the County Health Officer periodically. The whole thing was kept quiet, virtually ignored by the churches, city aldermen, and the "good" element in town. They felt that it was needed to take care of the basic needs of the "rough element" in town. A polite form of hypocrisy. However, they were well patronized and endured for years, finally just fading away. The single roughnecks, and I am sure a few married ones, went to "whore town" pretty often. They were working twelve hours a day, driving to and from work seven days a week, and this did not leave much time for social life. The married men had it much better. Sam Sikes was married, lived on a small 25-acre place northeast of town, kept a cow, a lot of chickens, and grew a big garden and lots of hay and cow feed. His wife and oldest son, who was twelve years old and taller than I was, kept up the work on the little farm, so Sam went home every night. Dee was a bachelor, thirty years old, had no car, lived in a boarding house, and made the "district" fairly often. So did my uncle, who was also single. They didn't think much about it, as it was just one of the things you did, and paid-for sex had no strings attached.

But the curious thing was that all the crew didn't want *me* to do the same things that they had always done. They warned me constantly about the bad things that could happen to me in the "houses": of fights, petty jealousies, the callousness of the "sporting ladies," and a host of other bad things. I can hear Dee Gregory even today, solemnly telling me to never indulge myself in "store-boughten pussy," because it was a bad, useless thing for a boy to get started to wasting his time and money for, and that no good could possibly happen. It was a queer kind of morality, and I felt as though I had four extra fathers, all telling me, "Do as I say, not as I do." But I liked and admired those guys because they meant well and were genuinely interested in me. So I promised them faithfully to stay away from the red-light district, and to never even consider spending money in the place.

It was an easy promise to keep. What none of the crew knew was that I was on first-name terms with every madam in whore town, and had been in each of their houses many times. For the last two years in high school, I had worked every afternoon and all day Saturday in the shoe department of a local department store. It was the biggest store in town, was owned by a prominent Jewish family—a very moral, strict bunch of people, and very orthodox, with a reputation to sustain.

The women in the red-light district were not allowed to leave the district. The city was adamant about this. Oh, they were useful, filled a need and all that, but could not come uptown and defile the city.

However, the women had money to spend, and they liked to spend it on clothes, pretty shoes, and other fripperies. The madams got together, called the owner of the store I worked in, and arranged for someone to come down into the district, bring all kinds of clothing and shoes, fit shoes, and act as a movable department store. No one in management and none of the married men would accept that job, so I, a single sixteen-year-old gentile kid, got the assignment. I could measure feet, knew shoes real well, and could keep my mouth shut about women's clothes, about which I knew nothing.

It worked pretty well. The women would call the store and give the boss a list of things. He and some of the lady clerks would pick out clothes. I would get about two dozen pair of our fanciest ladies' slippers and mules. We would load the boss's Studebaker and I would drive down to whichever house they were meeting in that day, and we would have a great "trying-on" session, and they always bought lots of stuff. The store kept up its image and I got a liberal education. It was lucrative for the store, and I learned a few things that stood me in good stead, and gave me an odd slant on "ladies of the evening."

That was the most uninhibited bunch of women I ever saw or listened to talk, and their language was, at first, very shocking to me. I really didn't know that women used that kind of language. The time was usually in the mid-afternoon. Most of the women were just waking up, drinking coffee and discussing the last night's work and customers—in most unflattering terms, I might add. The sexual perversities and tastes of some of the town's most respected men were talked about, analyzed, laughed at, and ridiculed, in language that would not have been used on the Galveston docks. Most of those women came from Dallas or Houston. They had lived a very tough life and had no illusions whatever. They paid me no more attention than a piece of furniture and called me "kid" while I fitted shoes, took orders, collected money, was polite, and kept my big mouth shut.

Those ladies also wore very few clothes. They would shuck out of a negligee and try something on, and pay me no mind at all, so I became very blasé about naked women. After awhile, nudity becomes commonplace. You don't pay it any attention.

But listening, especially to the unflattering, ugly talk about their customers, turned me off completely. I would sit and listen to the talk and tell myself that I would never, as long as I lived, spend a dime on a whore and give her an opportunity to say ugly, mean, brutal things about me, or to laugh at some habit of mine. I have kept that promise fifty-nine years. I didn't tell the crew, just listened to their warnings; but I did tell Dee about two years later. He thought it funny, them warning me about something I knew a lot about. And then, he told me *again* that they had been *right* to warn me.

The summer of 1926 was drawing to a close. We had been drilling in our little oil field a full year. "Crackshot's" rig moved out, as they had drilled up their lease. The rig moved to Kosse, Texas, about 25 miles south of Corsicana, and I lost touch with the Kessinger boys for two or three years. John Wilson and Grandpa Williamson were on their last well when they ran into trouble. They "stuck" a bit. It was hard to figure out, but our drillers thought someone went to sleep at the brake and the bit balled up, stopped the rotary, and the man woke up to find that he had "planted" his drill pipe and bit. Now John and Grandpa were both excellent, smarter than average drillers, but even good drillers get sleepy on a twelve-hour night, put some roughneck on the brake, and take a little nap. (Incidentally, Grandpa was thirty years old. He got his nickname from the way he moved around, not from his age.) Anyhow, they got stuck, we heard about it, and Sam and I got permission to walk up to their rig and watch John Wilson try to get loose. He was known to be a thinker, and since rotary drilling was still in its "teens," so to speak, everyone wanted to learn as much as possible. Shared knowledge *made* the drilling industry.

It was a revelation to listen to John's talk and to watch his work.

He still had partial circulation, and he felt that one of the two water courses in his bit was plugged. So he jetted some of his heavy mud out of his slush pit and ran water into the pit to thin the mud, hoping to dissolve at least part of his "ball." They were strung with four lines, and he decided to try to pull and work himself loose with just the four lines. His derrick was wooden, of course. It had been skidded a number of times, and re-nailed after each skid. But its strength was of unknown quantity. Bear in mind that he had no weight indicator and no accurate way to judge how hard he was pulling on his pipe. If he pulled too hard, two things could happen: he would pull the derrick in, or pull the drill pipe in two. So it behooved him to be very careful, make no sudden moves, be very patient, and never "jerk" on his pulling. Not an easy trick with a steam engine and a jaw-clutch rig.

Sam and I stayed two or three hours. John gave up on the four-line pull, shut down, and rigged a "luff line" which would give him a nine-line pull. Sam and I helped rig the line. I learned how to rig one, and it stood me in good stead later. In fact, that particular bit of lore earned me my first drilling job at the ripe old age of twenty-two years.

When we had finished the luff line, John called his fireman, told him to cut his fires down and let the steam pressure come down from 190 PSI to 90 PSI, explaining that he had to ease into his next pull, lest he jerk the derrick down on his head. He then made all of us go off away from the rig. He put his motor to barely turning, engaged the low clutch, and, while controlling the rig with the throttle, slowly pulled that damned bit loose. We went back to our rig in awe, feeling that we had been fortunate to watch a master driller at work. I worked derricks for John later and always looked up to him. He was a dandy. He neither smoked, drank, nor chased women, and I never heard him use bad language. He was a fine man and his life style earned him a very odd nickname. He was known throughout the Central Texas and East Texas oil fields as "Prick" Wilson. However, I called him Mr. John.

We drilled three more wells after both the other rigs moved out. Then in early March, we, too, ran out of work. Mr. Kent shut down his rig and stacked it, and we were "on the grass" again. Uncle Jim, who liked to save up, then lay off a few months, went into semi-retirement for awhile to, as he said, rest up a bit. Sam Sikes, too, welcomed the opportunity. But Dee and I wanted to keep working. I wasn't saving any money. I was buying lots of dress clothing that I rarely wore, and had traded my roadster for a Ford coupe, so I stayed short on money. Dee loved to drink, raise hell, and run around, and he stayed chronically broke. We immediately began to look for another job.

We found one. Grandpa Williamson took a job with the Simms Oil Company, a good small oil company, long since absorbed by a larger outfit. He hired me to work derricks and Dee as a floor hand. It was a fairly new Union Tool drilling rig with a 10-by-10 Acme engine and three 100-horsepower boilers: a real nice lash-up.

The spring of 1927 was with us. Our rig was a company rig, not a contractor's. Oh yes! There was, even then, a difference. Company rigs were much easier to work on and never seemed to pressure you. Contractors were a nervous lot.

We were drilling just outside the village of Mildred, 10 miles southeast of Corsicana. The Corsicana-Powell field had gone right through Mildred. Simms had some fringe, or "edge," leases there and we drilled two Woodbine wells to 3,000 feet. Then we moved onto a completed well that had a 400-foot "liner" or, as it was called then, a "screen" in it. Our job was to pull the liner, clean out to bottom, then deepen the well. Sounded simple, but did not turn out that way.

We had a tubular steel derrick on this job. It was made of 2-inch and 2$1/2$-inch pipe. Line pipe, I think, but it could have been tubing. The derrick legs were 4-inch outside diameter (OD) pipe, with welded lugs where the girts and braces bolted onto the legs. We were leery of it, mostly because it was different. We felt that derricks should be made of wood, so this thing was suspect.

Screens in those days were run into wells that had been completed "open hole." They were usually made of casing, smaller than the production string, and had long slits cut in them lengthwise to let oil into the well bore. Their primary purpose was to keep the hole clean and to prevent sloughing. They worked well, but occasionally they had to be pulled. This was one of those times. They were run in the hole with a simple J-slot device, gotten loose from, and left in place.

We picked up a retrieving head, went in the hole, latched into the screen, and found it firmly in place. We couldn't pull it, so Grandpa had steam pressure bled off and decided to take an upward strain, then try to turn the thing with the rotary table. Now in order to do this, you pulled up, got a good strain on the drill pipe, set the slips to hold the strain, then slacked off so that you could turn the rotary table without twisting up the traveling blocks, since when you slacked off, the elevators were loose and would not turn with the pipe. The only drawback was, you had to pick up again later to get the pipe off the slips. I was working derricks and was chosen to work the overhead clutch to engage the rotary, then jerk it loose when it bound up, stopped, and backed up. You had to have good timing and be quick on the draw. Grandpa and I did this a number of times with no apparent results. However, we persisted, since repeated efforts sometimes paid off in good results.

The last time we did it, I slammed the rotary clutch in and Grandpa wound it up tightly. The rotary stopped, groaned, and backed up slightly, I jerked the clutch out, the rotary ran backwards about six rounds, Grandpa picked up on the pipe, and all hell broke loose. There was a loud crack up in the derrick. Grandpa, who was looking up, hollered, "RUN!" He dropped the brake and ducked under the headboards right up against the No. 1 jack post. That damned pipe derrick came down on top of the headboards, with the crown and traveling blocks landing in front of the drum about 4 feet away, but we didn't get a scratch.

When things settled down and got quiet, Grandpa sighed and said, "Kid, quit hugging me. I'm having trouble breathing." So, I turned him loose. Dee and the other fellows helped us out from under that pile of junk, and Grandpa and I sat down and had a first-class case of the trembles. It literally scared the gizzard out of both of us.

We were finished with the Simms Oil Company. They shut down, stacked the rig, pulled in their horns, and laid everybody off.

I had one month to go to my nineteenth birthday. It was May of 1927. I had two years' experience, was a top hand, and was also out of a job, again!

Chapter Three

My First Boom:
Nigger Creek/Mexia

Things were quiet around Corsicana for awhile after we finished with the Simms Oil Company work. The Corsicana-Powell boom was over, but a few, very few, rigs were drilling, edge wells and semi-wildcats. Work was scarce and spasmodic, so we had lots of idle time on our hands.

The focal point for the oil-field hands in Corsicana was the Vogue Cafe on the corner of Collins and Beaton streets. It was a twenty-four-hour cafe, had all male waiters, catered to a 90 percent male, driller/roughneck clientele, and was a combination social club, hiring hall, and occasional boxing ring. We spent a goodly amount of time hanging around the Vogue, swapping gossip, rumors of jobs, a few lies, and lots of idle bullshit. But we were all "dough heavy" and it wasn't really a bad time. I was accepted as a full-fledged hand and thought myself a man among men.

After about a month of enforced idleness, bankrolls got slim and we began to want to go back to work. This was my first taste of the feast-and-famine episodes that I was to experience many times later in my life. But just before panic set in, the little city of Mexia (pronounced me-*hay*-ah) boomed for the second time.

Someone struck oil in a wildcat well on the bank of Darst Creek about 9 miles west of Mexia. Darst Creek was known locally as "Nigger Creek," and that little boom became forever known as "Nigger Creek boom."

It was a fairly short-lived boom. It flared up, raced ahead, tapered off, and died, within ten months. But it was a godsend to a whole bunch of broke or nearly broke roughnecks and drillers. There was a lot of rain that fall and winter after a dry, hot summer. The soil around Mexia was black and waxy, and it turned to gumbo when wet. The mud was ankle deep out in the fields. Stickup men were robbing people in town, in the oil fields, and around the honky-tonks on the outskirts of town. That boom was a going Jessie while it lasted. Hands flocked there from everywhere, and since it was the only game in town, nothing else really mattered.

Dee Gregory and I hired out to a driller named Walter Hauks. Walter was a mild-mannered man, a good driller, and a good man to work for. We all moved to Mexia, all of 36 miles from Corsicana, got rooms in a bowl and pitcher hotel, and ate our meals and got lunches put up in a cafe called Jimmie's Bakery. I had never lived away from Corsicana before, so it was a new, great feeling for me. Dee and Walter took it in stride. They had made many booms before this one.

The actual drilling was fairly routine. The wells presented no unusual problems. Most of the drilling rigs were modern for their time, and things, for the most part, went smoothly. I got an introduction then to something new to me, the "tooled joint."

Rotary drilling started out using plain thread pipe as drill pipe. It was ordinary collared pipe: not very thick-walled, and it had a high mortality rate. Under the two stresses of torque to turn the bit and strain to pull the drill pipe out of the hole, plus the heavy wear on the threads from making up and breaking out on trips, pipe failures were common. Expensive fishing jobs resulted. We needed a more durable pipe joint and got it.

The first tooled joint that I ever saw was devised and built by Colonel Lucey, who was an early manufacturer of drilling rigs and other oilfield tools. It was a machined, tempered-steel, tapered joint—a matching box and pin. Both box and pin were shouldered, and when the two shoulders jammed together when you made them up, you had a strong metal-to-metal seal. The tapered threads allowed you to make a joint up tight in just four rounds. It was a tremendous improvement. Therefore, it was highly suspect, since the oil fields have always resisted new things. It was admittedly better, but lots of the old-timers thought it was just a fad. Besides, the damned things were very expensive and who in the hell had money enough to put a tooled-joint box and pin on each joint of drill pipe? As a result, some odd practices came into general usage, and even the name took a corruption. They became "tool joints" and are called that today.

The rig that we were working on had some tool joints, but not on every joint of drill pipe. We had one joint of pipe with a box and pin; then we had a double with a box on one end, a pin on the other end, and a collar in the middle. These two were known as "Greyhound" joints because they were supposed to speed up connections. Incidentally, anytime you picked up another joint of pipe to deepen the hole, you "made a connection."

As we drilled deeper, we went through a procedure to enable us to utilize our tool joints. It would drive a driller out of his mind today to follow this method, but we thought nothing of it, since tool joints had proved their value while tripping. It went like this: First we made the kelly down; it was 38 feet long and had a tool-joint pin on the bottom. Then we picked up, broke the kelly off, and set it in the rat hole; picked up, made up and ran the single Greyhound in the hole. We then latched back onto the kelly and made it down again. That done, we pulled up, set the kelly back, laid down the single, picked up the Greyhound double, the kelly, and made it up again. This time we broke off the kelly, set it back, picked up the single again, and once more made the kelly down. That made four joints buried. So this time, we set the kelly back, laid down the single and double, and "made up a four-ble." The fourble had a tool-joint pin on the bottom joint, two collars in the middle, and a box on the top joint. Then we started over again. It was a bit tedious, but we thought it pretty modern. You could come out and go in the hole without breaking out a single collar, and it saved a hell of a lot of galled threads. Tool joints made a large difference in oil-field procedure. They brought Wilson tongs and front-latch elevators into general use, since we had to have stronger tools to make and break pipe. The old-time chain tongs and Hill tongs just couldn't handle tooled-joint threads and shoulders.

How the "kelly" got its name is a story from the long-ago past. The kelly is the square or hexagon-shaped joint that literally drives the drill pipe round and round. Today it is 48–60 feet long, but the first one I ever saw was hexagon shaped, 28 feet long, and had split drive bushings. Today the drive bushings are bolted around the kelly and are an integral part of the assembly. The drive bushings fit into a 5-inch-deep square in the center of the rotary. As the rotary turns, the bushings turn the kelly. Actually, the technical name of the kelly joint is "grief joint," and it does take lots of grief, but since the day that the very first one was put to work, it has been called the "kelly." Now to the story.

When the first rotary drilling rigs were put to work they were very primitive. Since they were new devices made from scratch, one of the problems was to be able to turn the pipe and still be able to move it down to keep weight on the bit at the same time. Most of the rigs were built in local machine shops, and were made by individuals new to the art of drilling, and feeling their way along. Some demented genius invented the grip ring to solve the problem, and the medieval "rack" never caused any more trouble. The rotary table sits in the exact center of the derrick floor. The rotaries had four 2½-inch diameter holes in a square pattern drilled in them. The grip ring had four 2½-inch dowels on the bottom of the thing. It also had four metal discs, 6 inches in diameter and ¾ of an inch wide. These discs were so positioned that they opposed each other. Each had a worm drive with a wheel to manipulate the thing in and out. The drive, or grief joint, was a thick-walled joint of round pipe. You used the wheels to push the discs up against the pipe. If they were too loose, they would slip and score the pipe badly. If you got them too tight, they gripped the pipe so tightly that it would not slide downward through the discs. So usually, the newest, greenest hand was assigned to the grip ring. He ran those damned discs in and out as the rotary turned, took a good chewing out from the driller for being such a dumb ass, and learned to hate that ring with a purple passion. When the first hexagon-shaped grief joint was field tested, they took it to a rig in the old Corsicana field and tried it out. It worked perfectly. So, being much like children with a brand-new toy, they ran it up and down the derrick several times.

The poor weevil who had been dancing attendant to the grip ring suddenly realized that he was forever free of that damned contraption. He watched the driller run that new gadget up and down the hole, and suddenly said out loud, "May the good God bless you, whatever you are, slide, Kelly, slide!" "Slide, Kelly, slide" was the name of a popular baseball song, and the grief joint has been a kelly joint ever since that day. And that is how the kelly got its name.

Which brings us to another fine oil-field name, rat hole! When the first kelly joints were used, they were too heavy to lay down when you made a trip, so we hung them in the corner of the derrick in a wireline, hook arrangement. This was clumsy, dangerous, and time-consuming, yet stayed in use for several years. Then some lazy, thinking man drilled a slightly slanted hole about 8 feet toward the corner of the derrick. He drilled it 25 feet deep and $8\frac{1}{2}$ inches in diameter, put a 6-inch OD pipe in the hole, and lo! the rat hole came into being. Now when making a connection or a trip, we simply broke the kelly off, set it in the rat hole, unlatched the bridle on the hook, got loose, then did the chore, whatever it was, as the kelly sat there out of the way. And believe me, it was a huge improvement since the kelly stuck up 10 feet above the derrick floor, out of the way, but easy to latch back onto. We thought it wonderful!

Mexia had lived through one big boom and was plenty able to cope with a new one. It was a raunchy, tough little town, and the towns-people as well as the merchants gave no quarter to the oil-field hands. They jacked up the price of everything: rooms, food, work clothes, boots, and shoes. You could like it or do without it. Because cars were not plentiful, roads were not good, and the hands were stuck with whatever the town offered. However, we were a clanny bunch and did not socialize with the people of the town. Mostly, after work, we would gang up in front of a popular cafe and talk, argue, brag, lie, and tell jokes. We were alien and knew it, so we kept mostly to ourselves. Those old days would seem tough today. The men were away from home, lonely, and working long, hard hours, but they did not complain. The money was good. A dollar went a long way. They were used to hard work, and the life wasn't all that bad. Since the average roughneck had a sixth-grade education, he was fortunate to be making as much money as he was, and knew it. So they counted themselves lucky.

All booms had their parasites. Mexia was no exception. She had 'em all: bootleggers, pimps, whores, gamblers, dance-hall girls, and thugs. We were their natural prey, and prey upon us they did, with results that were often funny, sometimes tragic, and once in a great while, a little bit of both comedy and sorrow.

There was a little lease broker from Pennsylvania in Mexia at that time. I never knew his last name, but the hands who hung out on "Roughneck Row" in front of the cafe called him Louie. He was smart and popular. He bought lots of coffee, came up with a pint of decent moonshine drinking whiskey occasionally, and generally made himself agreeable. Everyone liked him and it paid off for him. Most of the farms in the area were not large, and the farmers, both black and white, had a vast distrust of checks. Those roughnecks tipped Louie off to that fact and were constantly telling him to "Go see Mr. So and So. I think he is ready to lease, but don't offer him a check." Louie would thank them, go to the bank with a tired-looking old suitcase, and have them fill it with $1 and $5 bills. Then he would go out to see his prospect and try to get both the farmer and his wife into the kitchen, make his pitch, then start heaping all that lovely green cash out on the dining table. It made an impressive pile and was awfully hard to refuse. Louie did okay and began to really make money.

But he did show off a little and wore about a 2½-carat square-cut diamond on the left hand, a real flasher, and when the sun caught it, it really did shine.

We were all talking, joking, and kidding Louie about being a Damn Yankee when one of the hands said seriously, "Louie, if I were you, I'd quit wearing that big old diamond all the time. Some outlaw is gonna cave your head in some night and steal the thing."

Louie just laughed and said, "Hell, I've got big old knuckles and I have to soap it to get it off. It wouldn't be easy to steal."

About two weeks later one morning at breakfast, Louie came in just as we were leaving for work. He was a little pale around the gills and had a big bandage on his left hand. Somebody asked him, "What in the hell happened to your hand, Louie?"

Louie gave us a sick grin and said, "Well, I asked for trouble and got it. As I was going home to the hotel last night and passed by that alley about three blocks from here, someone conked me on the head. I woke up about an hour later and my ring and finger were both gone. The cops found my finger in the alley, but the ring had vanished. I guess that they were only interested in the ring since they left the finger! So now I don't have to worry about being robbed, since I am never going to carry more than ten dollars with me." Mexia was tough, but most boom towns were fairly salty. Times had been hard, and even the holdup men were having to work overtime.

Walter had bought a new pistol he was awfully proud of and carried it everywhere, even to work. Dee and I encouraged this, since there had been a few rig crews held up and robbed on the job. We felt fairly secure with a pistol in the dog house and didn't think we would be victimized, which turned out not to be necessarily true.

We all went out to a taxi dance one night—Walter, Dee, and myself. It was about half a mile outside the city limits—a popular place, and if you were known to the folks who ran the place, a bottle or two of home-brew beer or a pint of pop-skull whiskey was available. Of course, Walter wore his gun. He carried it in an underarm holster. We stayed until about eleven o'clock, danced a few times, had a couple of beers each, then started back to town since we had to be at work at six o'clock the next morning. We were all afoot, of course. The road was muddy and deeply rutted, but since we all wore knee-high laced boots, muddy roads were no problem.

I was in front, followed in the same set of ruts by Dee, while Walter brought up the rear. It was a single-file sort of a road. About halfway to town, we had to cross a wooden bridge over a small creek. There were many bushes and trees growing on both banks of the creek. The moon was dark and the little bridge was a gloomy-looking thing. About 30 yards before we reached it, I heard a rustling sound in the brush as though something was coming out from under the bridge, so I stopped to listen. Dee stopped, too, and whispered, "What did you hear, kid?" I answered, "I don't know, but I think something or somebody is under the bridge. We may get held up." Walter had stopped, too, and then he said, "Wait a minute," and we heard him walk back up the road a little way. He came back in a couple of minutes and said briskly, "Okay, let's go." We did—crossed the bridge and a half-grown calf ran out. Feeling greatly relieved, we started on to town, when Walter said again, "Hold up a minute." Then he turned and hurried back up the road, came back, and again said, "Okay, let's go."

Dee stopped and asked, "What in the hell was that for?" And Walter answered, "I went back and got my gun where I hid it. You don't think I was going to let those thieving bastards have it, do you? I paid forty hard-earned dollars for that damn gun!"

So much for toting a gun. We never felt safe with Walter again. He was a fine driller, but a damned poor gunman.

He finished up a well, then went home to Corsicana. Dee and I went to work for John Wilson, and that is where I met "Doc" Milligan, who figured rather large in my life a little later at Luling, Texas. Doc was a horse-faced old boy about thirty-five years old. He was a good driller and roughneck, but a heavy drinker. He and Dee were old drinking buddies. They even roomed together. Doc was roughnecking for John at that time, since drilling jobs weren't too plentiful right then as other people kept coming to Mexia from other places.

Most of the early hands in the Nigger Creek field were from Corsicana, my hometown. The Corsicana-Powell boom was about over, and that second boom dying turned lots of men loose. So they naturally gravitated to Mexia, which was close. They were a clanny bunch who favored each other for jobs and were very proud to be from Corsicana, though they never called the town by its name. All of the oil-field hands simply called Corsicana "The Blocks."

Back at the turn of the century, about 1905, six blocks of downtown Corsicana were paved with bois d'arc wood blocks, 4 inches square and 10 inches long, set deep with the 4-inch-square side up. When it rained those blocks turned yellow and boys running around town barefoot got their feet stained yellow. So in 1927 we were known away from home as "Yellow-heels" and always went home to "The Blocks." This endured for many years until all the old-timers retired or died. They were a proud, tough old bunch and to their dying day were loyal to "The Blocks" because it was where the first oil well in Texas was drilled and the first rotary drilling rig was devised and built. They thought themselves especially lucky to be natives of the old place. Strangely enough, I think so, too. I'm proud that I call it home, even today, though the old town is a farm–ranch–light-industry place, placid, stodgy, and slow. They still do a little drilling, and I still love to visit my two sisters who live there. Both Dotty and Jo love the old town and say it is still a most pleasant place to live.

Back in Mexia late that summer, Mr. John, Doc, Dee, and I decided we were rich enough to go home for a visit. Our rig was waiting for a location and we were all "dough heavy." We were in two Model T Ford roadsters. It was raining and had been doing so for two days. John Wilson and I were in one car; Dee and Doc were in the other Ford. John "Prick" Wilson did not tolerate drinking, and both Doc and Dee had been painfully sober for too long, so they invested in a half-gallon fruit jar of moonshine whiskey and took off just ahead of John and me, swigging heavily on the jug. Of course we weren't drinking, John and I. John was a teetotaler and I certainly didn't drink around him.

Doc and Dee did pretty well with Doc driving until they got to Richland Creek Bridge. It had a long, raised wooden approach over the bottomlands. The creek, a big one, was out of its banks, and there was about 2 feet of muddy water all over the bottomlands under the approach. About 50 feet up the approach, their Ford suddenly veered to the right, crashed through the railing, and disappeared.

Mr. John said, "Oh, my God! Those two hellions have killed themselves, kid. Half our crew is gone!" We drove up, stopped, jumped out, and looked down, expecting to see the worst. But sometimes God *does* look after fools and drunks. That Ford had landed upright, or at least it was sitting on its wheels, and we heard Doc say, "Dee, you son of a bitch, if you broke that jug I'll kill you!" And ole Dee said, "Didn't spill a drop. Here, have a swig and let's abandon ship. There is a foot of water running through this Flivver and we are still 20 miles from The Blocks."

We made 'em wade out, backed up, put them in the turtle seats in the rain, and went on to town. They finally rescued that Ford of Doc's, but I never learned exactly how they did the job. However, the odds were against their being sober.

I went back to Mexia alone. John Wilson's rig didn't get the location he was waiting on, and since the bird season opened and John was a quail and dove hunter, he decided to take a vacation and hunt. Doc and Dee wanted to carouse a bit, so they stayed at home to run and play.

But I had made up my mind to get a job firing boilers. First, because I had never had a firing job, and second, because, while it was demanding, it was still the easiest job on a drilling rig.

It wasn't easy to get a job. I was nineteen years old, slight, blond, looked awfully young, and had never really had a firing job. But I finally hired out, after three days of asking, to a driller I did not know. We were rigging up, and I lasted two days. My greenness showed and he fired me.

The very next morning I snagged another job because I could truthfully say I was an experienced fireman. This time, four days went by before they axed me. But the third time stuck. I became a full-fledged "pot fireman" and stayed on for three wells, when they stacked the rig and laid everyone off. The Nigger Creek boom was petering out rapidly. A few dry holes will do that to most booms. However, the experience I struggled to get really paid off later. I used it to ride out some tough days when work was hard to find.

Back to The Blocks. I went out to the farm and stayed with my stepdad, Mr. Andy, and Mother. My two youngest sisters were at home. Mary was two and Dorothy was ten years old. I paid for my room and board; it helped the folks; and staying at home was nice after a long time in little hotels. I coasted for about three weeks. Both my little sisters loved to be read to, and I did lots of reading and helped Mr. Andy, who was deep into the cotton harvest.

But this soon palled. Tom Sharp, who was actually a rig-building contractor, bought a drilling rig and ventured into the drilling business. He hired Staley Kessinger, "Crackshot's" son, as his daylight driller, and Staley hired me to work derricks. I got Mr. Andy a job working on the floor. He was green but willing, and six bucks per day in slack time on the farm looked good to him. We all helped him get started and he did well. It was early winter. The job was near the little village of Purdon. We drove my little Ford to work. It rained a lot, but we didn't mind. Jobs were scarce and we were happy to be working.

We made the winter working for Sharp Drilling Company. Drilled two dry holes to 3,300 feet deep, about 3 miles apart, just south of Purdon. Nothing but run-of-the-mill drilling; no problems. The other two members of Staley's crew were "Possum" Parker, the fireman, and a chunky, redheaded fellow named Joe Palmer. Joe was a brother of Tom Sharp's wife. He was a stolid fellow and very quiet, but didn't like to be touched from behind and was always jumpy when you walked up behind him. We couldn't understand this and avoided him. Later, much later, we learned why he was so touchy. He had been a part-time member, or at least a hanger-on, of the Raymond Hamilton, Clyde Barrow group. His brother, Leo Palmer, was arrested with Ray Hamilton while Joe was working with us. I never got the straight story, but I wasn't too interested in the Barrow-Hamilton gang, who were going strong at the time. They finally electrocuted Ray Hamilton, but I never knew just what became of the Palmer boys.

We finished up in early March, stacked the rig, and went on the grass again. This time roughnecking jobs were nonexistent. The doldrums had set in. No new booms were opening up and, while there was work in other parts of Texas and Oklahoma, local people were plentiful to do the work.

I stayed out at the farm and got a job clerking in a clothing store, making less than half of my roughneck wages. It was quite a comedown, but I had worked for the same store while I was in high school and we got along fine. Mother was delighted. She did not want me working in the oil fields. I didn't like to work in the store, but kept my mouth shut, worked hard, and even got a raise to $22.50 a week. My twentieth birthday came around, and a chance encounter with Doc Milligan changed my life forever.

Chapter Four

The Bruner Boom in Luling

The little town of Luling, Texas, east of San Antonio and southeast of Austin, got its first oil well that year. The wildcat that hit was drilled by a very eccentric gentleman from New York named Edgar B. Davis, who was called the "wildflower" man. He was said to have leased lots of land around Luling and staked his discovery well that spring by plucking a wildflower and saying, "Here is my oil well!" They drilled where he picked the flower and struck oil, or so the story went. Anyway, Luling boomed and caused an exodus of hungry hands to leave Corsicana, since they had endured a long, dry spell.

But I wasn't one of them. I had gotten a raise and had a fairly tempting job offer at an exclusive shoe store. I was just mulling it over, biding my time, barely twenty years old and not actually knowing just how I wanted to spend my life. Nineteen twenty-eight was not a bad year, and I was contented with my job and in no hurry to change my way of living. So I didn't go to Luling.

In fact, I sold my Ford, moved to town, and had just about decided to get out of the oil fields. Mother was begging me to quit roughnecking, and I had two girlfriends who had access to cars, so my social life had picked up and I was happy and content to just coast along for a time.

However, it all came unglued early that fall. The Big 4 Shoe Store played coy with me about the job that they had promised me. They wanted to see how the crops did, they *said,* and it spooked me, so I dropped them like a hot rock. Then one Saturday the wife of one of the owners of the store where I worked told me she had heard that I might go to work for the shoe store, and if I did, that they were forever through with me. I got angry and told her that they just employed me, did not own me, and that Mr. Abe Lincoln had freed us slaves years ago. Then I grabbed my hat and went to lunch. While I was eating, someone sat down on the stool beside me and said, "Kid, you look mad as hell. What is the matter?" I looked up, and it was Doc Milligan. He was grinning at me, and both gold teeth were shining. I said, "I *am* mad and in a damn bad humor. I'm having trouble on the job."

He said, "Ain't you working in a store?" I answered, "Yep, and I'm just about ready to quit."

Doc said, "Look, I've got a hell of a fine drilling job in Luling. It is a new rig, an angle-iron steel derrick, three 125-horsepower Broderick boilers, and an entire string of Acme tool-jointed drill pipe. Dee Gregory and "Possum" Parker are working for me. We have got at least a year's work ahead of us, and I need a derrickman. Quit that damned job tonight. It's Saturday, and I'm going back to Luling Monday. Come go with me."

I said, "Doc, if you are lying, I'll kill you. But damned if I don't believe I'll just take you up. I'm tired of being a ribbon clerk. I'll get my rags together and be at Mother's Monday morning, ready to go."

The store owners were very surprised people. They really didn't expect me to quit. Cotton harvest was in full swing, they were very busy, and experienced help was hard to find. They tried to talk me out of quitting, even offering me a small raise, but to no avail. I told 'em goodbye, took my paycheck, and went to Mother's. I told her where I was going and fluffed off her fears, checked out of my room in town the next morning, gathered up my oil-field clothes, and took off early Monday for Luling with Doc. I had forever thrown in my lot with the oil patch, for better or for worse. And, of course, it turned out to be both; yet I have never regretted the decision. I have done many things, lived in several states, met many people, done crazy and dangerous jobs, but it has never been dull. My world has certainly been different than it could ever possibly have been had I stayed in Corsicana.

Mr. Davis' little oil field was booming right along, and Luling was bursting at the seams. The main street of Luling was really half a street, as the railroad ran down one side of it, so downtown had a curious one-sided look. I haven't seen the place in fifty-four years but doubt that it has changed too much.

Rooms were at a premium, but I got lucky. Doc knew a Mrs. George who ran a rooming house. She was a large, middle-aged lady, and had a vacancy. So I shared a two-bed room with a big old boy named Jim Blank. A tall, quiet man, he was a roughneck, and his hobby was playing the stock market. He was as tight with money as the skin on a dead horse's belly. He saved every dime and drove over to Austin once a month to buy stocks, often on margin. I know he lost a lot of money in the market, but he was certain he would make a killing someday. We roomed together a year and never really knew each other. He was prone to be preoccupied, and I was having a love affair with a little redheaded waitress at the Topic Cafe. She was being kept by a tool pusher, and I was helping him with his "homework." She led a rather active sex life, and kept both of us busy. So I didn't lie about the room much, as I worked a twelve-hour tour every day. Work and my love life kept me well occupied.

Mr. Davis' oil company was called the United North and South Oil Company. He was a New York native, but had fallen in love with Texas. Had made and lost several fortunes, and finally had made the big strike in Texas. The people who worked for him—and he kept six drilling rigs busy for two years—admired him. Most of the rest of us thought he wasn't playing with a full deck. He was opinionated and very stubborn. He kept a failing stage play called *The Ladder* on Broadway for several years because, as he said, "I like it, and other people should, too." He paid the cast, hired the theater, paid all the other help, and folks stayed away in droves. He lost lots of money before he finally gave up and let the poor little play die.

We didn't criticize him openly because he had some guys working for him who would frail your knob if you low-rated Mr. Davis. So mostly, he just went his way, kept on making money, and all the other oil companies hustled to offset his wells. It really did make a rip-roaring boom.

People and oil companies from everywhere converged on Luling. There were many hands from The Blocks there. Doc finally rounded out our crew with another Corsicana roughneck, a tall, tough, funny old boy called "Polecat" Tomlin. He was a dandy, a good hand, and fun to work with since he looked at things with a different slant than most of us. He was given to saying things in a funny way, and we all liked Polecat and were glad he was in the crew.

Another fellow from Corsicana, a man named Penland Spencer, was drilling on a well near our location. He was short, redheaded, volatile, and pugnacious, but likable and a good man to work for. We visited his rig often, and he and some of his hands would slip up to our rig and drink coffee and gab. We called him "Penny" and enjoyed him.

I lived through my first tornado that summer. It was in June. Our rig was shut down. We had the only steel angle-iron derrick in use in the Bruner field. It was damaged, and we were shut down waiting for the Lee C. Moore Derrick Company to send a crew to repair the derrick.

Doc was working nights, 6:00 P.M. till 6:00 A.M. The day had been hot and sultry—one that the old-timers called a "weather breeder." We settled in for what appeared to be a long, dull night. Little did we know what was in store.

We were using three boilers. Possum Parker, the fireman, had cut the fire out of the middle boiler when we came on tour at 6:00 P.M. By 9:30

P.M., steam had gone down and he and I drained the boiler. Then we removed the handhole covers, the manhole cover, and prepared to wash the boiler. We did this periodically to remove accumulated scale and dirt. I usually helped with this chore since I had fired boilers.

Dee was asleep in the boiler shed, a 12-by-4-foot sheet-iron-roofed structure about 15 feet in front of the boilers. Doc was reading a book in the tool house. Polecat was somewhere about; he was a restless soul and roamed around a bit.

There were wooden derricks all round us, fairly close to us. Since spacing rules were practically nonexistent, everyone crowded his neighbor's lease as closely as possible.

Sometime after 10:30 P.M., the wind got really wild. Possum and I crawled into the firebox of the dead boiler, just in case it hailed. We had just finished refilling it with cold water, so we felt safe. Then we heard a roaring noise and all hell broke loose. Derricks began to crash down. Doc ran out of the tool house and jumped in his car, which promptly blew into a roadside ditch and turned over. Dee got up to run; then a 10-foot length of sheet iron caught him about the hips, flatwise. He sailed off into the woods like a big bird tiptoeing along the ground. Polecat was not in sight.

The storm was over in just a few minutes. Our boiler hadn't budged, so Possum and I crawled out. We could hear Doc yelling. His car was lying on its side, it was raining very hard, and the car was rapidly filling with water. Dee came out of the woods, wet and scratched up. Polecat also wandered up. He had crouched down behind the motor. He was wet but unhurt. We rescued Doc by setting his car upright so he could open the door. His little Chevrolet sedan wasn't badly damaged. In fact, he just kept on driving it, since it had never been pretty anyway. When we took stock, we were in good shape. Our derrick still standing, and our lights still burning.

But no other derricks were lit, and it was still raining very hard. Penny Spencer's rig, about 300 yards south of us, was obviously blown down, so we decided to go and see if he needed any help. As it turned out, he needed help badly. His derrick had blown down and crushed the front half of his wooden tool house, which was 25 feet long. Penny's left shoulder was dislocated, his left arm broken just above the wrist, and he was in great pain. He had two hands tearing into the back of that dog house because he had a man inside who had been sleeping off a drunk, and Penny was afraid that he was dead.

Dee and I splinted Pen's arm, but were afraid to tackle that shoulder. Doc fired up Pen's car to take him to the hospital in Luling, at about the time those two hands got the back end torn out of the tool house. They had to wake that drunk, who had slept through the whole storm.

He stumbled out, saying, "Whassamatta? Wha's goin' on?" And then little Mr. Spencer blew his top.

He yelled, "You son of a bitch! I was worried sick about you, and you slept through it all. I was afraid you were dead. Now if I wasn't crippled, I'd kill you myself!"

It was a wild, eerie night. Twenty-two derricks blew down, two men were killed, many were injured, and damage to rigs was tremendous. Doc and Dee took Penny to the clinic in town and got his shoulder back in place. Then they had to take him to his hotel, as the clinic was full. They stayed with him. Polecat, Possum, and I went back to our rig. We had lots of visitors from other rigs. They came to dry out at our boilers. Everyone was wet as drowned rats. Our crippled steel derrick was the only one left standing in that swath the storm cut through the Bruner oil field. I will always believe that the storm made believers out of a few drilling contractors. They had, as usual, resisted changing over from wooden derricks, for all manner of reasons. However, the steel ones came into more general use after that tornado, at least around Luling.

There wasn't much in the way of entertainment in those little old boom towns, but we always had a few real characters around who marched to very odd drummers. One old boy in Luling was a real jim-dandy. He was forty years old, wouldn't take a drilling job at all, but was a roughneck able to do anything, even drill in a pinch situation. But he would get drunk about every sixty days and become a practical joker. His name was Curtis Billingsly. He hailed from a small town just south of Corsicana, and he took life as casually as anyone that I ever knew and enjoyed each minute of it. One of his favorite stunts was to put a skin-tight, blood-red glove on his left hand. That glove made the hand look as though it had been freshly skinned. He would then put the hand in a black silk sling, just as though he had a broken arm. He would go down-town, and if he met some ladies on the street, that bloody-looking hand would accidentally slip out of the sling. It looked horrible. The ladies would gasp and squeal, and Billingsly would laugh and say, "Awful, ain't it?" He was a pleasant, funny guy when drinking, and sometimes when meeting a total stranger on the street, Curtis would stop him, shake hands, and say, "Hi, neighbor! I'm Curtis Billingsly and I never have believed that Old Man Noah did right when he kicked those cats off the Ark; 'cause I really don't think that those cats were fighting." Then he would walk on, leaving a puzzled person behind. We thought him very funny and applauded him. It didn't hurt his ego either, just egged him on. He was our funny man.

Luling began to die on the vine that spring and early summer of 1929. Doc's rig shut down. He, Dee, and Polecat headed for The

Blocks. I went to Refugio, Texas, with two young hands about my age, Norman Andrews from Corsicana and Alton Cox. We almost starved because work on the coast was very slow, too. In fact, we camped out without a tent on the banks of the little Mission Creek about one-half mile south of a Catholic nunnery for ten days, living on very slender rations including two chickens we stole from a farmer and roasted over an open fire. But I finally landed a derrick job on a rig belonging to Houston Gulf and Gas Company. The driller was from North Texas and knew nothing of the high pressure on the coast, and didn't know how to handle it. The drillers on the coast had to keep the mud as heavy as possible to lessen the possibility of blowouts. We were drilling along one night, and Jack, the driller, had me jet a quantity of mud out of the pits and run a stream of clear water into the mud system, thinking that the rate of penetration would improve. It didn't, and at about 4:00 A.M., Jack decided to pull out and change bits, so we started out of the hole. I was in the derrick and am not sure whether he was filling the hole or not, but all of a sudden mud began blowing up around the rotary table. I started down the ladder, then saw I could not make it. We had a lower set of guy wires on that old wooden derrick, and I grabbed one of them, folded my gloves over twice, slid to the ground, and hit the ground running, because it was really roaring by that time. I ran about 70 yards before looking back, and was just in time to see the derrick and rig disappear into the crater that was forming. I turned and ran 50 more yards, then saw all three boilers go into the crater. It scared the living hell out of me. I may have been as scared since, but I doubt it, and it cured my Gulf Coast fever. I quit and I didn't go back to South Texas for six long years. If there is anything that will bring out the rabbit in your soul, it's working in gas fields without blowout preventers, which were not in general use at that time.

Back in Luling, Doc Milligan had gotten a job on half pay. The other half was interest in the well. He needed a derrickman and talked me into taking the same deal. The promoter who was drilling the well had used up most of his money assembling the "block" of acreage, so he gave Doc 20 acres and me 10 acres, side by side. Since this well was a semi-wildcat or so-called "stepout," it really didn't look like a bad deal. So we drilled the well to the Edwards limestone and recovered a 2-inch core that looked good. You never drilled into the lime more than 5 feet because the water contact was close. Then we set pipe, casing that is, and drilled out the cement plug and drilled 3 feet of formation.

The promoter had all his investors out at the rig that night when we began to swab the well in, using the drilling-rig sand line and a casing swab. Doc and I spelled each other on the swabbing, a tedious job. I was going in the hole with the swab and hit fluid very high. In other words, the fluid began rising in the hole. I came back out of the hole very rapidly, and the fluids followed me out. The wells around Luling flowed, but more like an artesian water well with no pressure to speak of. We had laid 3-inch line from the control head to the pits. Doc and I ran out to the flowline and the fluid was oil!! Everybody went crazy. Men were hollering and yelling, and dipping their hands in the oil and smearing it on their clothes and faces. This went on for twenty minutes or so. The lights from those old-time steam generators were not too awfully bright, but the scene looked like a Roman orgy, without sex. Doc and I had congratulated each other about twenty times for being so smart. When I looked back to the flowline from the derrick floor, the fluid was still black, but now a dull, dead black. I stepped to the end of the line and caught a handful of black, salty sulphur water. The silence was so thick you could have cut it with a knife. Everyone's dream went glimmering, but *I* was rich *once,* for twenty minutes.

About that time, and I think it was in October, Mr. Edgar B. Davis sold his United North and South Oil Company to a major oil company. The story was that he got $12 million for it, a fabulous price in 1929. He promptly paid everyone working for him a bonus of 50 percent of every dollar they had earned from him. There were a bunch of instant rich roughnecks, drillers, and pumpers around Luling just then. Mr. Davis was the greatest man in the world and they loved him. Unfortunately, I didn't share in that deal, so I just kept on working. Mr. Davis left, but I heard later that he moved back to Texas and finally died there. He was a good, decent, but very odd man. We have seen all too few like him in the oil patch.

I had begun to fire the boilers for a tough old driller from home named "Cowboy" Sikes who had been working for Rowan Drilling Company for six months, and that is where I met Mr. Charlie Rowan, Stuttering Charlie. He had two small drilling rigs and was enduring hard times. He couldn't meet his payroll regularly, and Wilson Supply Company was financing him to some degree. It really paid off for them later, as Mr. Charlie was tough, practical, a good operator, and he finally made it *big.* Today, Rowan Drilling Company is a real biggie. Mr. Charlie is dead, but his name endures. He had a terrible stoppage in his speech, hence his nickname, but you didn't dare *help* him say a word, even though his face was purple and you thought he would choke to death, because he would knock the hell out of you if you did, and he was a big man.

We were working daylights on one of his rigs, a two-speed National. One day I wandered up from the boilers and noticed that Cowboy had a "hot box" on the line-shaft journal box just behind him. Babbitt was beginning to run out of the thing. I told him about it. He said he would shut down when he "got the kelly down" and for me to melt some babbitt and be ready to pour a new bearing. I headed for the boilers to do that, when Mr. Charlie drove up and got out of his car. He, too, noticed the hot box, mentioned it to Cowboy, and got the same answer, "I'll fix it when I get the kelly down." The old man gave him a cold-eyed stare and said, "Cowboy, you know that I am running on short money and can't afford trouble. If you gall that line shaft, I'm gonna fire your ass off this job."

Old Cowboy never batted an eye. He kicked the low clutch in gear and began to pick up off bottom. Then he told the boss, "Hell, Charlie, if that's the way you feel, I'll fix it right now." He knew the old man meant every word.

Little Jimmie Rodgers, "the Blue Yodeler," came to Luling that fall. He gave a performance at the Old Queen Theater. The tickets were $10 each, almost two days' wages, and he packed the house. He had 'em hanging from the rafters. They loved the little "singing brakeman." He sang the kind of songs that they understood. Entertainment was nonexistent in Luling, and Jimmie was a rare treat. I went, of course. He sang two hours, got encored so many times that he finally came out on stage and said, "Fellers, have mercy! I am a consumptive; I'll give out, and you are killing me. I love you all. Good night!" He died a few years later, but no one who heard him that night could ever forget him.

Luling petered out, so three of us (one of us owned a pretty good Model T Ford) decided to go to Pampa, where we heard there was still work. It was the winter of 1929–1930, and it was a bad one. We got as far as Abilene, where the radiator froze up. It was 350 miles to Pampa, and north of us at that, so we turned east and went home to Corsicana. That is how I wound up in the "Free State" of Van Zandt County. That was a very rough winter. I had a couple of jobs that winter. It took about twenty-five days to drill a well. I didn't make much money, and by spring I was ready to get with it.

Chapter Five

The Free State

The spring of 1930 was a tough one. The Depression was going strong, but it really had not hit the oil fields yet, and although work was slow, it wasn't too bad. Early in February, Tom Sharp got a wildcat well to drill near the little city of Canton, Texas. Canton was the county seat of Van Zandt County, known as the "Free State" because it had once seceded from the Republic of Texas and had to be reconquered. The natives were still a pretty independent bunch; they tended to their business and intended for you to tend to yours.

My Uncle Jim was the daylight driller for Tom, and Staley Kessinger was the night driller. All the hands were from Corsicana, and we all stayed in the old Dixie Hotel in Canton. A big old two-story frame hotel, painted, as the landlady often told me, "Sunny Yellow." She served family-style meals at a set price, and I doubt that she made any money off us. The food was southern style at its best, and we all ate as though famine was just around the corner, and believe me, we loved it. The food was really out of this world. In fact, on Sunday when church let out and townspeople swarmed to the noon meal, the landlady was threatening to charge admission to "watch the roughnecks eat."

We drilled two wells, both dry holes, at Canton. We plugged and abandoned them and Jimmie hired out to an old man named Scott. He was a one-rig, mostly broke, contractor, but a job was a job. The work was at Van, still in Van Zandt County. Van had been a quiet little town of about 200 souls when Pure brought in the discovery well. Pure owned most of the good acreage, and the other companies took what was left. Still, it turned out to be a Pure Oil boom, and Van boomed with it. The natives were Bible Belt rednecks. They did not approve of the four dance halls, the clapboard hotels, the noisy cafes, and the drunks, bootleggers, whore ladies, hell raisers, moonshiners, thugs, pimps, and all the low types who followed the booms. They all came to Van and stayed. The old Blue Moon Dance Hall was notorious. The townspeople hated it but they were badly outnumbered. Their views did not prevail and we went our rowdy way. I had heard many tales about the famous Texas Ranger "Lone Wolf Gonzales." I met him for the first time in Van, in the Blue Moon.

Our rig was on a townsite location, three blocks east of the dance hall and two blocks north of our hotel. We were working morning tour, from midnight until noon. One night Polecat and I wandered down to the Blue Moon at ten o'clock. We had two hours to kill before time to go to work, so we wanted to dance a few times. The joint was going full blast, music a'blaring, and folks kicking the splinters off the floor. We joined in, found a girl apiece, then began to tread a few measures.

A few minutes after eleven o'clock, two guys dressed in khaki uniforms burst in at both front and back doors of the dance hall. Both carried side arms. One man, the smaller, wore two pearl-handled six-shooters. The bigger man, who turned out to be Sergeant Gault, hollered as he came in the back door, "Texas Rangers! Everybody face the wall and put their hands on the wall above their head."

Nobody argued with him. We all did as we were told. I was quite sure they didn't want me or Polecat and so I was very curious as to just who they *did* want, and soon found out.

The "Lone Wolf" walked down the row of people, selected two rough-looking men, handcuffed them, hands behind their backs, then headed them toward the front door, and when he arrived there, turned and said pleasantly, "Go on with the dance, folks. I'm sorry we had to interrupt. We got the guys we wanted."

Those two Rangers impressed me. They were really tough. The men they picked up were two bank robbers who had escaped from the Oklahoma Prison at McAlester. Gault and Gonzales made it look easy. They were a hell of a pair of men, and they also ruined *that* dance.

One of the popular drinks at Van during that time—and, of course, Prohibition was still in effect—was a 90 percent grain alcohol solution of Jamaica Ginger, popularly known as "Jake." It was fiery, not pleasant to taste, had to be diluted with Coca Cola to be drinkable, and in roughneck eyes had only one virtue: it would get you drunk. The local bootleggers sold it, along with home-brewed beer and moonshine bottled-in-the-barn whiskey.

Some enterprising moonshiner made up and sold a huge quantity of "Jake" that was made of denatured alcohol, and he poisoned a bunch of people. Some died, and many came down with an ailment called "Jakeleg," which gave folks who had it a curious, jerky walk. A few people never really got over the disease and were crippled for life. Most recovered after a time, though many suffered bad effects for years. It scared me, and I never drank a drop of any kind of alcohol for two years.

Van didn't last long, but was a wild, rowdy little boom while it did last.

But we didn't last as long as the boom, and it happened this way: We finished our third townsite well in early June 1930. We were working morning tour. When we relieved the afternoon tour crew, they were preparing to install a device called a Tulsa control head on the casing collar in the cellar.

The cellar was 4 feet square and just about 3½ feet deep. We used earthen pits, and the cellar just had a ditch cut in the pit side, which left just about 2½ feet of slimy, gray rotary mud in the cellar. We used the catline to pick up the control head. The head was badly thread-worn and had been used too many times. However, Pure Oil furnished it and our job was to make it up in the casing collar. Polecat and I got down in the cellar. We had removed the rotary table, but did not take time to bail out the cellar. That damned head weighed at least 500 pounds and was very unwieldy. Starting to make up threaded joints is called "stabbing" in oil-field terms. Polecat and I immediately began to have a monumental amount of hell, trying to "stab" that damned control head. We would get it started, make it up a few rounds, and then the worn-out thing would jump cross-threaded. We would back it out, then start over again. This went on for an hour, which frayed mine and Polecat's good humor considerably. It had turned into a frustrating job, a mean one!

We were wet, miserable, and in a very bad humor when a young Pure Oil Company engineer drove up, got out of his car, and came up on the derrick floor. He was dressed in riding breeches and English riding boots, and looked very "dressed up." After watching about four of our futile attempts, he stepped down on a cross sill, which put his knees at shoulder level to Polecat and me. Then after one more unsuccessful try by us, he said very loudly, "My God, men. Can't you stab that damn thing? I could have done it myself by now."

It was the wrong thing to say. Polecat and I didn't hesitate. We each hooked an arm around his knees and dragged him off into the cellar with us. Then Polecat said, "Okay, Mr. Smart Son of a Bitch. Show us, don't tell us." That young man scrambled out of that cellar, got in his car, as muddy as he was, and headed for the office.

Our driller didn't like what we did, so Polecat tried to explain. "Hell, Jimmie. You would have done the same thing. That little pipsqueak in those swage-nipple britches and overshot boots was way out of line and you damn well know it. You'd'a done it yourself."

What we didn't know was that Pure was meeting Mr. Scott's payroll, and that morning when we came off tour, our checks were ready . . . We were fired! Mr. Scott said that he hated to fire us but Pure left him no choice since they insisted that we had threatened, intimidated, and insulted a very fine young engineer. Polecat was unrepentant. He maintained that we should have "kicked his ass."

Getting fired was no joke, but to this day I believe it was worth it. Polecat hired out to another outfit, and I lost touch with him for about two years. Jimmie and I went to Canton on a wildcat for a promoter. I worked for another driller because the man who had the rig leased, the promoter, promoted Jimmie, my driller, to pushing tools, which means just that. The tool pusher pushes *everybody* on a rig. Some of them, then and now, are known as "whopdowners" or "hard asses," and earned the name, but Jimmie wasn't one.

In the early days, the daylight driller was the head man. He answered only to the contractor or, in case of an oil-company-owned rig, to the drilling superintendent. Gradually, if a contractor acquired too many rigs, he simply couldn't make them all in a day. They began to put men into cars, to pick up daily drilling reports each morning and to get and deliver supplies to each rig. Usually these were young men with little or no experience. The drillers despised them as "know-nothings." Short pieces of pipe threaded on both ends sold in supply houses were called nipples. They still are so called. So the old drillers simply called those men "nipple chasers" and sent them on as many useless errands as they could.

But all things evolve, and some older drillers, some who had been injured and some just getting on in years, began to "chase nipples" and to get more involved in rig operations. As most of them were more experienced and, in many cases, smarter than the average driller, they gradually assumed more and more authority. Then the true "tool pusher" came into his own, "looking after" two or more rigs and with the "stroke" to hire and fire men. They are still at it to this day. Resourceful, tough, practical, skillful men, they, as much as any other group, make the oil fields "go."

When Jimmie made pusher, he hired an old friend to take his drilling job. The new man's name was Noma Wright. He was a small, dark man, and had the reputation of being high-tempered, but I had known Noma for years, had been on fishing trips with him, and he and I hit it right off. I was a good, competent derrickman, so he couldn't find too much fault with me. Experienced roughnecks were not plentiful around Canton.

It was a peculiar, "funny odd" job. The old man we were working for was a "mail-order promoter." He would work up a block of rank wildcat acreage, hire or, as in this case, lease a rig, then mail out glowing prospect brochures to people all over the United States, mostly in big cities, and his favorite prey was schoolteachers. I read some of those colored, gaudy brochures, and wondered how grown people could be so gullible. They not only were misleading; they were outright lies. Also, he had the nerve to sell the same acreage several times in New York, Boston, Chicago, Atlanta, and Dallas. Since people registered their leases in their hometowns, there was little chance of this scheme coming to light, unless . . . he made a well. If that had ever happened, that old rascal would have wound up so far back in jail that they would have had to pump sunlight to him. He had leased that terrible old rig from a pore-boy contractor. It was a real junkpile, but we were not choosy. The Depression was on, and we felt lucky to have any kind of a job.

Besides, he let us know he wasn't in a hurry. The longer it took to drill the well, the more mail-order leases he could sell. So as long as we made any hole at all, he was happy. Believe me, we took full advantage of it. In all my years in the oil patch, that was the only leisurely job I ever had. We were very careful, careful not to overdo, and the days passed peacefully. Each Sunday we had visitors; every farmer for miles around just knew we would make a fine oil well. They were very interested and would make a picnic lunch and come to the rig. We enjoyed the fried chicken and other food that they brought, and entertained them by explaining how the rig worked and telling ferocious lies about our lives in the oil fields.

Our rig, as I said, was a pile of junk. It was a "two-speed" National with a high and low gear. It was a "jack-post" rig, with a single-barreled steam engine, equipped with a flywheel—primitive even for 1930.

We had two 70-horsepower Broderick locomotive-type boilers for power, and on this job they were fired with wood. It was a mighty struggle to pull a bit out of the hole when we were 2,000 feet deep, and we had to pull them rather often, as we were still running fishtails, sharpened and tempered at a blacksmith shop. Believe me, some of them were of uncertain temper. In spite of everything—visitors, a poor rig, and a promoter for a contractor—we finally bottomed out the first well, but we were definitely *not* in the Woodbine sand. Our promoter simply couldn't afford to chance making a well, so he stopped short. But he did make money. His investors took the beating.

We moved about 5 miles south to another block of acreage. The old man sent out a new bunch of brochures while we rigged up. We had to do some rig repair, since the rig was about to fall apart.

One of the floor hands and I were pouring new babbitt bearings for both line and drum shafts. Noma, the fireman, and a weevil we had hired were trying to install new brass bushings and a bearing in the crosshead on that old single-barreled engine, and this was hard to do. Those old engines were obsolete. You had to line up two sets of machined holes with two square-shouldered steel bolts. There was absolutely no slack. They had to fit precisely. In order to align the things, you used the flywheel to move the crosshead ever so slightly, looked in the hole with a flashlight or mirror, then tried the bolts. If they were off as much as one one-thousandth of an inch, they simply would not go. It was frustrating, agonizing, and not a job for a man with a temper. Unfortunately, Noma had a temper. He had the weevil moving the flywheel. The kid was nervous. Noma was nipping at him and was rapidly running completely out of patience.

Now, one thing you never did was to put your finger in the holes to feel and see if the holes lined up. It was a big NO-NO. This time was an exception. Noma told that kid he was an idiot for about the twentieth time, stuck his second finger down the hole, and said, "I believe it's okay." That poor kid moved that flywheel a fraction and clipped the first joint off Noma's finger as neatly as any surgeon could have done the job.

We heard Noma yell, and I got there in time to take a ballpeen hammer away from him as he was trying to kill that poor boy. We took him to town to a doctor, and I, at the ripe old age of twenty-two, inherited his job. He quit, and Jimmie asked me to take the job and, of course, I jumped at the chance to drill. There is no doubt that at that moment, I was smarter than I have been in the entire fifty-three years since.

I hired a crew of fellows about my age, all but the fireman. He was a sawmill fireman about forty-five years old—a specialist, since firing with wood wasn't done in the oil fields, except in very rare instances.

We set and cemented 800 feet of 8-inch casing and drilled ahead; actually made pretty good time, as a matter of fact. Then the old man decided to lay off the night crew and just work days. So each night we pulled the bit up into the casing to keep from sticking it and shut down, then came out in the morning and ran back to bottom and began drilling again. This slowed up progress quite a bit, but we were in no hurry. We did not have any trouble, no fishing jobs, and finally got down to 2,500 feet.

One of the "marker zones" in that area is the "Austin chalk," so called because it comes to the surface, or "outcrops," near the city of Austin, Texas. It is a clear, grayish white chalk, easy to identify by biting into a little piece of it brought to the surface by the pump, then trapped in the cuttings box (a wooden box about 12 inches deep, 2 feet long, with a removable "end gate"), as it tasted chalky. We caught cuttings regularly every 20 feet in those days, to see what we were drilling through. The shales in that area are blue, or black, and chalk cuttings really stood out.

There was a middle-aged farmer who owned about a 300-acre farm half a mile east of the well. He was intensely interested in the well and visited us every day. He would ask a thousand questions about how deep we were, what we were drilling in, shale or whatever, and when we expected to strike oil. He was a nice old boy, and we liked him and tried to answer all his questions. But he really was a bit of a nuisance and was rapidly becoming a pest.

We were looking for the chalk, knew that we were close to it, and one morning I was squatting by the cuttings box and had washed out a handful of cuttings. There were a few gray flakes mixed with the shale. I picked one out and bit into it. No luck. It was a piece of oyster shell.

A voice behind me asked, "What are you doing, driller?"

I looked around. There stood that farmer. I said, "Harvey, I'm eating dirt. You want a bite?" He said, "No, but I do want to know why you bit that thing."

Like an idiot, I told him and had an instant geologist on my hands. From that day on, he would come walking through the woods each morning and head straight to the cuttings box. He would grab a handful of cuttings, inspect them, and bite any whitish specks, then talk to the derrickman, who caught, washed, and sacked the samples.

We did not make a great amount of hole each day, sometimes less than 40 feet, so this ritual went on for about a week.

Bob Roper, the derrickman, had a dry, wry sense of humor, but he got awfully tired of our visitor. One day he saw him coming through the woods, picked up an old white, dry dog turd, crushed it between his gloved hands, and stuck it down into the cuttings trapped in the box. Then he came up on the floor of the derrick. His victim headed, as usual, for the cuttings box, grabbed a handful of samples, and Eureka! There it was. He just knew we were in the chalk. He picked out several pieces, bit into them and shook his head. Came up on the floor and over to me at the brake, then said, "Driller, I sure thought you were in that chalk, but this stuff don't taste like chalk. I think it's 'magnisshy.'"

I didn't laugh. I didn't dare, and pretty soon he left. I chewed Bob out good, but he thought it funny. The next day we really did drill into the chalk, and everyone was happy, but we did not make a well, again. We worried that hole down to 3,100 feet and were just above the Woodbine sand, which was the producing zone, but the old man stopped us. He couldn't afford to make a producing well.

As we were tearing down the rig, I began to run a high temperature. By the time we had the old rig stacked, I was quite ill and had a raging fever. Still, I managed to drive to Corsicana. The doctor told me I had typhoid fever, put me in the hospital for ten days, and then I went out to the farm to stay with Mother. It was late summer. I was down to 110 pounds and it took me another month to regain enough strength to even think of working.

It wound me up in the Free State. I never got to work there again. Canton, the county seat, was small, built on a square around the courthouse, and was never in a hurry. I have always remembered Canton as a fine place to live. It had all the attributes of old-time southern living, including First Monday, which was and is an institution, bigger today than ever before.

On the first Monday of each month, Canton had "trades day." People came from Louisiana, Oklahoma, Arkansas, and all over Texas to swap mules, horses, wagons, or almost anything you could imagine. There were refreshments, pink lemonade, a bit of home brew, and just possibly a few nips of good locally made corn whiskey. It was a big day. Those folks traded everything. They even had a fenced enclosure half a mile out of town for trading dogs—all kinds of hunting dogs, coon hounds, fox hounds, possum dogs, and bird dogs. It was a real experience, and some of the lying was fantastic. Some of those dogs must have been supernatural, to hear their owners talk about them.

An odd thing happened one First Monday just before we left Canton. We, Bob Roper and I, had moved out of the Dixie Hotel. We had a large room on the northwest corner of the square, upstairs over a cafe. We played poker with the cafe owner, the sheriff, and several merchants almost every night. Not a real cutthroat game; we couldn't afford to gamble for high stakes, but it was fun, and Bob and I ate cheaply at Sam's Cafe, since he was a better cook than poker player.

Two families wandered into Canton that First Monday. Each man had an old wagon, a woman, and some kids. One man had five kids; the other had four. Both men were mule traders. They made their living traipsing around the countryside with a string of mules on a long lead line behind the wagon, or walking beside it. They would stop anywhere and swap, and did make a living of sorts, but were a down-at-heel, scruffy-looking lot. The men shaved every three or four days, whether they needed to or not, and chewed tobacco constantly. Whether they knew each other earlier was never known, but there was no doubt that they became well acquainted in Canton. The women were slatternly, and the kids were as wild as coyotes. They lived on the road, made as many First Mondays as possible, and were highly allergic to work. But they seemed to be content with the life that they had chosen to live.

We got into town late in the afternoon on that First Monday. We surveyed the hustle and bustle and decided to stay out of it. We had a poker game that night, and the sheriff told us this strange story: Those two couples left town at dusk. Then one of the lady members of a Church Aid Society came up to the sheriff's office and told him that those two men had, that day, swapped women and kids. She and her entire group were highly scandalized, and she demanded that he find those awful people and arrest them.

He went hunting them. They were not hard to find, since they were camped side by side, 10 miles north of town, by the side of the Wills Point road. His information was true—they *had* swapped! They also told him that it was none of his business—that they were not, and never had been, married, but had just "shacked up." They were unhappy with him for butting in, told him they had broken no laws, and he was sticking his nose in where he had no business putting it.

The sheriff was young, but he handled that crisis like a veteran. He thought of his four-cell jail, then imagined two men, two women, nine kids, four dogs, and nineteen assorted mules in it. He simply couldn't handle the job, so he apologized, asked them "pretty please," to be out of the county early in the morning. He then went back to Canton and told the church ladies he simply could not find those awful folks, that they must have left the county, and they accepted that. Solomon couldn't have handled it better. That sheriff was good, but he never told anyone but us, since he intended to run for re-election.

I finally got over my typhoid, and by the time I did, I was as broke as a convict, needed a job, and East Texas was booming. I headed for Kilgore.

Chapter Six

The East Texas Depression

I went to Kilgore with my uncle, Jimmie Colvin. He, too, had starved out and had taken a roughnecking job. He was working for a man named Herman Griffen, a Corsicana native, a good driller, and a man who became a lifelong friend of mine. Griff was ten years older than I was; he was a hard-headed, dogmatic, decent man, and a "yellow-dog" Democrat if one ever lived. I worked for and with Herman many times. We had some dandy arguments, but stayed friends until his death a few years ago.

I got a derrick job from a man I did not know, a small blond man named Henry Mann. We were staying at an oil-field hotel six blocks from downtown Kilgore named the Como Hotel. It was run by a formidable lady named Esther Owens, and she certainly ran a tight ship. No women were allowed to stay at the Como, not even wives of married men. It was strictly stag. She had a fine dining room, serving family-style meals. The cook was a large black woman, and she could *really* cook. We accepted the "no girl" rule in order to get to eat Beulah's cooking.

We didn't do badly. Room and board was $10.00 per week, a blue chambray work shirt cost you 98 cents, and good corn whiskey was $2.00 a half-gallon fruit jar. The Depression was in full swing. Times were bad, and it was early winter of 1931. Men worked twelve hours for $5.00 a day, sometimes for as little as $4.25 per day. Contractors were drilling wells for $3.00 per foot. Oil was selling for 10 cents a barrel, but somehow we managed to make a living and even had a little fun in the process.

I began to drink, since everyone else seemed to be doing a lot of drinking, but I never could keep up with the real dedicated drinkers. I just didn't like it that well.

Kilgore had three dance halls, and there were honky-tonks everywhere. We chased after the girls who worked in the cafes, beer joints, honky-tonks, and taxi dances. They didn't expect too much from us because most of them were even poorer than we were. It really wasn't too bad. We were lucky. Millions of people had no job and few prospects of getting one. We, at least, were working, making a scanty living. It beat the hell out of not working at all.

Uncle Jim stayed at the Como, too. He and I were kin, but you would never have known it. We did not room together, work together, or play together. Our tastes were altogether different, so we each went our own way.

Henry Mann, the driller I went to work for, was a tough little man from Fordyce, Arkansas. He had the reputation of being a gunman with a police record, and lots of roughnecks were afraid of him. He had trouble hiring hands because of his reputation. He drank a quart of whiskey every day, wore a pearl-handled pistol to work, and was known to sometimes sit at the brake and shoot light bulbs out of the derrick, eight girts up.

I liked to work for Henry. We hit it off immediately. I was a fast derrickman; he liked that. I wasn't the least bit impressed with his reputation; he liked that. And, last but not least, I was an excellent pistol shot; he *really* did like that, so I worked for him all that winter. We shot up lots of shells. The other crew members were sure that we were both crazy and gave us a damn good leaving alone. Henry called them his ribbon clerks, and me his "right bower." He really was reliving the Old West.

I finally got the story of his "record" and trouble with the law out of him. He wasn't at all proud of it, so I had to dig it out of him a little at a time. It went like this: Some years back in Seminole, Oklahoma, he got drunk, went into a small cafe to eat, did not like the food, and said as much. He and the cafe owner had words; Henry paid for his dinner and loudly informed the guy that his food was fit only for pigs. Then he went outside and began talking to some other men standing around outside the cafe. However, the proprietor called the police and told them that Henry was creating a disturbance in his place of business.

The police arrived, went into the place, then came right back outside and demanded to know which stander-around was Henry Mann. Henry said he was, and the cop grabbed him by the left arm and told him, "Okay, feller. I'm taking you to jail."

Henry said, "The hell you are! What for?" The cop said, "Disturbing the peace."

"Do I *look* like I'm disturbing the peace? Well, I'm not, and I'm NOT going to jail."

Here, in Henry's words, is how it went then: "He whipped out his pistol and hit me a slightly glancing blow from my hairline to about an inch above my right eyebrow; as you can see, I still have the scar. It knocked me to my knees, tore a flap of skin loose on my forehead about the size of a dollar bill. The damned thing fell down over my right eye, and blood poured down my face and blinded me.

"I was wearing my gun in a holster under my left arm. I grabbed it and shot upward where I thought he was, since I couldn't see him. Both he and the cowardly bastard with him ran around the corner. I held that flap of skin up with one hand and shot at 'em one more time and missed again.

"There was a bunch of crosslaid crossties stacked in front of the railroad freight office, about 100 yards away, so I got up and stumbled toward them. One of those cops took a shot at me, I whirled and he was not in sight, so I kept running. I made it to the pile of ties, crawled inside, wiped the blood out of my eyes again, and reloaded my gun. I had dropped ten shells in my pocket when I left home. I had fired three, which left me a total of thirteen shells to use in my war on the Seminole police force, all ten of them.

"I stood them off, all of 'em, for twenty minutes until I ran out of shells. Didn't hit anybody and didn't get shot. I had finally stopped bleeding, but saw myself in the mirror as they were booking me, and I was a fearsome-looking thing.

"They charged me with everything they could think of and threw me in a cell, after a doctor sewed up my forehead. Some friends went my bail, got me out, and I hired a lawyer. Luckily, I had saved a little money.

"They finally reduced all the charges to illegal firing of a pistol in town and resisting arrest. I paid a $300 fine, served fifteen days in their stinking jail, and then they turned me loose, but kept my pistol, confiscated it.

"When they gave me my wallet and other belongings, the clown who pistol-whipped me came up, stuck out his paw and said, 'Well, I hope you don't have any hard feelings. I was just doing my duty.'

"I got mad all over again, so I looked him in the eye and told him coldly and plainly, 'Feller, I'm leaving Seminole and I'm never coming back, so as long as you stay here you are safe, but stay away from boom towns because if I ever lay eyes on you again, I'll probably be wearing a gun, and you can give your heart to God because your ass will be mine. I'll kill you dead.'

"He stepped back, I walked out of that jail, caught a train out of town, and I'm never going back. But, if I ever do see him, I will keep that promise, and he damn well believes that I will keep it."

Henry was a cold-eyed little blond, and *I* believed him. But he never saw the guy, never killed anyone, and lived to a ripe old age. However, he wasn't the kind to push around because he *would* hurt you.

Henry also lived at the Como. He had a room five doors down the hall from the room I shared with Red Goldman. But Henry wasn't a mixer; he stuck close to his room, drank by himself, and didn't join the lobby bull sessions. He was a real loner.

We had lots of bull sessions that winter. We would finish a well about every six days, then we would be laid off three days, "cement time." The drilling contractors couldn't afford to keep you on the payroll. They were barely staying ahead of the wolves themselves. As a result, we had very little money to poop off, and many a rainy night was spent sitting in a semicircle in front of a big open-flame gas heater in the lobby of the Como, telling lies, bragging a little—neighboring, as we called the custom.

One cold, rainy night right after supper, seven or eight of us were sitting, as usual, in front of the fire. Supper had been a big meal. Everyone's belly was full, no one felt very talkative, and it was very quiet.

Then another fellow came in. He was new to the Como Hotel, and he was a loudmouth. He paced up and down in front of the fire, pausing often to stand directly in front of the flame to warm his backside. He took over the conversation. According to him, he had been everywhere, had done everything, and had worked in all the booms. We let him ramble for awhile, but he was tiresome. Finally, a big, rough old boy named Sam Langston asked this clod, "Man, where did you come from originally?"

"Kansas, why?"

Sam gave him a slow grin and answered, "No reason really. I just thought you might be from there."

"Why did you think it?"

"Because my first old lady was from Kansas. She was a lot like you. She had the loudest mouth and the coldest ass of anybody I ever saw."

That ended it. No comment, no more loud talk, and soon he faded away to his room.

We all gave Sambo a rousing vote of thanks and enjoyed the silence again.

Winter hung on in the early part of 1932. Roosevelt had been elected. The banks closed for awhile, scaring the hell out of lots of people, but not the roughnecks, who thought that all banks did was cash payroll checks. Then the President declared the eight-hour day and threw the oil patch into a tizzy. Some drilling contractors swore they couldn't afford the eight-hour day. They threatened to shut down, which caused panic in the patch. But the banks reopened, bankers asked the contractors how they would pay for the rigs they owned, and the Texas Railroad Commission clamped proration on producers. Oil began to come up considerably above the ten-cent-per-barrel low; the contractors got a little better price per foot. They also began to modernize those old "jack-post" rigs to "unitized rigs" as they were called. Unitization lopped a full day off rig-up time, so we survived. It was a fast-moving, scary time. The oil patch hasn't been the same since, and thank God for that, because during the first twenty years of rotary drilling, changes happened with glacial slowness, and even good improvements were resisted with a ferocity that would be astounding today.

East Texas became strictly a hurry-up place. We would start rigging up on say, a Monday, then be running casing on Saturday, 3,300 feet deep, be laid off three days' cement time, drill out, tear down, move, then do it all over again.

We had lots of leisure time and very little money. Being broke was chronic, so we shared what little we had and "made do," together.

Henry got laid off. He left Kilgore soon after, and I didn't see him again for four long years. But before he left, he gave the Como Hotel a memorable night and morning. It happened this way: We were at supper one night when Henry came in with a woman in tow and they went upstairs to his room. She was a hooker, about thirty-five years old, plain looking and ill at ease. I am sure that she had heard of the ways of the Como Hotel. Henry was drunk, of course, and the scar on his forehead seemed to be on fire.

I was coming down to supper and met them and said "Hello." Henry just grunted, and I knew he was looking for trouble.

During supper, someone told Esther that Henry had taken a woman upstairs. She called her husband, Roy Owens, and told him to tell Henry to "get that damned woman out of here." Roy was a nice, slow-moving guy, who did not crave trouble with anybody, much less a man as unpredictable as Henry Mann. He told her to cool it. She got huffy and got insulting about his nerve, so he started up the stairs very slowly. I got up from the table, caught up with him, and said, "Roy, don't do it. He is drunk, mean, and ready to hurt someone. It isn't a good idea at all, but if you feel you have to do this thing, knock on the door, and if he jerks it open with a gun in his hand, just say, 'Sorry, Henry,' and leave. He won't shoot you if you talk soft."

It happened just that way. Roy came back in about three minutes and told his wife, "You almost got me killed. He is crazy drunk, so leave him alone. We will talk to him tomorrow."

The next morning at breakfast, Henry brought his lady friend down to the dining room to a dead silence. He was openly wearing that damned pistol. Both he and the woman looked pale and sick. They must really have tied one on. They ate a few bites and left. We all heaved a sigh of relief.

Henry moved out a few days later, and I was at last glad to see him go. I liked him, but he was too unpredictable for me. I had begun to think he might kill someone.

Work was slack in early 1933. The slowdown in East Texas was on and off. Spasmodic, feast or famine. It kept you uneasy and also kept you broke.

I ran into Polecat Tomlin downtown in Kilgore one day in May, and was delighted to see him. It had been a long time. He had just hired out on a job and told me that his driller was looking for a derrickman. I wasn't working, so we hunted up the driller. He hired me on the spot. Polecat and I visited a bit. We really liked each other, and I was happy to get the chance to work with him again. The location was in the Sabine River bottom, 8 miles southeast of Gladewater. We went out to rig up the next morning. It was late May, hot and humid in the river bottom, in a glade completely ringed by tall trees. There wasn't a breath of a breeze, and by 9:30 A.M. it was deathly hot and even toughened men began to suffer.

To make matters worse, the rumor was out that it was a "hot job." The man who owned the rig was drilling the well for himself, and the grapevine said he was awfully hard to get your money out of, so Polecat and I got nervous. We sure as hell didn't intend to work that hard for nothing, and it was *hard* work. Everyone really "put out," and around 11:30 that morning, one of the men sidled up to his driller and asked, "Drill, what do we take off for lunch?" The driller glared at him and said, "One glove." That's the kind of job it was.

Polecat and I talked it over and pretty well decided to quit at the end of the day. We were "spooked," felt no obligation to our driller, whom we did not know, and felt that getting another job wouldn't be hard to do.

So we decided to make the day, carry our end of the log, and drag up at quitting time, with no hard feelings between us and the driller, tool pusher, or anybody. It didn't quite work out that way.

That afternoon about two o'clock, he and I were nailing down the derrick floor with 3-by-12-inch rough sawmill lumber. We were using thirty-penny nails. I would start them with a couple of licks with a rig builder's hatchet, then Polecat finished 'em off with a 10-pound sledge hammer. It was fast, but tiring. We had finished one side when a huge 300-pound man climbed up on the floor and sat down in the corner of the derrick on an empty nail keg. We didn't know him, so we ignored him.

Shortly thereafter, a supply store salesman came up on the floor and asked, "What's the name of this outfit?" Nobody knew, so nobody answered. He then came over and stood directly in front of Polecat and asked, "Hey fellow, what's the name of this outfit?"

Polecat didn't even look up, just growled, "The In and Out Oil Company." The salesman said, "I never heard of it; what does it stand for, really?"

Polecat still didn't look up, but said, "In a hurry, and out of money!" The fat man got off the nail keg and came over; he said, "This is my outfit, and I may be in a hurry, but I'm not out of money." He hauled out a checkbook and asked, "What is your name?" Polecat told him, and he wrote him a check for one day's work. I said, "You wouldn't happen to have another check handy, would you? My name is Gerald Lynch."

He never said a word, just wrote me a check and signed it. It was on a Kilgore bank.

We finished the day, and when that bank opened the next morning, we were there. We cashed 'em, they were good, and we were the only ones who got a dime out of that job. We had some real crooks in the patch in those days, but only one Polecat Tomlin. I finally lost touch with Polecat. He just drifted out of my life. I have never seen him since July of 1933, but I've never forgotten him. He was one in a million.

Two young men moved into the Como shortly after Henry left. One of them became my roommate. Red Goldman had moved to Longview, and Esther assigned Nolan Mosher to share my big corner room. Mose was from Dallas and had worked for Otis Elevator Company until the Depression "shutdown" got his job. He had a cousin who was a drilling contractor, so Mose got a job roughnecking on one of Bert Fields' rigs. Mose was my age, twenty-four, fun to be with, easygoing, and a hell of a good roommate. We became the best of friends. In fact, Mose was the best friend I ever had. More like a brother than a friend. He was open, sunny dispositioned, gutsy, and thoroughly dependable. I have never in all the long years since met his equal.

Harvey Holmes was just *Harvey*. When they made him, they threw away the mold. He was truly unique, fearless, funny, a good companion, a bit of a minor league philosopher, and still a bit of a loner. We three, Mose, Harvey, and I, became an unbreakable trio. We all worked for different contractors, but played, drank, and ran around together. We made the honky-tonks, chased girls, enjoyed Harvey's scrapes—and the Lord knows, he got into lots of situations.

Most of those girls who worked in the tonks and dance halls were pretty nice kids. They had starved out on the farm, and the Depression made them go to work. There were very few jobs for anyone, especially girls with little education, so they gravitated to the oil fields and made a living as best they could. They were not whores, and many of them got married, mostly to roughnecks and drillers, and made good wives.

We were young and feisty, and constantly begged them to spend a night with us, as we were a fairly horny bunch. Once in a while one would. It was greatly appreciated and remembered and, of course, we always wanted an encore.

Work had picked up and the price of oil had risen, so jobs were more plentiful. The Texas Railroad Commission had prorated the field, and wells were restricted as to how much they could produce, so naturally more wells were being drilled.

It was still a hurry-up deal with everyone trying to drill 'em faster, trying to out-drill the competition. They worked us like mules, but didn't treat us as well as mules. At that time, for us, it was a frantic world. We played just as hard as we worked, then sweated the booze out the next day. We were tough people in a tough business.

There was a lady of uncertain years who ran a taxi dance hall out between Kilgore and Longview. "Mattie's Dance Hall" was famous, or infamous, all over East Texas. You brought your own booze, and she would serve you ice and setups for a modest fee. The girls would dance with you for 10 cents a dance. The dances lasted all of three minutes, so the pace was fairly fast, and a $5.00 roll of tickets didn't last too long.

Some of the girls were very pretty, and all of them were tough enough to take good care of themselves. They knew the score. With many it was fun and just a part-time thing. With others it was their only way to make a living, and it was not an easy thing. Dancing from 8:00 P.M. till 1:00 A.M. every night, with about fifty different lead-footed, for the most part, clowns, being propositioned about fifty times a night, and fending off over-amorous drunks was not a bed of roses.

Mose, Harvey, and I would manage to make Mattie's joint once a week at least. We were not very good dancers, but liked to drink and watch other people dance. There were all kinds of dancers—the slow, the fast, the acrobats, and the falling-down drunks. It was like a one-ring circus.

One of the girls at Mattie's was a slender brunette about thirty-three years old. She was an old lady to us twenty-four-year-olds, but we liked her, and she called us her "kids." When we showed up, she always managed to sit with us in a booth by the dance floor, telling us about her love life, which was varied, and some of the odd things that happened to her. She was rather pretty, especially under the colored lights, and some of the older men, forty-five to fifty, really went for her. She would go to a motel with one once in a while, and if he was appreciative and just happened to leave fifteen or twenty dollars, she would take it. She wasn't exactly selling her favors, but did think they had value.

One night she dropped down by Harvey, who had one side of the booth to himself, then said, "For God's sake, give me a drink. I'm pooped." Her first name was Johnnie, but we called her "Iron Jaw" 'cause she sure could talk rough. Harvey asked, "What's the matter, Iron Jaw? Are you slipping?" She answered, "Hell no, but I had a rough night last night. Some clod about forty-five years old, big sailing drunk, wanted to shack up. I said 'no,' he persisted, then told me it was worth fifty. My Gawd! Fifty bucks is as much as I make in a week, so I said 'yes' and we got in his car and headed for Longview. He was very loving and had roving hands. You guys know I haven't got any more boobs than a fourteen-year-old boy and wear these big old falsies. Well, we got going and he kept pulling his right arm around me and feeling that false boob, getting hornier by the minute. I'd been dancing all night and was tired, and the thought of a night with that old goat was just too much, so I said, 'Lover Boy, if you will just wait till we get to the motel, I'll pull these damn things off and you can play with 'em all night.' He said, 'I'll be damned,' then dropped that thing like it was red hot. We went on to the motel, but he had lost all his fire, and it wasn't too bad after all."

We all laughed, then told her it served her right for flaunting those gorgeous false boobs before the public. She called us a bunch of "smart asses," then went back to her dancing. She was a funny, no-nonsense sort of old girl, and we all thought a lot of her. She married some guy about six months later and went to South Texas to live. Never saw her again, but we all wished her well. She was a dandy.

East Texas was going fast and furious. I would get an occasional drilling job and would be rich for a time, then go back to roughnecking. As I said before, Mose had been working for Otis Elevator Company as an installation and repair man when the Depression hit and he got laid off and drifted into the oil fields, so he had no desire to drill, and planned to go back to Otis as soon as he could. You couldn't have run fast enough to give Harvey a drilling job; the only thing he shied away from was responsibility. The world was his oyster; life was a ball, and work was a necessary evil. The girls liked him, and lots of men did, too. He was a playboy without money, and was having a hell of a time.

Salt water was infiltrating much of the surface water in the East Texas field by then. Oil producers had their tanks, and salt water got into the creeks and ponds. Salt water is death to boilers because it foams up so much when it is hot, you couldn't tell by your sight glasses or water cocks just how much water you had in your boiler. If it fell below the crown sheet, the crown sheet would get red hot; then if cool water hit it, the boiler would blow up, in most cases killing or badly burning the fireman. Quite a few firemen got killed and many injured, and anybody using water out of Rabbit Creek had trouble getting anyone to fire their boilers. That water was especially bad, so some outfits paid a bonus to firemen, and I took one of those big-money jobs. There was a big sweet gum tree about 30 feet in front of the three boilers I was firing. I never knew exactly how much water was over the crown sheet, so I would turn on the water injector, then run like hell and get behind the tree, stay there for three or four minutes, then go on with my job. I never blew up a boiler, but began to be very nervous; then I quit at the end of the second well. We had drilled both wells without moving the boilers and when we did move, I lost my safety blanket, the tree. The man who took my place blew up the middle boiler the second day and died in the explosion. My luck had held, but I didn't crowd it again for a long time.

Even though Mrs. Owens, our landlady, ran a tight ship with her "no girls" rule, she shut her eyes to drinking, and one or two of her roomers were real lushes. One was a mean drunk, a troublemaker. He got drunk one night and came down to supper in a vile mood. Mose and I had dates that night and were dressed in our best, which wasn't much, and this clod began to pick on Mose, verbally. Mose was a husky, tough, short little man and did not suffer fools gladly. He finally told the guy to get lost or he would knock him on his ass. He quieted for a while, but just as we got up to leave, ran at Mose yelling, "I'm gonna' beat hell out of you." Mose promptly floored him and—by then, mad as hell—grabbed him by the front of his collar to jerk him to his feet, when he came out of his pocket with a knife, and cut Mose to ribbons. Harvey kicked the knife out of his hand, breaking two of his fingers, but he had cut an artery in Mose's upper arm near the armpit. I reached into the slash and grabbed that artery with my bare fingers. It was slick as glass and as tough as rubber, but I managed to stay clamped onto it until we got to the hospital, where the doctor said Mose should have bled to death. Harvey and I both gave blood, and the doctor took 240 stitches in Mose's body, and that broke up the trio for a long while.

They took the drunk to jail and charged him with assault to do bodily harm. Mose didn't have much money and he faced a long time off work. The drunk's father paid Mose $5,000, a fortune in those days, so he didn't press charges and they turned the guy loose. He left town immediately, and we never heard of him again. Harvey and I had plans for him, but we never got to carry them out, which was just as well, since neither of us really needed a jail term.

Mose went home to recuperate and spend his money, and the Rangers came to town to clean up Kilgore. The pimps, bootleggers, gamblers, and whores all left town temporarily.

The working stiffs stood around and admired the Rangers, who were led by Sergeants Gonzales and Gault. Those two men were the toughest men I ever hope to see. Manuel "Lone Wolf" Gonzales had acquired the reputation of a man who shot first and asked questions later, and was both feared and admired. Gault was a famous pistol shot. He won many medals in competition, and he, too, was admired and feared. Kilgore quieted down in a hurry, and the townspeople were happy. We were, too. The folks they had run out of town weren't loved.

I never spoke to either of those two gentlemen, though I saw them quite a few times. They didn't mingle with people, but were very businesslike. This was their second trip to Kilgore. They had been there before in the early days of the boom, before I made the scene, and they created quite a furor. They filled the jail and had to handcuff a lot of thugs to a hitch rail in front of one of the churches. The rail was about 2 1/2 feet above ground and anchored in concrete. It was made of 2-inch pipe, about 40 feet long, and was very convenient. The Rangers would handcuff one arm to the pipe, and the thug would make himself as comfortable as he could. Some would be questioned and told to leave town; some would be taken to Longview, whenever it was feasible, and put in the county jail. Wrongdoers were not pampered in those days, and they feared the Rangers like the devil feared holy water.

A story was told and retold many times, about that first Ranger foray into Kilgore. It may or may not have been true, but it added to the legend of Lone Wolf Gonzales and was generally accepted as true by the oil-field folks. They had a very high regard for the Rangers. The tale went like this: Back in 1927–28 in Wink, Texas, a young Texas Ranger was killed by a shotgun blast as he was crossing the main street. The man who shot him was rumored to be the kingpin bootlegger in West Texas. He fled and, somehow, with a lot of legal finagling, beat the rap. Pled self-defense or something, and never went back to Wink. The Rangers vowed revenge, the story said, and swore if he ever made a false move for the rest of his life, he was a dead man.

He came to Kilgore and put in a joint about 2 miles east of town, kept his nose clean and caused no trouble. When the Rangers came into town, Gonzales was pulling a horse trailer. The yarn said that he unloaded the horse, saddled him, and set out for that particular joint. He arrested the killer and his bodyguard, and made them walk to town, wading Rabbit Creek in the process, then cuffed both of them to the hitch at the church in the late morning. It began to drizzle that afternoon. Just after dark, Gonzales rode up and asked this fellow, "Heavy, are you hungry? If you are, I'll take you down to the Blackstone Cafe and feed you." That street was unpaved and muddy, and the only streetlights were three blocks away. The fellow looked down that dark street from where he was squatting in the mud, looked at those two guys, then said, "Hell, Lone Wolf, I ain't the least bit hungry!" Thus the legend grew.

We settled back to what passed for normalcy after the Law left, drilling and completing oil wells, and the work went on, day and night. Kilgore had wells drilling downtown; they even tore out four rooms from the side of the LaSalle Hotel, a wooden structure, and put up a derrick in that space. The derrickman on morning tour was the most envied guy in Kilgore. It was summer and hot, and the girls would raise their windows, pull off most of their clothes and relax when they came in from work, generally about two o'clock in the morning when the tonks closed. It must have been something to see. Anyway, *he* swore it was wonderful, and even better when they came out of the bath.

I worked on my first directional drilling job that summer. We rigged up on a vacant lot, and our target to bottom out was under a street intersection about 70 yards away. Eastman did the job, and I'm afraid I made a nuisance of myself, for the damned thing fascinated me and I asked a thousand questions. Even learned something of the technique. Most of the hands looked on it as just a queer idea of some engineer, who were all crazy anyway. One of their favorite sayings was that engineers and O rings were ruining the oil fields. O rings are actually a modern version of precision sealers or gaskets. They are all sizes and look like O's.

A little later I was on a job and saw my first Schlumberger logging truck and crew. It, too, was new to our part of the oil fields. A real wonder. The crew was French, and they pronounced the company name "Slum-beir-jay." We had no French in our vocabulary, and their English was so heavily accented that we only understood a few words. My driller was almost illiterate, so I had to make out his reports. He was damned certain that the oil fields had gone to the dogs completely, and wanted no part of those new-fangled gizmos. However, engineers and geologists were here to stay, and all of us, or at least most of us, began to smarten up a little bit. Change still came with glacial slowness. We resist better than most folks.

But we did have a communication problem with that French engineer and his crew. He despised us as a bunch of ignorant louts, and we were pretty sure he wasn't playing with all his marbles. Hell! He couldn't even speak English.

The oil field was growing up, but for some stupid reason, the contractors, drillers, and tool pushers resisted any change. They fought new techniques and clung to the old ways. Some of the old-time contractors actually resisted themselves right out of business. Others saw the light and accepted the new ways, and engineers came to be grudgingly accepted as necessary evils. The oil patch continued to evolve. We drilled 'em deeper, faster, and straighter. The instruments to define deviation from the vertical were coming into general use, and "straight hole" became a virtue—much more so than even today.

I worked through the summer in East Texas roughnecking. There were a lot of rigs from Oklahoma in East Texas then, and they thought Oklahoma drillers were the best. I was having no luck getting a drilling job, and in December, when the weather turned cold, I headed for Southern Louisiana. Blew into Morgan City, where I hired out to a Cajun driller named Louie Firman and went to firing boilers. It was a good job. I liked Louie and he liked me, and we hit it off just fine.

It was a kinfolks crew. Louie had his son-in-law, his brother-in-law, and a nephew working for him. All of them had French names, and also a peculiar habit of not calling each other by name. If one of them needed some help, he would say, "Hey-Nephew, give me a hand," or "Bro-in-law, help me here a minute." So, I fell in with them and said the same things. Inside a week, all of them, driller and all, were calling me "brother-in-law," and I carried that nickname for twenty-six years. That was a fun winter. We worked hard, it rained an awful lot, and we drove to work over corduroy roads made of logs and sometimes planks. You needed to keep your mouth firmly shut on those roads or you would chip a tooth. Those roads were really rough.

There were lots of dances, dinners, and parties, and I was invited to many of them. I got along fine with the Cajuns. They couldn't speak English "too awful pretty good," but they were delightful folks.

Came spring, came mosquitoes, gnats, and every other flying insect you could name. We were working evening tour from 4 P.M. to midnight, and after dark it was usually dreadful. If the wind blew off the Gulf towards land it was bearable. When it blew off the marsh, it was very tough. Mosquitoes came in clouds and some of those big gallinipper mosquitoes could bite through two khaki shirts. They had bug fans on the derrick floor, which helped a lot, and mosquitoes didn't bother the Cajuns too much, but I had no fans at the boilers. I wore mosquito netting over my hat and face, but I suffered. Those damn bugs were eating me alive.

The alligators were mating, too, and those old bull gators roared all night, serenading their lady loves, and you haven't really lived until you have heard a bull gator sing his love song. It ain't pretty, but it's loud.

By the last week in March I had had it. I quit and went back to Kilgore, looking as though I had smallpox. The welts went away and the memory faded, but I never went back to Louisiana to work. It's a beautiful country, but not for this old Central Texas boy.

Chapter Seven

Fading Depression, Fading Boom

I came back to Kilgore and moved back into the Como, which had become "home" to me. Mose had also come back to the Como, and we roomed together again. Harvey Holmes, the "Healdton Flash," had stayed in Kilgore and had many stories to tell us, some of them tall, all of them funny. He, Mose, and I took up where we left off, and life was fun again.

East Texas turned out to be a proving ground. Speed was of the essence, and contractors had to hustle to keep up. The major oil companies became more demanding; they wanted straighter holes, drilled more cheaply. The straight-hole instrumentation was available, and much more instrumentation, weight indicators, records, and pump gauges came into general usage; then clear water came into the picture.

Change was everywhere, and it came to stay, never to leave the patch.

Weight indicators, which used strain on the drilling line, "dead line," to register the weight of the string, and recorders to record weight on bit and rate of penetration, also came into our lives. Then we began to try to drill holes more vertically, and found that it was not an easy thing to do. Still, we somehow managed to learn to put up with "company men's" strange ideas.

It was impossible to drill a perfectly vertical hole due to the fact that a bit turned to the right and twisted the well bore into a spiral. Also, there were huge oyster and clam shells to divert the bit from the true vertical. It was generally known that most finished oil and gas wells were spiral. "Drag bits," which had four or six blades, as opposed to the old fishtails, were supposed to drill a much straighter hole, and some companies demanded a hole 3 degrees from vertical, maximum—much to the dismay of the contractors, who got paid by the foot of hole drilled, since "holding up" or keeping weight off of the bit slowed drilling up a bunch. So "boilerhousing" became a way of life on the rigs. There were many more "slope tests" run in the tool house than were actually run in the hole, but the company men got wise to that, too; they would come out at odd times, demand a slope test be run, and stay and witness the job. So the war went on, and on. It still does, to this day—not about slope tests only, but a multitude of other things, drilling mud for one. "Mudding up" slows drilling, so watering back is done and geologists raise hell about the size of the samples. But the instruments of today monitor nearly everything down hole and are pretty reliable, so boilerhousing, in general, is a dying art.

But back in the old days, weight indicators and recorders were resisted, called "tattletales," and hated with a passion. But they had come to stay, and the bitching did no good. Drilling gradually became a science, and the old days of drilling "by guess and by gosh" were gone, never to return.

I had a problem back in the East Texas boom days. I was a good driller, but had a hell of a time getting a drilling job. I was twenty-four years old, with seven years' experience, but I was slight of build, weighed about 130 pounds, was a towhead, 5 feet 8 inches tall, and looked about seventeen years old. So all the contractors called me "kid" and advised me to grow up whenever I applied for a drilling job.

I resented it, but couldn't do anything about it. I had a size 6 foot and men's shoes, smallest size was 6½. I wore boys' shoes until I was twenty-five years old. It was a joyous day when I bought my first pair of men's oxfords. I had finally arrived at man's estate, and finally began to pick up an occasional drilling job, but I was twenty-eight years old before I became a full-time driller.

I didn't worry about it much; I was too busy working and helling around. We drank a lot, made all the honky-tonks, and were well known at all the dance halls, where Mose fell in and out of love regularly. Harvey, the "Healdton Flash," was an inveterate playboy. He specialized in other men's girlfriends and was in constant hot water. But he was a tough rooster and didn't get into too many fights, mainly because he was really tough. He was a real character, had no fear of man or devil, and, more than anyone that I ever knew, fully enjoyed life.

His main girlfriend was a little "whorelady" who had two men keeping her up. One owned a barbershop, the other was a driller, and she cost them both plenty of money. She was a very lovely little brunette, one of the most beautiful women I ever saw in my life. She met Harvey at a dance one night and fell for him, so he, as he said, began to help those two guys with their "homework." It was quite a deal, and Mose and I worried about him. We were afraid somebody would kill him over her, but he would just laugh and keep right on helping 'em out.

Besides that, he had the nerve of a Mississippi riverboat gambler. One night he and the gal had a fight and she tore his shirt to shreds. The next morning she gave him one of the driller's shirts to wear home. It was a beautiful, expensive shirt. The driller who owned that shirt also lived at the Como Hotel, and he was a tough hombre. So what happened? Harvey wore the shirt to breakfast; the driller was working morning tour; he had just come in, and he sat down next to Harvey, noticed the shirt, and said, "That's a pretty shirt. I used to have one just like it." I was across the table and almost choked on my toast. Harvey never turned a hair. He just grinned and said, "Is that so? I didn't think there was another shirt like this in the whole world."

As it turned out, the guy had left the thing at the girl's house one night when both he and the gal were drunk, and couldn't find it the next morning so went home shirtless. She found it under the bed, laundered it, and intended to give it back to him, but gave it to Harvey instead. Harvey wore it out, and that poor dumb driller never knew the difference. Harvey thought it was a big joke, and we laughed about it later. Mose and I envied him; we couldn't have gotten away with that stunt.

Work was holding up well; the price of oil had gone up; Hobbs, New Mexico, was beginning to come alive; and many of the Oklahoma rigs were going back to Oklahoma. Many of the men began drifting away to other oil fields. The rigs and people who stayed were kept fairly busy, and with more prosperity instead of being chronically broke, we had more money to spend, so we spent it, rapidly.

Drilling techniques had changed, too. Instead of completing wells with a rotary rig, well-servicing rigs were coming into general usage. We were drilling the wells, setting and cementing casing, then moving the rig to a new location. Since it wasn't uncommon to drill a well and case it in five days, the work was fast and furious. Tool pushers would say, "Sixteen hours a day are yours, so use 'em as you please, but the eight hours you are on the job are *mine,* and I'm gonna get a solid eight out of you," and they did!

The rigs were more streamlined, the pumps were bigger, the drill pipe was smaller. Instead of using 6-inch OD or 5⁹/₁₆-inch pipe, 4¹/₂-inch and 3¹/₂-inch OD (outside diameter) drill pipe were commonly used. The wells were relatively shallow, 3,100 feet, so the larger, more powerful draw works made trip time much faster. Most of those rigs were strung with just four lines, and those double-barreled engines were fast. A derrickman had to be on his toes. Those blocks just flew up that derrick, and he had to latch the elevators "on the fly." The double board he stood on was just 56 feet above the derrick floor. It took six seconds for the traveling block to go that distance, and he better not miss many latches, or he was fired. The saying went, "If you can't hack it, you can't stay." Time spent on trips made the boss no money, so you hurried to get the bit back on bottom, making hole.

We had our accidents, lost fingers and toes, broke arms and legs, and got busted up in many ways, and, of course, some men were killed. There were no compensation laws then. The contractor paid your doctor bill, and maybe you got a small settlement from his insurance company, but mostly, you just toughed it out, starved for a while, then went back to work. I broke two fingers on my left hand once and never lost a day. The doctor splinted them in an aluminum case, and I just kept on working.

Nobody thought too much about it. They just accepted the good and the bad luck as usual oil-field practice, and the work went on, with or without you. I sometimes think that the hands of today would run off screaming if they had to do once what we did every day, and I wouldn't blame them. I wouldn't even think of working like that again. It was brutal. But the old-timers fully believed they were a special breed and were confident that they were equal to the task, whatever it was, and they were right. They did it, and set a pattern for the men who followed them, were vastly scornful of "weak sisters," but would help you keep up if you were a little crippled from a job injury. They then expected you to do the same thing for someone else someday. They may have been "oil-field trash," but I loved 'em and am proud to have lived it with them. They were "much man." Most of them are dead now, but they left an indelible mark on the world.

Arabia, Africa, South America, Russia, Indonesia, and everywhere in the world that oil and gas wells are drilled benefited from the know-how we so painfully acquired. America led the way and made it all possible. We still lead the way. What they know, they learned from us, and while they don't love us, they still respect our knowledge. East Texas was the pivot. What we did there colored the future. The dumb old boys from Arkansas, Oklahoma, Texas, Louisiana, and New Mexico, fresh off the farms and ranches and with a few city slickers thrown in, made the oil fields go, and go they have. I'm glad I had a small part in those goings-on; it was a lot of fun.

Things changed with slowness. The motto for years was "Stick with the old, the tried and true, and distrust anything that's new." The contractors and company drilling superintendents liked things as they were. They hated change and what they called smart alecks. Drillers who were innovators kept their secrets to themselves and used their knowledge to outdo other drillers. I remember an old boy I worked derricks for in the days when drilling with "rotary mud" was the thing to do. Rotary mud, so called, was formed by drilling through Bentonitio and sticky shale formations. It was usually heavy with dissolved solids, gray in color, viscous, and slowed drilling rates a lot. But it "walled" the hole and was considered vital to a good, trouble-free operation. The fact that it was often a troublemaker, especially when drilling through what was then called "gumbo," was ignored. Then the bits would ball up, and sometimes had to be pulled out of the hole to clean them, a practice both time-consuming and costly.

This old driller (he was about forty-five years old) had somehow discovered that water, the thinner the better, was the best thing to drill with, and used that knowledge to out-drill any driller who ran tour opposite him. Since drillers were rated by the amount of hole they made each day, he was sought after and always had a job—no small feat in that day.

The twelve-hour day was still in effect when I worked for him.

My first day on the job, he asked me, "Kid, can you keep your mouth shut?" I said, "I sure can keep my mouth shut." Then he said, "Go down and taste the water in the ditch; if it ain't fittin' to drink, it ain't fittin' to drill with."

I took the hint, jetted the pits half empty, then turned a big stream of water into them. Drilling picked up almost immediately, and he drilled up a storm for about eight hours. Then, about four hours before relief time, he called me over to the brake and told me to cut out the water going to the pits, grinned a slow grin, and said, "We had better clabber up that mud a bit, or old John might make as much hole as we have drilled."

I never told anyone our trick, but neither did I ever forget it. It stood me in good stead later, when I began to drill.

Men like that were rare. They kept their secrets and stayed far ahead of most of their rivals, the ones who "went along to get along."

Still, inch by inch, progress crept into the drilling business, and in my fifty-eight years of perspective, I am amazed at the changes time has wrought.

It was the spring of 1934. East Texas was slowing down, and we had to drive greater distances to work. Rigs were scattered, and many "edge" wells were being drilled. Still, work was plentiful and we were seldom "on the grass." We made pretty good money and were not often broke.

The honky-tonks were still plentiful. Dance halls were sometimes hiring big-name bands, Ben Bernie, Glen Gray, and others, and night life was as active as ever. We all needed to relax. To put it bluntly, we played a great deal.

Mose, Harvey, and I had acquired the reputation of "top hands." We were all working days, a prized job. I even turned down a few morning and evening tour drilling jobs because they would interfere with my social life. We were having the time of our lives. Lots of drinking, dancing, and general hell raising. I was, and am, a terrible dancer, but I held the girls tightly while they danced and got along fairly well, or at least I thought that I did.

In early May that year, Glen Gray brought his orchestra to Kilgore, a Saturday night date at the Casa Loma dance hall, about 2 miles out of town on the Gladewater Highway. Everybody who wasn't working planned to attend. Big bands were a real treat, and Gray had a good third-rate band.

I was nearing my twenty-sixth birthday, footloose and fancy free, and the world was my oyster. I did not have a dime saved and didn't know any particular reason why I should save one. I could work as much as I pleased, and the "rainy day" everyone talked about seemed as though it would never materialize. All in all, I felt very cocky.

Mose and I bought tickets to the dance, blowing almost two days' pay, since they cost $10. We didn't take dates either because we figured that there would be plenty of girls in attendance. The girls were plentiful all right, and it looked like a real big night.

We had a bottle of whiskey, "bottled in the barn," real corn likker, that was about 100 proof. We had had a few nips, and after we were seated in our booth, took a few more. I wasn't really drunk, but wasn't feeling any pain and looked forward to one fine night.

A man and two girls came in and took a booth across from us about 25 feet away, and Mose turned to me and said, "I know one of those girls. I went to school with her. She got married about six years ago and moved to Shamrock, Texas, but the guy she's with isn't the one she married."

He got up, went over, and said "hello" to the trio. Sure enough, he did know the girl, and the man *was* her husband. She had been divorced and remarried, so they invited me over to get acquainted and, of course, I went. The other girl was a slender ash blonde with hazel eyes, and very pretty. Her name was Amy, and I thought she was lovely, but I was just drunk enough to be a little too loud, and when I asked her to dance, she gave me a very cold look and said, "I don't like to dance with drunks." That shut me up, and I also began to sober up, too. But after two more tries and two more refusals, as she was dancing with another fellow, I told Mose, "I'm leaving, and besides, I don't think I like that damned blonde with the ribbon in her hair."

Mose just grinned and said, "Go ahead. I'll stay awhile. The night is still young. Besides, I see a little redhead that I'm gonna try to spend the night with tonight."

I left, went to the hotel and went to bed. I wasn't very happy with the way the night had turned out and wasn't too proud of myself. It had been a bad deal.

Mose showed up at breakfast, a little worse for the wear, as he had spent the night with the redhead. He said, "That blonde that scalded you last night said you might be all right when you were sober. Maybe you could date her. She is staying with a married sister, and I know where the sister lives."

I was interested, called on her at her sister's, made a date, took her to dinner and the movies. We hit it off well, and after a few very circumspect dates, I began to court her in earnest.

She was a widow, two years out of an unhappy marriage. She was managing a magazine crew that traveled everywhere selling magazine subscriptions. She had two other girls working for her, and they were halfway on vacation, just selling a few subscriptions each day and visiting her sisters. She had three living in East Texas.

She was wary. Her first husband had been a woman chaser, and he had made her damned suspicious of men. I began to think of marriage, but she shied away from the idea. I was getting nowhere fast and began to think I was spinning my wheels, but then she began to stretch her so-called vacation. The other two girls joined another crew and moved on, but she lingered. Her father had just moved to Joinerville, about 20 miles south of Kilgore. She spent a week or two with him, and either she drove to Kilgore or I went to Joinerville nearly every night. Things were looking pretty good, from my viewpoint.

This situation rocked on for about three months. She was hesitant and cold to marriage, and I didn't like the idea of this deal continuing for the next year or two, so things were at a stalemate.

I got offered a job with a drilling company in Houston—an 8,000-foot well, which was deep in those days. Wanting to bring matters to a head, I took the job, told Amy goodbye, and said if she ever got to Houston to call me. She said she would, and I left town.

The job was just so-so, but I had never worked on a well that deep and enjoyed the experience. We were drilling in the Pierce Junction field southwest of Houston—at that time, a few miles out of town. That drilling is mostly shale, and the rate of penetration was just fair, because we were "mudded up," mostly because the unconsolidated shales in that area were known to slough or, as drillers spelled it, "sluff." Anyway, they would stick the drill pipe, causing costly "washover" jobs. It was interesting work, and I learned more about various drilling techniques.

I had been working about two weeks when Amy called me. She was in town and wanted to see me, so we went to dinner, then to her hotel room, and she finally said "yes," but if it didn't work out, she didn't want to be tied too tightly, so we began a trial marriage, rented an apartment, and set up housekeeping.

I suppose I was tired of being a bachelor. Anyway, I took to marriage, thought it was fine, and have never changed my mind. The nine years helling around the oil patch had matured me a lot, and I was ready to settle down. We were both in love and very, very happy. I took a great deal of rough kidding on the job, but didn't mind at all, because when you are young and happy, everything is nice. Even Houston in July.

It was a very hot summer, the summer of '34. The hurricane season came early, the humidity was around 90 percent, and it was before the days of air conditioning. We had an upstairs apartment on South Fannin Street with a sleeping porch, and with a fan, it was bearable, just barely. I got down to 124 pounds, and being newly married didn't help me gain weight. I sweated more that summer than ever before or since. To this day the very thought of living in Houston gives me cold chills.

But we were young, and it didn't seem at all bad. I was working days, got home each afternoon about five o'clock, and we adjusted to married life pretty well.

Mose showed up in Houston in August. He said East Texas was slowing down. We had a two-bedroom apartment, and he stayed with us. Took a job with the afternoon-tour driller on the rig I was working on, and we both enjoyed having him back with us. Mose was the dearest friend I ever had. He and Amy liked each other and joked and teased each other a lot. He called her "Tish" for some obscure reason, and since she was a fanatically "clean" housekeeper, kept telling her that sanitation could be a vice, too.

We had a hurricane that late August. It almost blew Freeport away. We had knee-deep water all around the rig that afternoon when we waded out to the car, which had been parked on a paved, raised road about 1½ miles away, during the lull when the "eye" passed over. Got home just as the wind came back up, and rode it out. It was my first and last hurricane and I never want to see another one. That one scared the devil out of me. When rain comes at you sideways and stings like sleet, it "ain't fittin' out fer man or beast." The storm blew out that night, but left its mark on Houston. Signs blown around, windows blown out, and trees lying across residential streets. We decided that if another hurricane warning was posted, we would get the hell out of Houston.

The storm shut down the rig, and we were off work. I took Amy to Corsicana to meet my family. She had never met any of them and was a little nervous. I was, too, since I had not written home, nor told anyone at home that I was married. Mose rode with us as far as Corsicana, then took an interurban car on to his home in Dallas.

Mother gave Amy and me a coolish reception, since a wife was a big surprise. She asked me all sorts of questions about Amy and her family. I answered as best I could, since I did not know Amy's family any too well. But my stepfather and two sisters at home hit it off immediately with Amy. It made things easier during our visit, which, due to Mother's attitude, was a bit strained. We stayed three days; then the company called and said the water had drained off the drilling location and they were ready to start the rig up again, so we loaded up and left. Mose had come down the day before from Dallas. He made a big and lasting hit with my family. Even Mother was taken with him, and my stepfather, Mr. Andy, was fond of him, too. All in all, it was a fairly successful visit, though I don't think Mother ever completely forgave me for not marrying a hometown girl.

Anyway, Mr. Andy gave us a 50-pound sack of stone-ground cornmeal and 20 pounds of dried pinto beans he had raised to take home with us, and they sure came in handy later. We got back to Houston okay, and went back to drilling, and things returned to normal, except that the owner of the drilling company had gone to Europe on vacation with his family. He had not empowered anyone to sign checks, and consequently we couldn't get paid. It wasn't bad when we missed the first payday, but by the time the second one came and went without a check, things began to get difficult. We still had a little, a very little, money left, but had no credit established anywhere, since we had always paid cash for everything we purchased.

Mose hocked his watch, I hocked mine, and Amy still had a few subscription cards left, so she got out and sold some magazines. Three paydays went by without a dime in pay. Mose and I were mad as hell, but couldn't do anything about our anger. We had resolved to quit as soon as we got paid, but it had begun to look as though we never would get paid.

We ran out of everything except coffee, pinto beans, and cornbread. We ate beans and cornbread morning, noon, and night. Believe me, you can get real tired of them after a week. Amy and Mose took the deprivation much better than I did. I'm Irish, and the Black Moods descended upon me. One day in the fourth checkless week, we drove out to LaPorte. Mose and Amy waded in the bay and splashed around like two kids, but I sat in the car and sulked and brooded. I wasn't very pleasant to be around, but they seemed to understand.

The boss came back. His brother was pushing tools and said he would have the checks at the rig the next day, but he never showed on our tour of duty. By quitting time, I was beside myself with anger, and when we got to town, Mose and I walked out to the pusher's house, a good 2^1/$_2$ miles. We rang the doorbell and, when he came to the door, demanded our money. He then told us that he never paid hands at his home, but I jerked the door out by the roots, latch and all. We grabbed that portly gentleman by the arms and informed him that he was going to have a brand new experience; either we got our checks, right then, or we stomped a mudhole in his ass. We got the checks, walked back to town, cashed the checks at a grocery store, got Amy, bought some gas, went nightclubbing, ate dinner at a good restaurant, and got about two-thirds drunk. Amy drove the car, since she wasn't drinking, and said later that she felt sure we were all crazy. Maybe we were, but we still had enough sense to pay everything we owed and get out of town. We went back to Kilgore, and I've never been fond of Houston since that day. The Gulf Coast is fine, but not my cup of tea. I had three hitches there, and all three ended unpleasantly.

I went to work for DeArman Bros., a drilling contracting firm. Mr. Ed DeArman and his brother owned three rigs and were one of the best small contract drilling firms in East Texas. They sent us to Fairfield, Texas, to drill a wildcat gas well. There was a small gas field about 2 miles from where we were supposed to drill, and the wells were, for that day and time, very high-pressure wells.

We laid a 2-inch line from our location through the Piney Woods to one of those completed wells to obtain gas to fire our boilers. That was the largest Christmas tree on that well any of us had ever seen. It was about 8 feet tall, had three master gate valves and double wing valves, and the pressure gauge read 4,500 pounds per square inch. We were all leery of it, but the company switcher who operated the well showed us how to regulate the pressure down to 100 pounds so we wouldn't blow up our 2-inch line. We took off from one side of the tree; used five regulators, in sequence, to reduce the pressure to 100 pounds; hooked the line into the last regulator; and I very slowly opened the master gates and wing gates. Everything looked fine until a summertime hand, a college student from Clemson, took a notion to lift the weighted control arm on the first regulator, throwing the full 4,500 pounds on the next regulator, which was only weighted to 3,000 pounds. The pressure went through the rest of those regulators like a dose of Epsom Salts; that old 2-inch line we had just laid began to crawl all over the place, then blew in two pieces, about half a mile from us. I dived for the master gate and closed it faster than I ever have closed a valve before or since. It isn't easy to close a gate valve against high pressure, but I was scared to death and didn't even think about it. After all the noise died down and we all quit trembling, we started down the line to see how much damage had occurred. It was awful; small trees had been slashed off; the line had whipped itself around the big trees and was in about thirty pieces. All this occurred in less than one minute. Believe me, it was a good thing everyone there was fully grown, because the fright we had endured would have stunted growing boys.

We sent the college student back to Tyler because we thought he might yet kill someone, for he had too much curiosity and not enough caution. We heard later that he was studying for the ministry, and there was no doubt that the good Lord was on his side, because we had thought of killing him when he blew up that line. I hope he made a good preacher, because he was a lousy roughneck.

We drilled that well without incident and moved to Longview. Amy and I had never lived in Longview and had trouble finding a decent place to rent. We finally rented a raw, new shotgun house in a so-called court. The old boy who owned that court had pared those little places down to the bare essentials: a bed, a stove, a table, four chairs, a sink, and an outside bathhouse. Not a cupboard or any kind of storage whatsoever, and you could take it or leave it, and we took it. I was working evening tour, from 4:00 P.M. to midnight. The crew picked me up at 3:15 and I went to work, leaving Amy with our few household goods on the floor of the cabin.

Amy's dad was a carpenter, and she had learned a lot from him as she grew up. She had our car, and we were in fairly good shape money-wise, so she took the car, bought some lumber, and began to upgrade that cabin.

When I got back to that little house that night, the crew let me out of the car, and one of the men said, "I hear someone hammering." Sure enough, he did, and it was coming from my new abode. I knocked, and Amy asked, "Who is it?" I told her and she let me in. It was hot and humid, and she was stripped to panties and bra and was busy building a cupboard and shelves in the kitchen, wringing wet with sweat, and determined to finish that night. I jumped in and helped. By 2:00 A.M., we were finished and both took a shower and went to bed. Life wasn't too easy in boom towns, but those shelves and that cupboard helped a bunch, even though we only lived there two months.

Jobs played out fast in those days. We drilled four wells in the Longview area, then moved back to Kilgore. Found a pretty nice little four-room house, and for a wonder it was decently furnished. I took a daylight drilling job.

I was drilling for a one-rig contractor. The firm name was King and Stegall. I never saw Stegall, but King, first name Bill, pushed tools. He was a pretty good well man, and they were doing very well, even though they were new to contracting. I liked the job, and we drilled several wells without any trouble and made good time on each one.

I was enjoying drilling days. Even then, in 1935, the daylight driller was the lead-off man.

The morning-tour driller had a fireman called Shorty. If he had any other name, I never heard it. The little fellow, and he *was* short, was a very good fireman, but was totally illiterate; couldn't even read figures. We marked the pressure gauges on each boiler at the desired working pressure and, believe it or not, Shorty kept that pressure very, very close to the mark.

The locomotive-type boilers in use in those days had two holes drilled in the crown sheet at the top of the firebox. These holes were threaded to accept a plug. The center of these two plugs was full of babbitt, a metal with a much lower melting point than steel. It was a safety device. If the water level in the boiler dropped below the crown sheet and it would begin to overheat, the babbitt would melt and steam would spray into the firebox and put out the fire, thus preventing damage to the boiler and saving life, too, as firemen were often killed when a boiler blew up.

The plugs were called "soft" plugs and really worked very well. They saved many boilers from blowing up and saved many men from injury and sudden death.

On this particular well, we were using "live oil" as boiler fuel. This was high-quality crude oil, and was almost as volatile as gasoline, and it was housed in a 100-barrel tank about 50 yards from the boilers on a slight hill.

Our water for the boilers was contained in an earthen tank just about 35 feet in front of the three boilers, which was filled by pumping water from a small creek about a quarter-mile away. The contractors did not have a steel tank for water.

One morning when we arrived at the job, we were faced with real disaster. The boiler shed was burned down, the 3-by-12-inch board where the lights were placed across the front of the boilers was burned, and there had obviously been a big fire all around the boilers. Everyone's work clothes, which had been drying on a line hung between the boilers, were burned up as well, and it looked like a cross section of hell. Bill King, the pusher, and the morning-tour crew were trying to bring some order to things. The rig was shut down and the boilers were dead, of course, but the driller had managed to pull the bit about 40 feet off bottom before he ran out of steam.

I asked, "What in the hell happened?" and Bill King said, "That idiot pumping oil ran the oil tank over, and oil ran down the hill and got in the water supply pit. Shorty couldn't see the oil in the dark and pumped some oil into the middle boiler when he replenished the water in the boiler. When the plugs melted, hot live oil instead of steam went into the firebox and everything caught fire. Thank God, nobody got killed."

I asked Shorty how he felt when the plugs blew, and he said, "Hell, Gerald, I didn't have time to think, but I'll tell you one thing, I had more fire *around* those little bastards for awhile than I've ever been able to get *in* them."

Shorty was lucky he hadn't gotten burned. If he had been in front of that boiler when the plugs went, he would have been instantly killed when the fire belched out the firebox door. At the very least he could have gotten badly burned, but the little devil hadn't even scorched an eyebrow. The boilers were manifolded together, and steam from the other two boilers had put the fire out.

We fired up the two good boilers and got back to drilling. Bill got the boilermakers to check the middle boiler, which turned out to be undamaged. Then we put it on the line and tried to make up for lost time. Profit margins were very thin in those days. As for the danger, it was over, and everyone forgot it. Just another crazy incident in an altogether crazy business.

We finished that well without any more trouble, then moved the rig about 10 miles south of Kilgore on a well being drilled by the Kilgore Refinery. They had a good deal of production and refined their own oil, as well as other people's. They were just starting a new drilling program, and King and Stegall were happy to get a chance to drill a well for them.

I am Irish and also prone to be quick-tongued. It had gotten me in trouble before, and did so again on this well. On about the third day, after we spudded this well, I relieved the morning-tour driller a few minutes late, and he left in a hurry, quite irritated. I was irritated, too. My derrickman had overslept, causing us to be late to work.

I was at the brake, drilling ahead, and the other driller hadn't told me how deep we were or anything else—just said, "Here it is; I'm in a hurry," got in his car, and left without telling me the score.

Just about the time everything settled down, I decided to go ahead and make the kelly down before I shut down to service the rig, to grease up, when a big black Cadillac drove up to the rig. The driver stayed in the car, and a boy about twelve years old got out, came up through the tool house, and out to me at the brake.

He didn't say "Good morning" or introduce himself, just said very abruptly, "Driller, what are you drilling in?" I looked at that kid pretty sharply, but did answer him. I said, "Sonny, I'm drilling in a man's cornfield."

He glared at me and said, "You don't know very much, do you?" And I glared back and said, "No I don't, but I do know not to ask a busy man a bunch of damn fool questions." He whirled around, went back to the car, got in, and the car drove away.

The driver of that car was the owner of the Kilgore Refinery and the kid was his son, and the upshot was that Papa told Bill King to get rid of his day driller. Poor Bill didn't have much choice. He needed to keep that rig working, so he let me go. He eventually went broke, but I didn't cause it because I was long gone. Bill drilled for me later at Odessa when I was pushing tools. We stayed friends.

I just never had the proper reverence for employers, and I'm sure it hurt me in many ways, but I'm still that way. I'm just not a hero worshipper. If a man asks me what I think, I tell him, and it often isn't what he wants to hear.

I worked through the late summer and fall around East Texas. Things were slow, but so many rigs and hands had gone elsewhere, jobs were reasonably plentiful. But in early December of that year, 1935, I let a fellow talk me into going to Hobbs, New Mexico, with him. He was a driller I knew slightly, and told me if I went with him, when we got to Hobbs he would be given a tool pushing job and would then hire me as a driller. I took him up on the deal, not really believing it, as I was bored with East Texas.

We went to Hobbs in our car, and Curley, the driller, rode with us, which should have warned me.

The weather was rainy and cold when we left Kilgore, but just barely freezing, and was fairly typical for that time of year in East Texas. The further west we went, the colder and drier it became.

We got into Hobbs and checked into a small hotel. Got up the next morning and started up the street going west to a cafe for breakfast. Amy had on a light coat and I a short light jacket. The sun was bright, and we were on the north side of the street. It seemed quite cool, but not unpleasant, until we came to the first street crossing. The wind was brisk, out of the north, and we nearly froze getting across the street. We hurried to the cafe, rushed inside, and I asked the cashier how cold it was, and she said 10 degrees above zero. It was our first experience with dry, very cold, sunny weather, and we both immediately bought some heavier clothing. I got ready to go to work. We were on afternoon tour. Amy took the car and started to look for an apartment. The hotel we had checked into was strictly a fourth-rate one, and we intended to move out of it as quickly as possible.

Chapter Eight

Hard Rock Drilling in Hobbs and Oklahoma City; Leaving East Texas

I went to work that first night, completed the first tour, got back to the hotel about 1:30 in the morning, knocked on the door of our room, and Amy asked in a shaky voice, "Who is it?"

I said, "Your husband. Let me in, I'm cold." She answered, "Wait a minute," and I heard her moving furniture around, which was a real surprise to me; Amy was not a timorous soul.

When the door opened, I could see that she had pushed the small dresser up against the door, and that was what she had to move to let me in the room.

I asked her, "What is the matter? Are you afraid?"

She said, "A little, but mostly I am angry."

The room we had rented in that little hotel had just been vacated by a very popular whore. She had left suddenly, and her clients had been trying to get into that room all evening. Amy had barricaded herself in and cussed a few of the men out, but was a bit frightened since some of the guys persisted.

I went up and had a heart-to-heart talk with the night clerk of the hotel. I told him the next clown who knocked on our door would earn him a fat lip, to fend those people off, and that ended the harassment.

I was roughnecking, which was the agreement: that I would fire the boilers until Curley's pushing job showed up. Amy and I had already decided we had been flimflammed, but since we were in New Mexico, we intended to find out all we could about the town and working conditions, knowing we could always go back to East Texas and work.

That rig had three things on it that I had never seen before: wind walls around the derrick floor, a motor shed, and a water softener at the boilers.

The fireman that I relieved showed me how to service the water-softening unit, and said that the water in that area was so hard and carried so many minerals that it formed thick scale in the boilers very rapidly. When the flues and hull of a boiler become thickly coated with scale, the efficiency of that boiler is greatly reduced, more fuel is used, and the boiler doesn't function at all well, hence the water softener. I was interested. I've always had a lot of curiosity about new things, and that damned softener was new to me.

It was a cold December, and the thermometer stayed well below freezing for most of the month. Amy was having no luck at all finding a place to live. We were awfully tired of that dingy little hotel and began to think of going back to Kilgore. Hobbs had boomed and faded several times, but was on a boom then. It was a raw, rowdy, uncurried town. Prices were high, it was cold as the devil, and we couldn't find a decent place to live. I was still sore at Curley for lying to me about that job, and let him know it. It didn't make for pleasant working relations. We were barely speaking to each other.

Amy and I ran into Harvey Holmes' old girlfriend downtown in Hobbs one day—the one who tore his shirt off that time, long ago in Kilgore. She had married a rig builder and moved to Hobbs, and when she heard that we were thinking of returning to Kilgore, she offered to sell us her little house there. It was a pretty little three-room place, and she said we could have it for $300 cash.

It took all of forty seconds for us to make up our minds. We bought that little house, then and there. We felt lucky. The house was furnished, too, which made it a real bargain.

I quit my job the next day. Curley and I got into an argument about a gas line valve about a mile from the rig. The valve off the main line kept freezing and pinching down the supply to the boilers. Curley said it was my job to keep it working, and my Irish boiled over. I told him one of the roughnecks could at least help, that I couldn't keep up steam, and run a mile to work that damned valve. One word led to another, and I checked it to him. Since I was driving that day, I refused to let him ride to town with me. He was pretty unhappy about no ride, but I told him it would be after the fight, if he rode with me, and he decided not to try me. I don't, to this day, know how he got to town, but I saw him later in Illinois, when he was broke and hungry.

Amy and I checked out of that little hotel the next morning and headed for Kilgore. We had been in Hobbs one month and both agreed that it wouldn't have been a bad place if we could have found a place to live. Hobbs wasn't building; it had boomed and died before and nobody wanted to invest in rental property.

I had learned one thing, for sure, on this foray into the Permian Basin. The work was easier because this was "hard rock drilling," quite different from the predominantly shale or "snowbank" drilling in Central, East, and South Texas. Snowbank drilling was faster, and easier on the rigs, but hard rock drilling was easier on the hands. I liked the idea of easy work, and I liked the country. The climate was different, cold and dry in winter, hot and dry in summer, but dry nearly all of the time. We would have stayed probably, but housing was practically nonexistent, and we had bought a house in Kilgore.

We stopped off in Corsicana December 24, 1935, Christmas Eve, spent Christmas with my family, then went on to Kilgore. I was awfully glad to be back on familiar grounds, and we loved the little house we had bought. It was about ten blocks from downtown, and there was a small park just across the street. There were a few other houses on that block, but it was a quiet neighborhood, not a thickly settled street, and we had few neighbors.

However, Kilgore was definitely on the downgrade as far as drilling was concerned. The boom was gone. Most of the drilling was "inside" locations, and I found that a great many of the people that I knew had also left town. Harvey had gone back to Oklahoma. We never heard from him, or of him, again, but I have never forgotten him for all these many years. He was a "oner," and both Amy and I remembered the fun it was to be around him. Mose was leaving also. He was going back to his first love, the elevator business. Otis Elevator had begun to hire people back, and the Depression was fading away, so I was the only one of the original trio left. Amy and I had a good winter through January, February, and into April. Then work began to really slow up, and I was only working about half the time. If we hadn't owned that little house, we would have been in trouble. Money was scarce, and we did not have very much saved. We hung on, since we didn't want to leave Kilgore. I even spaded up a pretty good sized plot in the backyard and planted a garden. Even toyed with the idea of taking a job in "production" as opposed to "drilling," but drilling was in my blood and I couldn't make myself take a pumping or gauging job.

There was a strange little interlude that happened about that time. I had snagged a drilling job on a well just about one mile above the Gladewater-Longview Highway. We were working daylights, and each afternoon when we got off work, we would stop and drink a beer at a joint on that highway. It was on the way home, and the old girl who ran it was known to all the crew. She was a big, blowsy blonde, known all over East Texas as "Crying Blanche." She got tearful when drunk, and she drank every day. We teased her a lot about carrying the world's woes on her shoulders.

One day when we stopped, a slim, plain, small girl waited on us. She had no banter, just took our order, then served us, silently. Blanche called her Nelda, and she stayed and worked about three weeks, but never joked with the boys, who quit trying to kid with her. She was very quiet, and if some fellow tried to flirt, she would just walk away from him.

She left as she came. One day we stopped and she was gone. We paid no attention. Girls came and went fast around beer joints.

One day months later, two friends and I stopped by Blanche's Place to have a beer. Blanche was bawling loudly. She was really letting out all the stops.

I asked, "Blanche, what in the hell has happened?"

She kept blubbering, but said to me, "Do you remember little Nelda who worked here a while back?"

"I think so, vaguely. Wasn't she the silent one?"

"That's right, you do remember. Well, she is dead. The 'Law' just shot her and Clyde to rags over in Louisiana."

I said, "Her and who?"

"Clyde Barrow, that's who, and she was such a sweet little girl. She just got mixed up with a bad bunch of friends. Oh, boo hoo!"

I couldn't believe it. That little girl was Bonnie Parker. She had been on the run with Barrow and had stopped off with Blanche to rest up a bit. She surely didn't look like an outlaw. She looked like somebody's kid sister!

Oklahoma City boomed that spring. The famous "Capitol boom." They even drilled a well on the Capitol grounds, and most of the rigs were running right in the middle of residential neighborhoods. A frantic, wild, and woolly boom in the very center of a good-sized city.

A man I knew wrote me a letter asking me to come up to Oklahoma and take a job firing boilers. You had to have a steam engineer's license to fire boilers inside the city limits, and in order to get a license, you had to take a fairly rigid oral and written exam. Lots of good, competent firemen were failing that examination, mostly because they didn't have enough education to really understand some of the written questions, and could not express themselves on paper.

Leon Farmer, the man who wrote to me, was an old "Yellow-heel" from Corsicana. He and I had worked together many times, and he said the job paid a little more than a derrick job, and you couldn't leave the boilers, which made a very cushy job. His fireman had failed the test and he was desperate for a fireman. I wasn't working, so Amy and I talked it over and decided I should take the job, because work around Kilgore was sure to slow down even more than it was then, and it was painfully slow.

Work in East Texas did not come to a full stop. Wells continued to be drilled for several more years. Many roughnecks and drillers had bought homes there and settled down to stay, boom or no boom. They figured that even if they were only able to work part time, they would be better off than if they moved with the rigs.

I was tempted. We owned our house and I felt confident that I could stay tolerably busy, but wanderlust got us again, and I decided to take the firing job for Leon. I have often wondered what would have happened to Amy and me, had we kept on living in Kilgore.

A funny thing happened just before I left Kilgore. I ran into the sheriff of Van Zandt County in downtown Tyler. He was attending some sort of lawman's convention. He was my old poker-playing friend from Canton, had been re-elected, we were glad to see each other, and he had a story to tell me.

We went into a cafe, drank a cup of coffee, and he asked me if I knew a driller from Corsicana named Pen Spencer. I told him that I surely did know Penny, that, in fact, he was a friend of mine. He said that Pen and his wife were driving along a country lane somewhere between Lindale and Canton. They were returning to Corsicana from Gladewater. Pen had drilled a well there and Mrs. Spencer had gone to Gladewater with him. They took that secondary road, hoping to find some produce for her to take home and can for the winter.

Two boys in a souped-up, glossy Ford coupe passed them, then slowed down to about 10 miles per hour. The road was narrow, with a fairly steep barrow ditch on each side. Pen pulled out to re-pass the Ford, and the boy who was driving pulled over in front of him, so that Pen couldn't get by the Ford. They played that game for 10 solid miles, while Mrs. Spencer's blood pressure rose higher and higher. Those two young men thought it great sport, and it was obvious that they had done this trick many times before that day.

Pen finally passed them, and jerked his 1934 model Chevrolet crossways across the road, bringing those kids to a sudden halt. They jumped out of their car, ready for battle, just as Penny came out of his car with a 2 1/2-pound ballpeen hammer in his right hand. He hit the boy in front on the meaty part of his left shoulder, knocking him down. The boy began yelling that his arm was broken, but he scrambled out of Pen's way, and the second boy turned and ran. Pen had gone berserk. He ran over to their shiny Ford and began beating on it with his hammer. He knocked out the headlights, tail lights, windshield, and side glass, drove big dents into the body, and then threw up both sides of the hood and beat hell out of the motor. The boy with the lame shoulder who owned the car was crying and begging Penny to stop, but Pen just said, "Let me get in reach of you and I'll beat your damn skull in. You little bastards are a menace."

He finished, got in his car, and drove into Canton—went to the sheriff's office and told him what happened out on the road, what he had done, and where those two kids were stranded.

That sheriff told Pen that he knew those kids; that one's father was a banker in Wills Point, who had spoiled the boy; to go on home to Corsicana; and that he, the sheriff, would go find the boys, take them home, and hope they had learned their lesson.

Pen soothed his wife, who was *very* upset, and then went home. He never heard from the sheriff, and assumed everything was okay.

The sheriff said those kids were still scared when he found them. The one lad's shoulder was not broken, but had a huge purple bruise on it. The car was a total wreck, and they never tried to pull that harassment stunt again. He closed the books on the caper and said the country needed more citizens like Mr. Spencer.

I laughed and went back home. I never saw that sheriff again, but he was a hell of a man.

I caught a ride to Oklahoma City, leaving the car for Amy to use, since we did live some distance from downtown. There were many fellows going to Oklahoma City, and if you helped to pay expenses, a ride was easy to obtain.

The examination was not really hard. I made 96 on the written test and got my license. The job was a breeze: new, big boilers and a large boiler shed. I could not go 30 feet from the boilers, so I had a lot of leisure time. We were still on the 4:00 till midnight tour and were about ten blocks north of the Capitol building. I had the afternoon newspaper delivered to the boiler shed, and the Good Humor Man always stopped. It was the damndest job I ever had. A fellow I knew well named Dexter Hoover was firing a set of boilers about two blocks east of our rig. He carved and painted an elaborate checkerboard on the bench in his boiler shed and ran a nonstop checker game. He was a really good player, and roughnecks and drillers from rigs around him were constantly challenging him.

They had moved a house so they could erect our derrick. The lady who had once lived there had nice flower beds. It was funny to watch the roughnecks watering and weeding the flowers, but they took care of the flowers and really raised some beautiful roses. There never was a boom to equal that one. It was totally different. Roughnecks were even riding streetcars to work, and housing was plentiful; apartments were easy to find and were nicely furnished. All in all, it was an oil-field worker's dream.

EXCEPT: The weather. It was a hot, dry summer, with high humidity, but no rain. Amy had come up about three weeks behind me, and we had rented a very nice two-bedroom apartment on Northwest 23rd Street, in a fairly large apartment building. It was only about a mile from my job, which made it nice. She could drive me to work and still have use of our car.

But this was long before the days of air conditioning, and the heat was ferocious. People were leaving their houses at night and sleeping in the parks and on the front lawns. Water was rationed: no watering of trees, flowers, or lawns. Trees were dying in the esplanade on Classen Boulevard, and the heat held on, day and night. We had two large electric fans, but about all they did was stir the hot air around. People talked about the summer of '36 for years afterward in Oklahoma.

But if memory serves me correctly, we made it pretty well. Two good friends of ours, Herman and Stella Griffen, lived not far away. They were about ten years older than Amy and I were, but I had known Herman for many years, had worked for him several times, and he, too, was a "Yellow-heel." They had recently adopted a tiny baby girl; Stell's health was a bit fragile at that time, so we kept the baby a lot of the time. Amy had a wonderful time with the child and thoroughly enjoyed keeping her. The little girl was about fourteen months old and it was a full-time job keeping up with her. Kay, the baby, was a joy to all of us. She was a lively handful.

Oklahoma City was an oil-field town, as well as the state capital. It was a hell of a fine town to work in. We drilled wells in residential sections of town. It was noisy and was bound to be a big nuisance, but there was practically no friction between us and the townspeople. I have worked out of Oklahoma City twice and still remember it as one of, if not *the* best town in the U.S.A. to work in. There are very few that can compare with "The City."

The Capitol boom was short lived, too short. By fall, the rigs began to move out as they finished a well. We were working for the Falcon-Seaboard Company and had a brand new rig. When we finished our second well, they just shut down, and we were all out of work.

I learned a lot that summer, because I had always worked in "snowbank country," shale and shell drilling. Rock bits were in general use in Oklahoma City, as opposed to the "drag bits" we used in East and South Texas. We had used rock bits very sparingly in East Texas, mainly to drill the Pecan Gap and Austin chalks, but the relatively new, three-coned Hughes Tool Company bits were in general use in Oklahoma, West Texas, and Southeastern New Mexico.

They were a tremendous improvement over anything seen in the oil fields thus far, and revolutionized hard rock drilling. I was glad to get a chance to familiarize myself with them. Reed Roller Bit Company had also come out with a new type of rock bit, but was not able at that time to really compete with Hughes. Hughes Tool Company called itself the "Standard of the Industry." It was, but Reed was trying to outdo Hughes, and it made for a great deal of rivalry, which continued for many years. Reed claimed that its "flat-bottomed" bit with two large side cutters drilled a straighter hole, which made for lively controversy among contractors and drillers.

When work shut down, we decided to try West Texas. Amy and I went to East Texas to visit her family, then on to Corsicana to spend a few days with my folks. We were going to Wink. I had a job with the Uscan Oil Company, which had a rig running in the Cheyenne Draw field, just north of Kermit. We planned to stay in Wink, which was just 7 miles from Kermit, because we could rent a better apartment there.

We were driving a brand new Chevrolet car. I had, for the first and only time in my life, succumbed to "new car fever." The car was silver gray, and we were loaded down with housekeeping plunder. We, as most oil-field trash did, kept our belongings culled to what a car could hold: dishes, linens, and clothes. Moving too much stuff was more than could be managed on short notice, and when you followed the rigs, you sometimes made a 200-mile trip and went to work the next day. It made for great mobility, but pretty lean living.

The weather turned rainy after we left Fort Worth. It was a gray, misty September day. Not a downpour, but visibility was not good. About 10 miles west of Abilene, at a little town called Tye, we met a long line of cars. They had stacked up behind an elderly man and his wife in an old Ford car. He was driving at about 30 miles per hour. It was a two-lane road, not much room to pass, and he had quite a few impatient drivers stacked up behind him.

Just as I came abreast of the Ford, the fourth car behind him suddenly pulled out to pass. I turned toward the ditch, but did not quite get out of the way. A woman was driving, and her left rear bumper hooked my left rear bumper. Bumpers were wider than cars in those days. We slewed around just enough for the car behind the woman to hit me almost head on, and both Amy and I and the occupants of the second car wound up in the hospital. Amy's left hand had all the tendons severed, her nose was almost cut off, and she had a bad concussion, as she had gone through the windshield. I had three broken ribs, a punctured lung, and a concussion. Luckily, the surgeon who worked on Amy was a wonderfully skilled man. He repaired her hand, did a beautiful job on her face, and she eventually recovered full use of her hand. Her face was slightly scarred, but she was still a pretty woman.

However, that wreck did more than just butcher us up. It also broke us flat. We spent everything we had trying to get well, including the money from the sale of the little house in Kilgore.

Amy went to Lewisville to stay with her sister, while I went on to Wink in about a month. My job was gone, but Herman Griffen was drilling on a well near Kermit, and I went to firing boilers for him, since I wasn't able to do too much physical labor. We sorely needed the money.

The second well we drilled after I got to Wink was up in Cheyenne Draw, which was a dry wash about 8 or 9 miles north of Kermit. It ran east and west and was about 10 miles long overall. It is really more of a shallow valley than a draw. There were quite a few rigs running there at that time, and soon after we got surface pipe set and cemented, and were drilling ahead, an offset well to us blew out.

It blew out with a hell of a roar, and mud and drill pipe flew up into the air. That was the first time I ever saw drill pipe blown out of the hole, and I almost had a heart attack trying to shut the fire out of our boilers. I really hurried because I thought the blowout was caused by gas. It turned out to be air. There was no fire, of course, since air isn't flammable, but there were some very nervous people around for awhile until things got settled down.

We found out that compressed air pockets were not too unusual in that field. There was no way to control them, so they let 'em blow. They generally blew themselves out in six or eight hours, but if you don't think you get nervous and edgy when you are drilling in a place like that, let me tell you that you do; it's something you cannot get used to experiencing.

You didn't get air pockets in all of the wells. I think there were a total of six in that whole field, but you always wonder if the well you are on may be the next one to go up, and it is a very hairy deal to hit an air pocket. Everything happens at once, and all you can do is run like hell. Usually the damage is bad, too, since the drill pipe falls and tears out at least one side of the derrick, and the derrick falls. It makes quite a mess. Usually those pockets were caused by a fold in the earth's crust millions of years ago, probably by an earthquake. They are found at relatively shallow depths, and thank God are rare.

We drilled several wells, and I saved enough money to get my poor repaired Chevy out of hock and go to East Texas to get Amy. She was only able to use her left hand a little, but didn't want to stay in East Texas any longer. So we found a house in an old company camp, just outside Wink, that was only partially in use. Most of the people had moved out of the camps. The house had four rooms, was well furnished, and the rent was cheap, which was a blessing, 'cause we were broke.

It was a bad time, but we toughed it out. I kept working steadily, and we slowly began to accumulate a little money after paying off our debts, which had been large.

Learning is a never-ending process. That early winter I got to work on a well that a major oil company was completing with a drilling rig, in a new process called "under pressure drilling." This involved using live oil as a fluid medium, and we had the first "drilling head" I had ever seen. The drill pipe had inserted tool joints and a smooth surface. You had to really look for the breaks when tripping the drill pipe or even when making a connection. And, of course, the oil had to be returned to an enclosed tank. It was dangerous as the devil. Lots of men absolutely refused to work on rigs that used that method. I was, as usual, firing the boilers, so felt reasonably safe, and had lots of company. The roughnecks didn't exactly hang around the derrick floor. They did what they had to do, then got the hell away from that rig. It aged the drillers considerably, since they had to stay with the brake. Fortunately, this type of drilling did not last long. Some engineer or geologist had an idea that keeping mud or water off the formation while drilling into a pay zone would make much better wells. So, drilling "under pressure" was devised. It was very expensive, required special equipment, and was dangerous. So it was phased out soon, but it did prove that drilling under pressure could be done. Many years later, it came back, without the oil, as under balanced drilling.

So, we learned a little at a time and stored the knowledge away in our minds to use later, and it *was* used later. Maybe not in its original form, but if an idea had merit, it usually stayed in use in the field.

Those were the days when wells were "shot" with nitroglycerin. Pipe, casing that is, was set and cemented just above a pay zone, then the well "drilled in" with a smaller bit. Then the open hole would be "shot," have nitro lowered into the open interval and exploded by a time-set device—generally eight hours after being put into position, as the "shooters" tried to give themselves as much time as possible, because they started out using liquid nitro, which was very unstable and exploded prematurely quite often. The stuff was treated with great fear. Shooters were highly paid, and earned every penny of their pay. Quite a few were killed in the line of duty. Even when the cans that nitro came in were empty, they were dangerous. We used to carry them very gingerly about 300 feet away, set them down very, very carefully, then detonate them from a safe distance by shooting them with a .22-caliber rifle. They made a big bang and blew a sizable hole in the ground. Believe me, lots of roughnecks were too sick to go to work on days when the wells were to be shot. I always dreaded that time, even after solidified nitro came into use, because I've always been an active, working coward, and while "solidified" was supposed to be stable, I never really believed that it was.

We, Amy and I, and Arnold and Grace Holcomb, were sitting in our car one Saturday afternoon in Kermit waiting for a movie house to open for a matinee. We heard a heavy, thunderous explosion; it seemed to be north of town, so we drove out that way. About 5 miles north of town on the Jal Highway, a Gardner Brothers drilling rig was just off the highway. Twenty quarts of nitro had exploded in the cellar and above the derrick floor. Both the shooter and his helper were dead. The helper had his hands on a torpedo guiding it into the hole when it exploded, and we found shreds of him hanging on bushes 200 feet away from that rig, and shreds were all that were ever found. The man had vanished. We have always lived with danger in the patch; it was built into the business.

I think that everyone was happy when shooting went out of style. I know that I was glad to never be around nitroglycerin again. It scared the hell out of me.

We made that summer in the Kermit/Wink area; then as always in the oil field, things slowed up. So we moved to Hobbs and found a place to live right away, a rare happenchance.

There were many rigs running at Monument, Eunice, and Jal, three communities within driving distance of Hobbs. Naturally, everyone wanted to live in the larger town. Hobbs was then and is now pure oil field. Oil made it originally, and the oil business kept it going, so all the hands felt right at home in Hobbs. They knew everyone, told each other about jobs, and stood around on the streets around Pinky Tidwell's cafe, or the Turf Club, which was a pool and domino parlor. Told lots of lies and drilled a million oil wells. Somehow, the wells drilled much faster and had less trouble in town. I like Hobbs. I've lived there three times, made lots of friends, most of whom are dead now, and always thought the town was a good place to live and work. Hobbs boomed and died many times, yet always managed to keep a few rigs running even when down in the dumps. It is growing and going now, after all those ups and downs.

The only fly in the ointment that winter was caused by union organization. The rig builders were the target, and when they decided to go union, most of them did join, but a hefty minority did not. They were very strong, tough men and feelings ran high that winter of 1937–38, and there were fights in town and on the job. Unionization had never been the least bit successful in the oil fields, for many reasons—many drilling contractors, extreme mobility, moving from town to town, plus the fact that the work force was native American, fiercely independent and unruly. They didn't want *anybody* telling them what to do, or when or where they could work. It had been tried before and failed. Union organizers usually gave up after being rebuffed a lot of times. It is still that way. Those damn roughnecks are just as unorganized as they were in the beginning.

Drilling suffered. The fighting, the delays in getting derricks built, and the unpleasantness in general made many companies put off drilling, and Hobbs began to slowly grind to a halt.

I wasn't affected much just then. I had gotten badly injured early in December. We had rigged up a drilling rig over a completed well. The idea was to deepen the thing, so we killed the well with brine water, opened all the valves to be sure there was no pressure anywhere, and started to remove the tubing head. The seals around the tubing were held in place by a threaded ring. It appeared to be cross-threaded. The derrickman and I were just over the thing, and he tapped the ring with a hammer to jar the threads loose, when the damned thing exploded right in our faces. Someone had put two packing elements in that head, opposed to each other. They had trapped 1,800 pounds of pressure between them, and caused the blowout. I got hit a glancing blow by a half-moon steel plate. It broke my jaw, sheared off thirteen teeth, made a tiny puncture wound in my palate, and it took nineteen stitches to put my mouth back together.

To make bad matters worse, the idiot that started to town with me ran out of gas about 20 miles out of Hobbs. We were on Highway 18 about 2 miles south of Eunice when his tank went dry. I got out of his car somehow and stood up on the roadside. I was bleeding like a stuck hog and must have looked like walking death. A big Buick passed, slammed on its brakes, then backed up to where I was standing. A big, black-haired man jumped out of that car, grabbed me up in his arms as though I was a child, put me in the back seat, then held me steady all the way to the hospital. Then he picked me up, ran into the emergency room, and in loud, commanding tones said, "We need a doctor, immediately. I think this man is dying." He got me admitted, got in the car, and left. I never saw him again, but he saved my life. I *was* bleeding to death. I have often wondered who he was, and have always been grateful that there are men like him in this world. He was one hell of a man.

Needless to say, I was out of action for over two and a half months. My jaws were wired together and I was fed through a glass tube. My thirteen sheared teeth were giving me hell, and it was a bad time. Poor Amy had seen me the night I got hurt, and I was not very pretty. Still, she took it well and tried to keep up my spirits. And they surely needed to be kept up since I hurt all the time.

Finally, it all ended. I got out of the hospital, got those teeth out and bridgework installed. I felt fairly good and couldn't find a job. The rig builders were on strike, and the oil fields around Hobbs were shut down. There were no compensation laws in New Mexico in 1938. The drilling company had paid my hospital and dental bills. That was all I got. Amy had lived off our savings, and I had not earned a dime for three months. We were pretty close to the bottom of the bucket, and nobody knew when the strike would end, so we decided to leave Hobbs. When we paid our bills and loaded the car, we had twenty dollars. Total! When we crossed the state line into Texas, Amy said, "I hope to God I never see Hobbs again. It has always been a bad luck town for us."

The rig builders went union after a large amount of trouble, and in the process managed to antagonize every drilling contractor in the oil fields. The contractors accepted higher prices and some arrogance, because they had to do it in order to keep in business, but the resentment stayed. Many contractors began to look for ways to do without rig builders. They importuned the manufacturers of derricks to devise something different from the "standard derrick." It took a few years, but the rig builders had given themselves the "kiss of death." The old-time derrick builder is no longer with us. He got phased out by his final employer, the drilling contractor. The old-time standard derrick that had to be bolted together on location is as dead as the dodo bird. So much for unionizing the oil fields!

It was and still is an impossible task. The union "local" is the foundation of a union. Most of their appeal is to protect jobs and wages at a given locale. The oil fields simply won't "stay put." About the time a local got organized, the work moved right out from under them and went to another town, or even another state. The unions have had some luck in refineries and petrochemical plants, but the roughneck is still as free as the breeze. He always was hard to keep in one place. There was forever another boom he just had to make, and he did not want to wait for the union to find him a job.

But the strike damn near ruined Hobbs. Amy and I just led a general exodus. Contractors stacked rigs, laid off people, and generally pulled in their horns. The people left, and the town dwindled, but never for long. Hobbs, New Mexico, is a survivor. It *always* comes back.

Chapter Nine

Cayuga and Mabank, Then on to Illinois and a New World

The strike, on top of the accident, finished me in Hobbs. I had to find work. We went to Corsicana and I looked for a job in that vicinity. We stayed at Mother's and Mr. Andy's while I hunted a job. I found one the third day. It was in the Cayuga field, about 10 miles south of Malakoff, Texas. We drove from Corsicana, about 35 miles, and I was awfully glad to get back on the payroll. We had just run completely out of money. We were working for Fred Allison, a drilling contractor based in Corsicana. He was an Aggie, and that summer one of the hands on our tour was Big John Kimbrough, who later was famous as "Jarring John," the All-American from Texas A&M. He was just out of his freshman year, a nice quiet boy. I was roughnecking, of course, beggars not being able to be choosers, and my driller was the son of an old friend. His name was Bell White, Jr., and he was about three or four years older than I and weighed 220 pounds. He, John, and Tiny Moorman, who weighed in at about 290 and was 6 feet 6 inches tall, spent most of the day playing with a football, while I ran the rig. They kicked, threw, ran, and tackled, all without pads. It was rough as hell, and those three big lunkheads loved it. I think John made All-American on that summer's conditioning. After what Bell and Tiny put him through, football practice at A&M was child's play. After an all-day session at the rig, all three of those guys looked like mules that had been wearing chain harness without a collar: skinned, scraped, and bruised, but ready to go at it again the next day.

The job was okay. It was not a problem area to drill, and I began to get back in better shape financially, after a few paydays. Amy and I had a pretty nice apartment that we rented from a former schoolteacher of mine, Mrs. Boltz, who was a nice lady. She and Amy got along fine, and it was just 3 miles out to the farm where my folks lived. So Amy wasn't lonely, and I was home every night.

The oil in Cayuga was asphaltic-based oil. When it came out of the well, it was gassy, light brown in color, and was real "live oil." But spill some on the ground, and in an hour you could almost skate on it. It was peculiar stuff to me, as I was familiar with paraffin-based oil. I never really did get used to the characteristics of the stuff, though we drilled three wells there that late spring and early summer. But the work played out rather suddenly. It wasn't a very big field, and a few dry holes spooked everyone who had planned to drill, so our rig was shut down and we were on the grass again.

A friend of mine got a job to drill two wells on the east side of the Trinity River, near the little town of Mabank, about 80 miles southeast of Dallas. He asked me to fire the boilers for him, and since I was not working, I took the job. Amy and I moved to Mabank. We got a room and took meals in an old lady's home, as she also ran a small dining room. She had about six or seven regular boarders and set an excellent table. She was a fixture in Mabank. The bedroom we had was a huge room. The house was an old-fashioned two-story one built about 1905, and was comfortable and homey. We liked it fine, and Amy got acquainted all over town, so things were pretty nice again.

The job was an easy one. The contractor was "Tip" DeArman, youngest of the DeArman brothers. He had split with his brothers and was operating one rig. He was a small man, but pretty salty, and ran a good rig.

These were gas wells that we were drilling, and were not the usual thing for that part of Texas. Most of the wells were oil wells, and gas was a by-product, with not too much value. It was often flared, that is, was burned to get rid of it.

Tip had gotten these two contracts from a gas company that had a gathering system in the area. The field was a small one, and if I ever knew what the producing zone was, I have forgotten it. But it was a lively little zone and produced with about 2,000 PSI surface pressure.

We drilled and completed the first well without incident, then drilled the second one and brought it in when we had a small disaster. While rigging down, someone either dropped something on, or hit, a small 3/8-inch connection in a "tapped" bull plug which was screwed into the wellhead.

This was an extra heavy bull plug, made to withstand high pressure. It had a 3/8-inch threaded hole in it to accommodate a pressure gauge. Whatever caused it, the needle valve which was screwed into the plug broke off and turned 2,000 pounds of pressure loose. The noise was indescribable—a shrill, piercing scream, and you literally couldn't hear yourself think. That plug was screwed into the side of the wellhead, and the stream of gas was pointed right at a derrick leg foundation and immediately began to cut the wooden side of the cellar away.

Tip had acquired, at some time, a flat 2-inch pipe thread die. It was very unusual to see one around a drilling rig, but since a bull plug is only 3½ inches long, it was the only thing we could have possibly used to thread the outside of that damned plug. He got the die, and everyone began to try to come up with a way to get it on the plug, in order to thread it. No easy task with 2,000 pounds of gas blowing out of a small hole in the center. Finally, they wired two chains to the thing, which was about 3½ inches square and ¾ inch thick. After many, many attempts, they finally worried it upon the plug. Tip, the driller, and two hands. Of course, it was dangerous as all hell. One spark could have set the thing afire and killed every man in that cellar instantly. I really do believe that not one of those men even thought of that possibility. We all had cotton stuffed in our ears and were using signs to communicate, and the gas had cut through the cellar board finally, and was beginning to undermine the derrick leg. Everyone was concentrating on what was going on, and didn't have time to worry about danger.

The derrickman and I were rigging a deal to get a valve onto that plug when, and if they ever got it threaded, and it was a Rube Goldberg–looking gizmo. We had found a four-way 2-inch cross and rigged it on the valve with two long 2-inch nipples out each side to enable us to turn the valve against the pressure.

They got the plug threaded, but as they tried to get the die off, somebody lost his hold, and the thing blew completely away and Tip never did find it.

We, all six of us, began to try to install that valve, but it was one hell of a job. We finally got it centered on the gas stream, which was getting bigger all the time as it cut the hole in the bull plug larger. We walked it down that jet stream, keeping it centered, and finally stabbed it onto the threaded plug and made it tight. When Tippy finally closed that valve, the silence was wonderful. We were all deaf from long exposure to all that horrible noise.

The derrick leg was undermined, but three legs were intact and so the danger of the derrick falling was slight. We were all completely wrung out from three hours of tension, danger, and fear. It was 1:00 P.M., but we shut it down and went to town because we had had enough for one day. Nobody thought he was crazy or a hero; he had just done an unpleasant job of work, and still had to tear a rig down the next day. Roughnecks, drillers, and pushers are very peculiar animals. They still are peculiar, but not as dumb as we were, nor quite as proud.

We were finished in Mabank, and work was very scarce around that part of Texas.

Amy and I went to Lewisville to visit her sister, Essie, and I hunted a job. There just wasn't any work going on, and though I looked pretty hard, I found nothing. We stayed a week in Lewisville, then went to Gladewater. Amy's father lived there, and we stayed with him a couple of weeks. It was October of 1938, and East Texas was very dead. We ran into an old friend of mine named Henry Yancey, who had quit drilling and had taken a pumping job. He told us that his sister's husband was in Illinois; that Illinois was booming and that in his sister's last letter, she said good hands were very scarce up there, and work was plentiful; in fact, that Dick, her husband, was looking for a derrickman as she was writing the letter.

We were running out of money and decided to go to Illinois. We had about $16.00 when we left Gladewater. We also had a letter of introduction to Dick Hodges, Henry's brother-in-law, as well as his address in Salem, Illinois. That was about it. I know it was a crazy thing to do, but as it turned out, it was a blessing.

We left Gladewater on the second of November. We got out of town late and only got as far as Rogers, Arkansas, where we spent the night in a motel. The next day we crossed the Mississippi River at Cape Girardeau, Missouri, over a toll bridge. I remember it vividly, since the toll fee was $1.00. When I paid it, we had $3.00 left to live on, in a strange state. It was about three in the afternoon, and night came early in Illinois in the fall, a scary deal.

We drove into Salem and met the Hodges, Dick and Martha. Dick told me to report to work in two days, since he had to lay a man off in order to hire me. So we had a job, but needed a place to live, and with no money. It presented quite a problem. We ate dinner with the Hodges, then tried to find a place to spend the night. We couldn't find any accommodations at all in Salem. One lady we tried to rent a room from told us we could find a room in Mount Vernon, 20 miles away, so we started to Mount Vernon, but 10 miles out of Salem, I drove over a small hill and came to a little village. The road sign said "Dix." There was a red neon sign that said "cabins" over a garage. We stopped, asked the price, and were told $1.00. It was the first stroke of luck we had in a long, long time. We took the cabin on the spot.

The weather was cool, just about freezing, so I drained the radiator in the car. We built a fire in the small wood-burning stove, and looked at each other and began to laugh. Never in our wildest imagination had we dreamed of a day like the one we had just lived through. It was weird. You don't really have to be crazy to work in the oil fields, but it doesn't do any harm to be a bit "touched."

The next morning it was cold, about 25°. We woke up in a strange little town in a northern state, looked out to see if there was a place in town where we could get coffee, and just across the street in what looked like an addition to a residence, was a sign, "Eats." We went over and saw that coffee was 5 cents a cup, and doughnuts three for a dime. That was breakfast. We were down to $1.75, and a quarter of a tank of gas.

The woman who ran that little eatery was a small, red-headed woman about forty years old. She and Amy began to talk. She asked where we were from, and when we told her, she said that there were several families from Oklahoma and Texas who had moved into Dix. Most of them were employed in production, none in drilling. Anyhow, Amy asked if there were any apartments in town, and the lady said, "Why, I have a two-room apartment behind mine, and it is vacant." We asked about the rent; she said $18.50 a month. Amy told her we were broke, but needed a place to live, because I had to go to work the next morning. She let us have the little bedroom, bath, and kitchenette apartment, on credit, and also said we could eat in the cafe until I got a payday.

That was the day our bad luck vanished. I went down to the garage where we had rented the cabin, explained that I had a job and would be living in Dix, got my gas tank filled on credit, and we were ready for anything.

The drilling company that I went to work for the next morning was the Schoenfeld-Hunter-Kitch Drilling Company. I worked for them from 1938 to 1958, with four years out for World War II: a grand total of sixteen years. They were a good outfit, small, efficient; their rigs were in excellent shape and were a pleasure to work on. I had lucked out once again.

These were gas-motor-powered rigs. The days of steam had ended for me. They were good days while they lasted, but steam was being phased out in the oil fields. It simply couldn't compete with power rigs.

S-H-K didn't hire drillers. They promoted roughnecks who had worked for them a long while. I could not see why they didn't want to hire me as a driller. I had considerable experience and tried to talk them into it, but the answer was no. I had to roughneck to ever drill for them. Of course, at that time, I needed a job so badly that a derrick job looked good, so I signed on and went to work.

They paid off at the end of every well, instead of every two weeks, and we drilled those little shallow wells about every eight or ten days. I got my first paycheck from them seven days from the day I went to work. Amy went up to the little bank in Dix and opened a checking account. We never were broke again, for I had learned a good lesson. A man's best friend is a bank account, not a dog.

The weather turned bad in late November; rain, freezing rain, sleet, and snow, and the whole of Southern Illinois turned into a sea of mud. The mud would thaw during the day, then freeze solid at night. Getting to work was a problem; cars got stuck, and sometimes you would have to leave the car, then walk a mile or two to the rig. That was merely unpleasant, but when you had to move a drilling rig, unpleasantness turned into a nightmare. The mud seemed bottomless. Pumps, draw works, and other rig equipment are heavy; so we mounted them on what looked like a flat-bottomed metal scow. In other words, they were floored with iron, and we moved them into position with Caterpillars, as trucks were useless on location. They bogged down completely and had to be pulled to the pavement by "cats." But somehow we managed, by main strength, bull-headedness, and perseverance, to move 'em and keep them running, and it took a great deal of "doing" to keep things moving. I had never seen anything like it before, and to me it was a miracle that we worked that winter and never missed a day's work. I never got used to the winter weather in Illinois, but Amy had a ball. The weather didn't bother her. She had met several wives from Oklahoma, and they used our landlady's little cafe as a kind of club, kaffee klatch there each day, and even some native ladies came to listen. The landlady's name was Minnie Webb, and she was a sweet and gentle soul, so at least one-half of my family was contented, the better half.

Drilling wells in Illinois was a breeze. All the difficulty was caused by weather. I learned about gas-powered rigs, and needed the experience. I don't suppose that any of us are ever as smart as we think we are, and I also learned that you can keep drilling rigs running under very adverse conditions. It was a discipline I needed and rounded out my education.

Most of the oil-field folks in Southern Illinois were from Oklahoma, Texas, or Arkansas. Very few, if any, Cajuns were there; it was too cold for them. Dix, where we lived, was very small. It had a population of about 250 people. It was a farm community, and the oil-field trash, most of them Okies, were a nine-day wonder to the natives, who looked upon them as beings about as alien as Martians. They liked us, but thought us very odd. It was incomprehensible to them that people would move all over the country to work. Most of them regarded 30 miles as a great distance to travel, to visit, not to work.

Dix had two filling stations, the bank, two cafes, a large general store, the village square, and that was it. The general store carried almost anything you could think of, since it was the only store in town.

Canvas gloves had come into general use in the oil fields by 1938, and the old slick leather gloves were gone, never to return. The best gloves were made by the Boss Glove Company in Kewanee, Illinois. They were excellent gloves, 12-ounce duck, and had the trade name "Wallopers." Kewanee wasn't too far from Dix. I needed gloves soon after going to work, and went up to the Dix general store to buy some. In my ignorance, I assumed that Virgil, the proprietor, carried Boss Gloves.

It was the first time in the store for me. I asked if he had canvas work gloves. He said, "Sure I do," and threw a pair down on the counter. I looked at them and they had six fingers on each glove. I looked again and still saw six fingers, so I said to him, "Feller, I haven't been in Illinois very long and don't know many of the people here, but where I came from down in Texas, nearly everyone just had five fingers." He stared at me and said, "Those are corn huskers' gloves." I wasn't sure just what he meant, so I asked, "Do corn huskers have six fingers?" He laughed and said that they didn't; that the extra finger was a thumb; when the palm wore out on one side, they just turned them over. He had never stocked Boss gloves, but said that he would, and we talked for awhile. He was a pretty nice fellow, willing and anxious to please his customers. Later on when we knew each other a little better, he asked me why oil-field women demanded that he stock Folger's coffee, pinto beans, Faultless starch, and other staples new to him. They were not in use in that part of Illinois. I told him we were all a little odd, but nice, and did pay in cash. So he humored our women, and they, in turn, enlarged his knowledge of how people lived and ate in Texas and Oklahoma, and oddly, it turned out that people around Dix developed a taste for Folger's coffee and pinto beans, and found out that powdered Faultless starch beat lump starch hollow.

We, all of us, enjoyed Dix. It was a good little town, and we learned to love Southern Illinois people. But I never got used to their weather, which must be the worst weather in the whole world. It was certainly rough on the drilling people because drilling rigs run twenty-four hours a day, seven days a week. You had to get to work over half-frozen dirt roads that sometimes thawed enough to bog you down in the daytime, then froze solid again at night. You struggled, and the weather always fought you to a standstill. Anybody who has hauled a pair of six-buckle overshoes through two winters and springs in Illinois can qualify as extra tough. The farm folks take it easy in the winter, but we didn't have that privilege. Our work continued, rain or shine, and that spring and winter it was more rain than shine. Illinois posed no problems as far as actually drilling a well was concerned—routine stuff and no real challenges, except "movement." You can't imagine the effort it took to move anything. That black muck was real goo; we used to say that in the spring, buzzards wouldn't fly over that country because it would bog a shadow. And if you can imagine cementing a string of casing, with the Halliburton pump truck, a quarter of a mile away from the location, having gotten that far mounted on a flat-bottomed metal boat, pulled by a Caterpillar tractor, you can see what we were forced to do, to just keep moving. We laid a 2-inch line to the rig, then cemented the casing and ran up the line, pulling bull plugs, to drain the line, when the job was done. That just about tells the story. It was mean, tough work. We endured it, but did not enjoy the experience.

We struggled through March and April; then in May the sun came out. It looked slightly mildewed at first, but warmed things up considerably. Our jobs became progressively easier, and the sun brightened everyone's spirits.

Schoenfeld-Hunter-Kitch Drilling Company was in many ways a peculiar lash-up. Bill Schoenfeld's training and background was banking. He didn't understand the ins and outs of drilling, but he sure as hell understood money and how to manage it. "Skinny" Hunter had been a tool pusher for some years before the company was formed. He was probably the best manipulator of men that I ever knew, and an excellent well man. Bill Kitch was a Pennsylvania Dutch cable tool man. He owned and was operating several cable tool rigs when he, Hunter, and Schoenfeld formed S-H-K Drilling Company. Bill Kitch was married to Bill Schoenfeld's sister, but was as independent as a hog on ice.

The three men were totally different, but together they were an excellent combination. And the company was different from any drilling contracting firm I had known, up until the time I went to work for them.

They never "gave" you anything. You had to earn it. But they were scrupulously fair to their people and were far ahead of their time in labor relations. They kept their rigs and people busy and were slow to lay people off when the rigs were down. It was the only reason I stayed with them, and I stayed for many years. It was the first security I had ever felt; I had always worked "catch as catch can," and it had not always been a good system, since it was full of ups and downs. Promotion was slow with S-H-K, but paydays were regular. Amy loved it, and our bank account grew steadily. It needed to grow; we had endured some very lean years.

It was a beautiful spring and early summer that year of 1939. Dix was in the midst of a fruit-growing area, mostly peaches and apples. The orchards were lovely and the air was sweet-scented and all Southern Illinois was in bloom.

I was on morning tour from midnight till 8:00 A.M., as I was doing some substitute drilling for vacations and sick leave, and morning tour was the logical solution. Boredom set in, so I organized a teenage baseball team. Those kids had absolutely nothing to do, so we gave them a reason for staying home. Amy and I, along with a few other oil-field trash, raised enough money from our local people and ourselves to buy a catcher's mitt, chest protector, bats, and a couple of dozen baseballs. Those kids ate it up. They were gung-ho about the game, and really did practice.

Then the townspeople caught afire. A farmer donated a pasture for a diamond. Another gave posts and wire for a backstop, and we were in business. Games were matched with other villages and I learned that baseball was serious in Illinois. As manager, I got involved in several arguments, and two fights. We had a hell of a lot of fun. The kids loved it, and I was a local hero for a very short time. It was a lively summer.

Summer ended and in mid-October, just as the apple harvest was in full swing, we got transferred to Frederick, Oklahoma. The company had made some deal with Cities Service Oil Company to drill a number of wells in a field southwest of Frederick, and they moved two rigs to Oklahoma. I jumped at the chance to get out of Illinois before winter set in, but Amy was a little less than thrilled. We had made many friends up there, and she was loath to leave them. Besides, she liked Illinois. I told her that if she had to work through one winter up there, she would run back to Texas screaming bloody murder. True, we had made some good friends up there, friendships that endured for a lifetime. Still, I had a living to make and did not fancy another winter in "Little Egypt," as Southern Illinois is called.

We loaded the car and set out for Frederick. We had a brand new Chevrolet four-door, a 1939 model. We went through Missouri and spent the night in Claremore, Oklahoma, then arrived in Frederick about noon the next day. The company had given us two days to move, and we needed all of that time, since Frederick was in Southwestern Oklahoma.

Apartments were available in Frederick, and by late afternoon we had settled in our new town. And a nice town it was; a quiet farm town, prosperous, and the county seat of Tillman County, just above the Texas state line. The town was quiet and the greatest single pastime was going to church on Sunday.

Amy and Martha Hodges became involved in church work at the First Baptist Church. Most of the social life of Frederick revolved around the church, which had at that time a very magnetic minister. So they stayed happy and felt useful, even though Amy was raised a Methodist.

We men worked. There is an old saying in the oil fields that "There is no bad weather, no Sundays, no holidays, and no time off for good behavior in the oil fields." We didn't disturb Frederick any at all. After all, we only had two rigs and sixteen people. We didn't even make a ripple in the even tenor of their lives. They were set in their ways, and we were aliens.

The field we were drilling in was about 7 or 8 miles southwest of town. Cities Service had a camp there. There were about fifty pumping wells, and we set in to drill some "edge" wells. There were no problems that I can remember, just an occasional "twist-off" fishing job. Bill Kitch was our tool pusher. He lived in Oklahoma City, 150 miles away. Such problems as arose were taken care of by the daylight drillers. Both men had been with the company since it was founded in 1930. Dick Hodges went on to become drilling superintendent after World War II started. Joe Jones kept on pushing tools. Bill came down to Frederick about once a month because the jobs went so smoothly that it was actually boring. We felt more like ribbon clerks than oil-field hands. Frederick was a "dry" town, so the boys who liked to drink, carouse, and dance had to go to Electra, Texas, about 30 miles from Frederick.

We all saved money. Hell, there wasn't anything to spend it on. I joined a bowling league. The bowling alley and two movie theaters were "it" in Frederick, and I never was fond of movies.

Amy and I moved to a better apartment. It was upstairs over a funeral home. It gave you a bit of an eerie feeling at first, and took a little getting used to, but turned out to be an ideal place to live. It was just across the street from the Baptist Church, which suited Amy just fine. I teased her, told everyone that she moved just to be closer to that preacher.

Mose stopped by on his way back to Dallas from Denver. He was working for Otis Elevator Company and was happy to be back in his first love, the elevator business. He had married and was living in Dallas. We were delighted with his visit. He stayed two days, went to the rig with me one tour, morning, of course, and it was just like old times. Amy told him to just wait until she met his wife; that she would tell her lots that the wife might not know about Mose. We had a great time, talked till all hours, and dreaded to see him leave.

That was a nice winter, but spring was turbulent. Frederick is in "Tornado Alley," and the little town of Snyder, 25 miles north of Frederick, was badly damaged by a tornado that spring. All the people around Frederick had storm cellars and ran to them from every cloud. Amy was an Okie, too, and she ran with them. It would infuriate her that I wouldn't share her fear of storms, but I was trying to sleep in the daylight hours and couldn't be bothered running to a storm cellar every day.

Summer came and it, too, was nice and not too hot. We had been in Frederick a year and a half, a long time to work in a small, almost forgotten oil field.

Tragedy hit our lives in late June. Mose got killed. I was working morning tour and had just awakened. Amy was cooking my breakfast and I turned the radio to the five o'clock news from Dallas. Right near the end of the newscast, the announcer said that a man named Nolan Mosher had been killed in a fall; a scaffold had given way, and he fell nine stories down an elevator shaft. I couldn't or wouldn't believe it, so I called Mose's mother, Mary, and she said it was true, he was dead. I called Dick Hodges and he arranged for me to be off. Amy and I went to Dallas, attended the funeral, and closed a chapter in our lives. I've never forgotten the little guy. I can see him plainly right this minute. He was one in a million.

Our work played out in the spring of 1941, and Cities Service moved us to Oklahoma City. We began to drill some east edge wells on the extreme eastern edge of the city. Our home yard was there on East Twenty-Ninth Street, the office was situated at the yard, and it made it very convenient for everyone.

We, all of the crews, moved into the part of Oklahoma City called locally "Capitol Hill." It was oil-field oriented; had been through two drilling booms. It was all south of the Canadian River and was a town in itself, and a fine place for oil-field trash to live.

The job was easy, trouble-free drilling, so the summer went pleasantly. We went back to Illinois in September. I came very near not going, but we had become kind of like a family in the past two years. The two rigs and their crews had been together all that time, so naturally we were familiar with each other and the job, which made for good working conditions.

We drilled two wells at Newton, Illinois, then moved into Fairfield. Made a trip to Dix to visit friends and renew news of each other. But in late October, it began to rain and we were back in the mud again. We drilled two more wells, and I had about all of Little Egypt I could stand again. I told Dick Hodges that one more well was about the size of my sojourn in Illinois, but I never got to make that well. On the morning of December 7, 1941, we were moving a rig in on a very muddy location, when Skinny Hunter came out and told us that we had *volunteered* to go to Hominy, Oklahoma, to drill a well—that they were moving one of the rigs out of the Oklahoma City yard to Hominy, that it was a hurry-up job, and for us to take off then and get ready to move. He added casually that there had been a rumor on the radio that the Japanese had bombed Pearl Harbor.

The "rumor" was true. I loaded the car that noon with the radio blaring out the Pearl Harbor story. Roosevelt went before Congress, and they declared war on Japan. We pulled out of Fairfield about 2:00 P.M., and I was out of Illinois forever. I have never been back to the state.

Hominy is the heart of the Osage Nation. It is an Indian town, and the Osages are big Indians. It's nice that they are friendly. We drilled that well for Cities Service; it was out on Grey Bull Creek about 15 miles northeast of Hominy. We finished up in early January of 1942. Bill Kitch told us that they were shutting down temporarily because of uncertainty about the war.

Amy and I packed up, went to Oklahoma City, picked up my last paycheck, told everyone "goodbye," and headed for Dallas where I was going to enlist in the Sea Bees.

Time out for World War II—four solid years, completely out of the oil fields, a first for me, as I had been born and grown up in the grease patch. My Daddy was working for Magnolia Petroleum Company when I was born, and two of my uncles on Mother's side of the family were drillers. I was really an oil-field brat! The war years would be a strange four years for me.

I came back to Texas to the Permian Basin in April of 1945. Amy was in Winnsboro, Texas, staying with a sister, Ruth Kerr. Her health had begun to go bad and she had come back to Texas to go to Scott and White's Clinic at Temple, and since she knew I would be along, she stayed with Ruth until I arrived. She had kept in touch with some of our S-H-K friends and had told me that Dick and Martha Hodges, and Ray (Sonny) and Abby Saak, whom we had known in Illinois, were living in Odessa. Dick was drilling superintendent for S-H-K, and she asked me to say "hello" to them as I came through town.

When I pulled into Odessa, hauling a luggage trailer behind me, it was 4:00 P.M. I called Dick's place, and Martha told me to come on out. They had rented a two-room motel deal with a kitchenette, and a colonnaded living and bedroom. Odessa was crowded from the air base and the oil fields. Housing was at a premium, hard to find and not much when you found it, but Martha was like Amy. She could always find something decent.

Dick came home; we were awfully glad to see each other and had a lot of gossip to catch up on. He had been my teacher as well as my driller, and down through the years I had learned a great deal from him. He was the finest driller I have ever known, and I learned more from him than any other man I ever worked for or with.

The Hodges insisted that I stay the night with them, and I did. It wasn't a tough decision to make. There were no hotel rooms available in Odessa. Dick and I argued all night. He wanted me to come back to work for S-H-K Drilling Company. I told him that promotions were too slow and seniority was too strong in the company for me to get trapped in "that" mess again. He swore that I had not lost any seniority since I had had some time in the service, and that they were moving two more rigs to Odessa from the West Edmonds field in Oklahoma. When they arrived, I would be the tool pusher on one of them. He assured me that as drilling superintendent he had that much stroke. In the meantime, I would be daylight driller on the first rig. It wasn't what I wanted, and I was none too anxious to hire back out to S-H-K. We debated it into the wee hours, and I finally agreed to go to Winnsboro, talk it over with Amy, and let him know what I decided.

Amy wanted me to take the job. She was afraid that we would run out of money. I told her that good men were scarce and I could pick and choose any job that I wanted, but she had been told in Scott and White that she might need back surgery, that there was a ruptured disc in her spine.

I took her to Dallas to an orthopedic specialist, got her a room in a small, family-type hotel, went back to Odessa and took the job. I still don't know if I did the right thing.

Chapter Ten

West Texas—S-H-K and Big Lake

But the decision had been made and I was stuck with it. Dick put me to drilling days on a National "75" rig running in the Fullerton Field. We were drilling for Phillips Petroleum Company, which had superceded Cities Service with S-H-K. Our company man was Blackie Gaines. He was destined to play that role for me again in other fields. Phillips moved their people around, just as S-H-K moved their folks.

Ray and Abby Saak were living in a small hotel on North Grant Street in Odessa, on the corner of Grant and 7th Street. It is long gone now, and a big bank has been erected where it stood. Abby got me a room there, since Amy had stayed in Dallas and I couldn't use an apartment. She, Ray, and their little nine-year-old daughter had a room on the ground floor, while I was on the second floor. I often took the little girl, Freda, to dinner, since Abby had been feeling poorly, and Ray was working evening tour. Abby was frustrated because she couldn't find an apartment. She was dreadfully tired of living in one room. Three people are one too many for even a big room. It was a hot summer, fans were inadequate, and we all suffered, especially me, who had to try to sleep days. I almost gave up, quit the job, and left, but I had promised Dick to stay, for awhile at least, so I kept working. Drilling is like swimming; you never forget how to do it; so I took up where I had left off four years before, and immediately fell into an old familiar groove. I had told Amy that good men were scarce when we discussed working for S-H-K again, and I found out that it was true when I hired my first crew after the war years. What a crew! My derrickman was my only real roughneck, and he had been invalided out of the Army because he had asthma. He was Tommy Farmer from Corsicana, and I had helped break him in roughnecking years before in East Texas. He turned out to be a real godsend.

My pipe racker was a skinny eighteen-year-old boy who tried to work in tennis shoes, but I vetoed tennis shoes and made him buy safety shoes.

My backup man was a sixty-two-year-old ex-cowboy. He worked in cowboy boots and strove mightily to keep up his end of the work, but he was no longer young, and the adjustment to roughnecking was hard for him to make, though he certainly made the effort.

But my motor man was a real foul ball. He was one of a breed in the oil fields known as "pool hall bums" who hung around domino parlors or pool halls to gamble on the games. They only worked when they were broke, and as soon as they got a little money ahead, they would quit and hang around the pool halls until they were flat broke again and had to hunt another job. The one that I hired *looked* like a hand. He dressed neatly, seemed to be sharp and alert, and he made a good impression on me. He turned out to be a sorry, lazy no-good, who wanted to sleep on the job, just so he could hang around the dives in town during the day. He helped make connections, trips to change bits, gave the motors a half-assed check, and that was about all the work I could get out of him. I hated him and longed for the day to come that I could fire him, but hands were scarce, so I kept him.

Things had changed during the war years. The old spinning ropes that we had used to make up drill pipe had been replaced by chains, and automatic cat heads had come into general use. They were run by the driller, were safer, and the driller had better control of the make-up process.

Another change had taken place, too. Open-hole completions were being phased out except for rare occasions. Now, instead of setting casing *above* a pay zone, we drilled *through* the zone, then set and cemented the casing. The casing then had to be perforated in order to reach the oil or gas zone. At that time, perforating companies were using sharp-pointed, bullet-shaped hunks of high-carbon steel, shot from subsurface guns, electrically.

The position of the shots was determined by running a gamma ray correlation log inside the casing, then matching it to an open-hole log which had been run prior to setting pipe. A much more sophisticated set of logs are used to do the same thing today. They really work, and today you can pinpoint a shot 20,000 feet deep, within an inch or two of where you want it. I still think it is a form of magic.

We use jet charges to perforate today, but those old bullets gave us some problems. The companies, and I'm speaking of major oil companies, would shoot so many holes in the casing that it looked like a sieve. The very first well I drilled on coming back to the patch had about 300 feet of scattered producing zones, and the company shot 1,200 holes over the interval. Some of those bullets didn't go all the way through the casing. Many would stick in the walls. They had to be gotten loose, so we would pick up a bit and a spring-loaded blade casing scraper and go in the hole. Then we would rotate the tubing string and start knocking bullets loose, and some of 'em didn't give up easily. We had to be mighty careful and also have luck to keep from twisting off. All drillers hated a bullet clean-up job with a purple passion. No credit if you did it right, but lots of blame if you didn't. Constant vigilance was the watchword, and even that didn't always work.

I was knocking bullets out of the casing walls one morning on morning tour. The casing scraper was hanging up, snapping and popping, and I wasn't in a good mood since I was making a double. My motor man had checked his motors when we changed tours and was sprawled in the tool house asleep. Dick Hodges drove up, got out of his car, and came through the tool house to the brake where I was standing. It was 2:00 A.M. He had been careful not to step on that lazy clown asleep in the dog house, because he was aware that hands were scarce and hard to replace.

Dick asked me if I had listened to the radio that day on the way to work, and I told him that I had not. So he said, "Well, I'm sure you will be glad to hear that Germany has surrendered. It is all on the newscasts."

I looked in the tool house at that lazy, sorry son of a bitch on the floor, latched the brake down, walked to the tool house door, and kicked that clod on the sole of his shoe. He sat up, startled, and said, "Whassa matter, connection already?" And I answered, "No connection. Roll up your doll rags, Sport. You are fired. The war is over."

I was a bit previous it turned out, as I worked short-handed for ten days before I could find another hand. Then he was a weevil, a boy of twenty off a farm at Dublin, Texas. I put Tommy Farmer, my derrickman, to working motors, and we made a derrickman out of the weevil. Tommy was a "Yellow-heel" and one hell of a hand. He took that raw kid under his wing and made a roughneck out of him, practically overnight. The boy was eager to learn. He said that he was very tired of working on peanut farms around Dublin. Roughnecking was a pleasure to him.

We were drilling Clearfork wells at that time, 14 miles west and about 5 miles north of Andrews, Texas. It was a 60-mile drive from Odessa. The field was called the Fullerton field, and the wells were 6,700 to 7,000 feet deep. The wells were prolific, and many of them are still producing today. There was a small community called Frankel City. It was named after the Frankel Brothers who pioneered drilling in that area. It had two cafes, two filling stations, three supply houses, and about twenty dwellings, and even though they are all long gone except one small cafe, Frankel City is still on the highway signs, still classified as a town.

I have never understood the reason for all those perforations that companies put in their wells. It began suddenly and ended the same way. Obviously, some engineer dreamed it up, God knows why, and he convinced someone in authority that it was "the way" to complete wells. It only lasted about a year, but dealt a lot of grief to a lot of people. It was very costly; the casing guns held a maximum of twenty shots; to make 1,600 holes took eighty gun runs with an electric line, and you were looking at thirty to forty hours rig time, plus the perforating costs. Besides, it was a dangerous practice. The perforating crews were loading guns on the derrick floors, and several men were killed by premature firings. The rig crews were barred from the floor while all this was going on, and were glad not to be involved. But all things come to an end. Finally someone realized that the excessive perforations were not improving production, that the cost and trouble that it caused was not justified, and they dropped the practice like a hot rock. Finished, Kaput! It went the way of the dodo bird, never to return, and went unmourned.

We drilled and completed two wells, then got the word that our rig was moving to Big Lake, Texas. Tommy quit me and went to work for McCullough Tool Company, a perforating company. I surely missed him as he was a real, old-time top hand, but he didn't want to move to Big Lake. It was 100 miles from Odessa by road at that time, so I couldn't blame him, and McCullough made him a good offer of a job.

I wasn't too thrilled about the move either. Amy was still in Dallas undergoing back therapy at the Carroll-Driver Clinic. Skinny Hunter had come into the picture in Odessa, back out of the Sea Bees. He deferred my tool pushing job, and I was sore about that, but Dick Hodges, who was really a good friend, talked me into the move.

We went to Big Lake: three drillers, Sonny Saak, Red Reed, and myself. I took two hands with me, and Red and Sonny had one or two men apiece with them. We had to flesh out the crews with local people. The locations we were drilling were 35 miles southeast of town, over dirt roads. Dick Hodges was our tool pusher and he lived in Odessa, so we were really unsupervised. Not that it made any difference to us, since all our supplies and repair parts had to come from Odessa. So, if we needed parts or anything in the form of supplies, we had to call Dick, and we didn't need to be told how to drill. We knew how. Since Sonny, Red, and I had all roughnecked for Dick long ago, he trusted us to do our jobs.

Big Lake at that time had a population of approximately 2,500 people. It was the county seat of Reagan County, had experienced one boom back in the 20's, and since it was the only town of any size in that vicinity, it had a few oil-field people living there, and consequently, we were able to hire help. There was one old-fashioned hotel and two cafes, a hamburger joint, and a few stores and automobile dealers, with about six filling stations thrown in. Not a metropolis by any standard, but still a pretty good little town.

I got into Big Lake at eleven o'clock in the evening. Late, because I had gotten delayed in Odessa. I had called the Big Lake Hotel for a reservation, but when I got to the hotel, the night clerk had given up on me and rented my room to a traveling salesman. I was mad as hell, but couldn't do anything about it. The night marshal came into the lobby as I was raising hell with the clerk. He suggested that I could sleep in my car, which was parked in front of the hotel, and he would see that no one disturbed me.

That is what I did, finally drifting off to sleep, only to be awakened about two hours later by two gunshots. I sat up startled and scared, and saw the marshal standing over someone lying on the sidewalk, half a block away from my car. I stayed in my car because I didn't know what would happen next. In a few minutes the marshal came by me and entered the hotel. I went in behind him and heard him tell the clerk to call Dr. Patterson, as he had just killed a man. He looked up, saw me, and advised me to spend the rest of the night on a couch in the hotel lobby. I took his advice, lay down on the leatherette couch, wondered what in hell would happen next, but *didn't* go to sleep. That was my introduction to Big Lake, and it certainly impressed me. I resolved to be a good boy while I lived in that salty little town.

The story the marshal told was that he tried to arrest the man for drunkenness, that the guy drew a knife and lunged at him, so he shot him. I don't know about the reason, but I know that he shot him. I saw the body.

We settled in Big Lake. It wasn't hard to do, since the local men we hired turned out okay. My two, J. N. Clark and Prestige Kane, both proved to be excellent hands. Clark went on to become a driller with S-H-K. Prestige wouldn't leave Big Lake, but both men were a big help to me.

I stayed on at the Big Lake Hotel at weekly rates and we all got acquainted with the townspeople and really felt welcome in Big Lake. It was a friendly town.

The field we were drilling in was known as the Todd field. Besides S-H-K there were three other drilling contractors who had one rig each in that field. All of us lived in Big Lake, even though Ozona was much closer to the Todd field. Ozona did not like oil-field people, and oil-field people didn't care for Ozona. It was years before the feud between

Ozona and bona fide oil-field trash died, though it finally did expire. We shunned Ozona, just as Ozona shunned us, back when we were drilling the Todd.

Our job went well. We were working in "live oak" country, hilly, with many live oak trees. The terrain was rough, but the Edwards escarpment was part of our field, and it made for some rather different things in our manner of drilling.

We were drilling Ellenburger wells, and the drilling was routine. We used clear water to drill with, down to 300 or 400 feet above pipe setting point, then mixed mud to drill into the Ellenburger. Had few problems since the rig we had was fairly new. It was a National "75" and was in excellent mechanical shape. We had an occasional twist-off, but had our own fishing tools and did our own fishing. Dick came down each week or ten days, usually bringing supplies from Odessa. The wells were good ones. We completed them with the drilling rig. The wells were owned by a company called Callery and Hurt. They were somehow affiliated with Southland Royalty, and we always had a Southland Royalty geologist on the job at the last of every well. He ran samples, picked the casing point; then when we completed the well, he came back out and supervised the bringing in of the well. In other words, he was our "company man" as well as our geologist. I have forgotten his name, but he knew his business. As I remember the procedure we used to complete those wells, it went thus: We set pipe well into the Ellenburger sand, drilled out the float that was positioned one joint above the guide shoe, then drilled the cement out of the bottom joint of casing, which had a metal disc positioned in the guide shoe which was supposed to rotate and keep you from drilling the guide shoe. The only way you could drill out the shoe was to pick the bit up and "spud" it, set it down suddenly and hard to break the disc. We did not to my knowledge ever drill a production guide shoe, and we drilled twenty-two wells in the Todd field before we moved out.

We drilled out with drilling mud as a fluid medium, came out of the hole, then ran the tubing back to bottom, then displaced the mud, which weighed 9.2 pounds per gallon, with clear water, which weighs 8.35 pounds per gallon. That was it. The well would sit there sometimes for forty minutes, then slowly water would begin to trickle out of the tubing, gradually getting stronger, then unloading the water in the well to the reserve pits. Quite a deal. Fine for everyone, but especially fine for the well owner. Cheap, quick, and efficient.

There was another peculiar thing done in the Todd field. It was on the edge of the Edwards escarpment and the Edwards lime "outcropped" in the Todd field. This limestone formation extends for hundreds of miles to the southeast. San Antonio and many other towns get most, if not all, of their drinking water from the Edwards aquifer, but it is full of cracks, crevices, and fissures where it lies, and is very difficult to drill through, since all your drilling fluids are lost into the formation. So, in the Todd field, the companies usually set and cemented 8⅝-inch OD casing below 700 feet with cable tools, which did not require water, then moved them off and moved a rotary rig over the hole to finish the well. This was cheaper and much faster than to try to drill the surface hole with a rotary rig.

On the third well we drilled, Sonny Saak drilled out the casing shoe on the surface casing and lost returns, completely—pumped away all the water in the slush pits and reserve tank, with no fluid back to the surface. Evidently, the cable tool driller had not drilled entirely through the limestone. I relieved Sonny about that time, and we were really in a quandary—one hundred and thirty miles from the nearest outlet for drilling mud and lost-circulation material, with no assurance that we would regain returns with the lost-circulation materials that we had available to us on location.

What to do? We had to do *something* to regain circulation, even though we didn't know the size of the crevices we had opened up.

Sonny and I talked it over at length. Then someone had the bright idea that we might use dry wood that would absorb water, swell, and seal the crevices.

We had a standard derrick. The floor was supported by 3-by-12-inch boards nailed to 6-by-8-inch sills laid across the derrick substructure about 4 feet apart. Sonny and his crew stayed overtime to help. We pulled nails out of the floor and tugged a 28-foot-long sill out from under the floor, then hewed it into a semblance of roundness with hatchets and an axe. We then dropped it into the well, which was dry, after first pulling the drill pipe and drill collars out of the hole, and it fell right to bottom. Sonny had "dry-drilled" about 50 feet while pumping all the water away, so we were pretty sure the sill was below the lost-circulation zone.

We had been pumping water while all this was going on, so the steel pits were again full. I ran the bit back in the hole and began to drill on that sill. I had never drilled wood before and didn't know what to expect, but it drilled easily, though I still had no returns. I had made about 16 feet when my derrickman, who was watching the flow line, came up on the floor and said, "You are getting partial returns." It was true; by the time I started drilling formation, I had full returns. Those chunks of wood had gone into the crevices, swelled tight, and sealed off the loss. We finished that well and never lost a drop of fluid. Sonny and I kept it to ourselves, and the roughnecks didn't care. They *knew* we were crazy.

I never used wood on lost circulation again, but it surely worked fine the one time that I did use it. Once in a great while, improvising beats planning.

By the time we had finished our fourth well, S-H-K moved another rig to the Todd field and also a tool pusher, Joe Jones, who had started out with them many years ago. I got ready to quit, but Dick talked me out of it again. He finally made good on his promise to me, but it took him almost another year.

Joe and I got along all right, but I seemed to be getting nowhere fast and wasn't too happy with my work, and I blamed Skinny Hunter.

I went to Dallas and got Amy, who had finally finished her therapy course at Carroll-Driver. We found a fairly nice apartment and, even though her health was poor, got along fairly well. There just wasn't much social life in Big Lake. Mostly, wives in the company stuck together, as they had nothing in common with the ranchers and towns-people. We were a clanny bunch, kept to ourselves, and really did not try to enter into the life of the town. Amy and Abby Saak were close friends, which helped Amy get settled into Big Lake.

The coming to Big Lake of Joe Jones, the tool pusher, changed our lives very little. He was an old cable tool driller and did not like rotary drilling. He and I preserved an armed neutrality. I thought him an old fuddy-duddy, and he thought me a young smart aleck. We were proba-bly both right about each other. There still, at that late date, existed some rivalry between the two drilling methods. We called them "jarheads" or "ropechokers," which was a contemptuous term. They, in turn, called us "swivelnecks" and "mud hogs." Joe left us to our own devices most of the time, and we had to tolerate him. After all, *he* was the boss. However, the work went well, the company was making money, and everyone was fairly content with their lot.

There had always been a great deal of rivalry among drillers. From the very beginning of rotary drilling, drilling contractors have been paid per foot of hole drilled. Consequently, the driller who produced the most footage drilled per tour of duty was the most valuable to his company. It was an odd thing, since the rig had to be maintained in tip-top shape, usually by the daylight driller. He tried to foresee trou-ble and prevent it whenever possible, but his primary job was to make as much hole as he could possibly drill, and his prestige depended upon footage drilled. Oh yes, many contractors would often say, "Old John does keep a good rig, but . . ." and pretty soon old John would be gone and a new daylight driller had his job. It was a mean, cutthroat system, but it worked, almost perfectly, for the contractor.

Sonny, Red Reed, and I were friends. We liked and trusted each other and for a long time had done things our way. This all changed when the other rig moved into the field and Joe Jones took charge of the two rigs. Joe brought three drillers with him, two old S-H-K drillers and one new one. He took Red Reed off our rig and placed him on the other rig, then put the new driller with Sonny and me. I have forgotten that man's name, but he was lazy, slow, and a backbiter. Sonny and I decided very quickly that he was going to be a real problem to us, because he was always whining to Joe. He had more excuses for shoddy work than "Carter had liver pills."

This was in the days before automatic drillers, so in order to keep an even weight on the bit, a driller had to stand at the brake and feed off weight by slacking off on the brake, and good drillers did this, but lazy ones "gouge-drilled." They would slack off a fairly large amount of weight at one time, then let it "drill off." It was a bad method. Too much weight would damage the bit and when it drilled off, the lesser weight slowed your rate of penetration. This guy was bone lazy and that was the way he tried to drill, so bits he ran didn't last long. He wore them out much too quickly. I was relieving him and soon learned that he always left me a very dull bit.

I had a fast rig and an excellent crew, and he wouldn't be out of sight before I would trip the pipe to change bits, get back on bottom as quickly as I could with a new bit, then make up for lost time. Both Sonny and I were "out-holing" him pretty badly, and he would complain to me that Sonny was leaving him in bad shape every day. It was a lie, and I knew it and paid no attention to his carping. But he began to whine to Joe, who liked him, mostly because the guy flattered him and pretended to look up to him. Joe questioned Sonny and me sharply and made both of us mad as the devil. We wondered how he could be so blind to this clown. Then Joe complained to the office, and that tore it wide open.

Dick Hodges and his wife, Martha, came to Big Lake. They checked into the hotel and took Amy, myself, Sonny, and Abby to dinner—told us that Joe had complained about us and demanded to know what in the hell was going on out at the rig. Now Sonny, Red, and I had roughnecked for Dick years ago when he was drilling, and were known in the company as "Dick's men." Sonny and I knew he would listen, so we told him that man was a lazy, no-good son of a bitch who didn't do his work and blamed his failure on other people. The old man listened. He knew we were telling the truth, and so he finally said, "Joe likes him and is protecting him, and if I fire him, it will cause a big stink in the company. Skinny Hunter won't like it if I go over Joe's head, so you boys get rid of him *for* me, ride him off the job."

We had a free hand, and he never knew what hit him. I would leave Sonny with a sharp bit; he would gut it, have both pumps down and be repairing them, then leave the guy low on water. The poor bastard didn't have a prayer. He had nothing but trouble from that day forward. Nobody felt sorry for him, and finally even Joe turned against him and fired him. Everyone was glad. We got another driller and things returned to normal. It doesn't pay to fight with other drillers. Cooperation pays off much better and it makes a better job.

By now, nearly all of our crew were local boys and most of them made top hands. Many had worked for little money and thought that roughnecking was a good deal. Some were married, some single, and most all of them were young men. One exception was a man of about forty years, an old cow-and-sheep-ranch hand. Everyone called him "Turkey," as he was an expert turkey caller. He loved to hunt and was an expert woodsman. He had a wife who adored him, and six or seven kids, all as wild as goats. His ambition was to save enough money to go back to Rock Springs, Texas, as he had been born there in the hill country, then spend the rest of his life hunting, trapping, and guiding deer hunters in the fall of the year. I asked old Dr. Patterson, who was the county health officer, how Turkey could ever save any money when he had to pay for a baby delivery each year. Doc just laughed and said, "Hell, I delivered the first one with Turkey's help. But he has delivered all the others, so I just check on her and the new baby the next day. He always does a good job, so I just charge him $10.00." Turkey was a funny old boy, a good hand, and he did, at last, get to go back home. I never saw or heard of him again, but wished him well. He was a real character and not a bad midwife.

There were eight rigs running in the Todd field at that time—six besides our two rigs. We had a real "shirttail" boom going, and Big Lake began to grow until it was bulging at the seams. Hands began to drift into town from other places, housing got scarce, and a small supply company moved into town. One local man built a motel and filled it up overnight. The young bucks needed a place to blow off steam, so a couple of beer joints came into the picture. There wasn't any bad trouble. Sheriff Billingsly kept things under control, but the jail began to do a very nice business in overnight drunks.

Amy and I had a problem. Her health was failing, and she felt ill most of the time. She went to Dr. Patterson, who was past seventy years old, and he told her frankly that he didn't know what was wrong with her. He said, "Gal, I can't be sure; you are either pregnant or have a tumor in your uterus." He got her an appointment with a Dr. Rape in San Angelo. We went to Dr. Rape, who was a specialist in gynecology. After many tests, he told her she needed an operation, since she *did* have a tumor. It scared us both, but after talking it over, we decided to go to Dallas to the doctor who had been treating her prior to her coming to Big Lake.

We went to Dallas. Joe Jones was reluctant to let me off the job, so I went over his head to the main office. They said go ahead and not to worry about my job. We got the second opinion from doctors in Dallas, and Amy had a hysterectomy at St. Paul's Hospital. She came through the operation with no problems and the tumor was benign—a great relief, since we had both been greatly worried about it being malignant.

My Uncle Jim had married and lived in Dallas, and he and his wife promised to see after Amy's welfare when she left the hospital. I made arrangements with an elderly widow lady who lived across the street from Uncle Jim for Amy to live with her during her convalescence. Mrs. Frost was a dear old friend I had known for years, so I knew Amy would be well cared for since Uncle Jim and his wife lived just across the street.

I stayed in Dallas one week. Amy did well and was progressing okay, so I had to go back to work, since money was necessary and medical bills were high even in those days. So I came back alone to live a bachelor's existence for an indefinite time. A bachelor's life isn't something that I like. I prefer married life, but what you get, you live with.

One of the longtime drawbacks of life in the oil fields has always been a lamentable lack of medical services. Most of the towns near a boom were small, usually less than 6,000 people, with only a few doctors in town, maybe a small clinic, but rarely ever a hospital. When the boom hit, the population often doubled or tripled, which overloaded the doctors, who were sadly overworked, and this made a very bad situation. Also, many doctors who were incompetent or drunks followed the booms, for with a large floating population, they could practice much better than they could have in an old, settled town.

We were in the same shape in Big Lake. There were a total of two doctors in town. Dr. Patterson was a good, honest doctor, but he was past seventy years old and had begun to limit his practice. The other doctor was new in town and was a drunk, totally unreliable, and often unavailable to his patients. It was 80 miles to San Angelo and 100 to Odessa; consequently, anyone who became ill or was injured was in real trouble. However, most oil-field trash are a hardy bunch and did not consider an 80-mile drive a big thing. We were inured to a hard life, including poor housing, long drives to work over terrible roads, greasy-spoon cafes, being ostracized by townspeople, and took it all pretty much in stride.

Wives stayed put, especially if they had children in school. The men were footloose, away from home, and it was a vagabond existence. Childless couples usually stayed together, but it was rough on wives—lots of moving and a succession of not-too-good apartments. Still, we were well paid. Wages in the oil patch usually were much higher than the prevailing wages in other lines of work, so we stuck with the job.

We had been in Big Lake for more than a year that summer of 1947. We had drilled with our rig eight wells in the Todd field. We had made good time on each of them, and felt that we had done an exceptional job. The other company rig had drilled four wells. None of us had a bad fishing job, and no disasters, so we felt very pleased with ourselves. Our crews were about 80 percent local people. Some of them were a bit different from run-of-the-mill folk. One little guy in particular, named Sid Schwabe, was a real character. He was thirty-five or thirty-six years old, stood 5 feet 7 inches tall in his stocking feet, weighed a solid 125 pounds, and did not have a thumb on either hand. A real "he-man," and I'm not joking, for the little man was fearless. He had lost both his thumbs in rig accidents before he came to work for us, and even though being thumbless was a real handicap, Sid never let it bother him. He was a good roughneck.

Sid and his wife were divorced, and they had two teenaged daughters whom Sid adored. He never missed an opportunity to see those kids. They lived in Ozona with their mother, and each payday Sid would go to Ozona to see the girls and pay his ex-wife child support. For Sid, it was a labor of love, and he never let those children down. They were the lights of his life.

It was his one virtue. He loved to drink, play poker, and get into fights. He never won a fight that I remember, but he never stopped trying to win one. His fists without thumbs were pitiful and kept him from being able to hit really hard, but he operated on the theory that someday his foe's foot would slip and he would beat hell out of him. But it never happened, not even one time.

Sid was working for Louis Hood, who was relieving me on the job. One day he didn't show up and I asked where he was and Louis said he wasn't feeling well, but would be back at work the next day. He did come to work the next day, and he looked like hell struck with a club. Both eyes were black, his nose was about twice its usual size, and he had a generous bunch of bruises, yellow, green, black, and blue. I looked at him, blinked, and asked, "Sid, what in the hell happened to you?"

"Stud," he said, "you will never believe it, knowing what a peaceable man I am. I went to Ozona day before yesterday to see the kids and pay the wife off, then took the kids to lunch. After lunch, I drove out to the county line to buy a drink as Ozona is in a dry county. No sooner was I in the joint, when this loudmouth at the bar started telling everyone how tough he was. I looked at him. He was about 6 foot 3 inches, weighed about 215 pounds, and looked able to do all the things he said he had done, so I accepted his story. I had a few drinks. I knew the old gal who owned the joint, and we visited a bit, but old loudmouth just kept on telling the world how tough he was, and it began to get on my nerves. I got up and told the woman who ran the place to wrap up a pint of whiskey to go, since I might need fortification later when I got to Ozona. Then old tough guy invited himself to ride back to Ozona with me. I let him, since I had no real reason to refuse, and as you know, I am a peaceful soul. We got into the car and started to town. He immediately began where he left off, telling me all about how tough he was, and I finally got a bellyful of him. We were about 7 miles west of Ozona when I pulled over to the shoulder of the road and stopped. This ape asked what was the matter, and I told him I thought I had a low tire. I walked around the car and came up on his side, then jerked the door open on him. He squared around and said, "What's going on here?" I brought my fist up out of the bar ditch and hit that big son of a bitch right between the eyes, with every ounce of me behind my fist, and he didn't even *blink!* I knew right off that he was just as tough as he said he was, and after a little while I asked him, "Feller, can you see?" He said he could see fine, so I asked him to drive us to Ozona, since both my eyes were swelled shut. He did. I finally got to Big Lake today, and that's why I missed yesterday." Sid was a gritty little cuss and never gave an inch to people bigger than he was. He really believed that God created men equal, and spent his life trying to prove that it was true.

Summer went into fall, and we had two floods. We had to cross Howard's Draw about 10 miles south of town to get to the job. One afternoon I was on evening tour and it rained hard. When we got to the draw, it was flooding, so we turned around and went to work by way of Barnhart and Ozona, and came up from the south. We had to cross Howard's Draw twice by that route. We made the first crossing fine, but when we got to the second one, about 5 miles upstream, the water was 15 feet over the crossing. We knew we were in trouble and turned around to try to get back across the first ford, but just as we arrived back at the ford, a 10-foot head rise just beat us to the crossing. We were trapped, spent six hours sitting in the car in the rain, and finally made our way out to the highway across pastures. Never did get to the job, and got home about two o'clock in the morning. The oil fields could, and did, get cantankerous once in awhile, just to keep you on your toes, and to remind you that nothing came to you easily all of the time.

The winter of 1947–1948 wasn't bad at all. We enjoyed good weather most of the winter. We were on the northwest edge of the Edwards Plateau in the beginning of the hill and live oak country. We were drilling on a portion of the old Shannon Ranch empire, which the heirs had leased to a man named Joe Myers. Mr. Myers' family lived in San Angelo, but he stayed close to his ranch headquarters, ate in the bunkhouse with his hands, and lived a bachelor's life most of the time. He often came by the rig to drink coffee and talk. We thought him lonely, and since all of us liked him, we always made him welcome, listened to his stories, then told him a few of our own yarns. It always pays rig crews to get on good terms with the landowner, since they are actually guests on his land. Joe Myers made it easy for us, and we enjoyed our days on the Myers' spread.

Joe invited Sonny and me over to see a sheep shearing that spring. Neither of us knew anything at all about ranching, so we thought it would be a good experience. We went, and it was a real revelation. We had an enjoyable time and learned a lot about sheep handling.

Sheep shearing crews are nomadic and follow the seasons, just like the harvest hands. They start in deep South Texas early in the spring of the year, then gradually work their way northward to the Canadian border.

The boss man or *jefe* usually owns the shearing machine and furnishes the crew. The crew on Myers' job consisted of six men and a boy of thirteen or fourteen years of age. They were all Mexican-Americans and came from Laredo, Texas. There were five shearers and one cook, who was a part-time shearer. The boy was there to pick up and sack fleeces. The work was fast, efficient, and a little brutal, since the men were paid by the number of fleeces they sheared in a day. They handled the sheep roughly and brooked no stubbornness from them. If the power shears skinned a furrow down a sheep's back, the boy who gathered fleeces dabbed a creosote tar compound on the cut and turned it loose. Each time the boy picked up a fleece, he gave the shearer a brass check, and the number of checks determined the size of the shearer's day's pay. So the work was fast and furious and interesting to watch.

Joe introduced us to the shearers, and we all shook hands very formally. These men were very polite, and I noticed as I shook hands with each man how soft and silky the skin on his hands was, and I wondered about it, since these were strong, rough men who looked like bandits, and had hands that would have been envied by a movie star. Joe laughed when I mentioned the amazing hands and said if I handled wool all day, that my hands would become just as soft, since the lanolin in the wool was responsible. I never saw another shearing, but I also never forgot the one I did see. It was a dandy.

Spring eased into summer. Our cable tool people who were drilling and setting pipe in our surface holes got behind. We finished a well, and they did not have another one ready for us to drill. So we had to wait for a few days on them. We welcomed the shutdown, as we planned to do some needed repairs on the rig, which had been in continuous use for almost two years.

Some of the fellows wanted to take a few days off, go down to Ojinaga, Mexico, get drunk, and go whoring, and since the work on the rig wasn't pressing, we let them off. Four of them went and brought back a very odd story.

Louis Hood had hired a boy about six months before this incident. He was from Brady, Texas, and was as green as grass in the spring, so, naturally, everybody called him "Worm." I am quite sure that he had another name, but I never knew what it was. He was just "Worm," and the name fit him. He was about twenty years old, 6 feet 3 inches tall, and about as big around as a telephone pole. He ran largely to hands, feet, and ears, and was a little slow on the uptake. He was easygoing, the butt of many jokes, and a likable kid. We overlooked his slowness because he was a good lad who tried his best to be a good hand.

He was one of the four who took off to Mexico. He had never been to a border town and felt very daring to be going to Mexico with old experienced men. I didn't hear from them for three days. Then they came back, and told us what a hell of a time they had. The story was told by one of the guys and went like this: "We got to Ojinaga, stopped in a cantina and had a few drinks, then we wound up in a crib house to drink some more and screw some of the gals. They were all young, some were pretty, and we finally got down to the real reason we came to Mexico. We all picked out a girl to spend the night with and separated. Worm was drunk enough to shed his shyness and had cavorted, danced, and drank like us older fellows, so he felt like a man of the world. Me and my girl went to her room and took along a quart of tequila in case we got thirsty. We poured ourselves drinks and began to undress.

"About that time, a lot of loud talk broke out in the next room. It is hot as the devil in Ojinaga all of the time, and this was late summer. The partitions between those cribs did not go all the way to the ceiling. They stopped about 18 inches below the ceiling for more ventilation. It didn't do much for the privacy, not that we cared for privacy. The noise next door went on, so I pushed a chair over near the wall, got up on it, and peeked over the partition. There stood Worm and his gal, both naked as jaybirds, except Worm had on his knee-high cowboy boots. I could tell he was big sailing drunk, and that little whore kept pointing at those boots and yelling at him in Spanish. He didn't understand a word of it, but it finally dawned on him that she wanted him to pull off those damn boots. He glared at her and said in English, 'What in hell's the matter with you, gal? You want me to catch athlete's foot?' I almost exploded. There are many things you can catch in a crib house, but athlete's foot isn't one of them. She finally quieted down, he did *not* pull off the boots, and they finally went to bed. We all woke up with a monstrous hangover and came back to Texas and home. The road back was three times as long as the road down, but we made it, finally. Worm suffered but didn't die, and sure as hell isn't in a hurry to go back to Mexico. I think we broke him into the Bordertown fraternity too quickly and he will probably never be the same again."

Big Lake back in those days got its water from a bored well out on the edge of town. That water was highly mineralized and contained, among other minerals, 3 percent magnesium sulphate—Epsom salts to you. We all went through an indoctrination and it lost its effect on us, but newcomers to town, especially salesmen, drank the water and immediately thought they had come down with a virulent disease. Old Doc Patterson told them that it would pass and wasn't at all serious. Still, some folks got mighty upset, as it isn't funny to come into a town feeling fine, then spend half the night awake with the green-apple trots. Big Lake wasn't a striking town, but if you ever lived there, you never forgot the place. It was just—well—different. It had a poker game nearly every night—ranchers, tool pushers, and townsmen. Sheriff Billingsly never played, but never interfered either. It was a tough, hard game, played for blood, and without mercy for a loser. I played occasionally when Amy was in the hospital in Dallas, but gave it up when she came home. She hated gambling, with one exception. She would bet on a horse race, something I never understood.

Our days in Big Lake were coming to an end. We had been living there for almost two years. We had drilled twenty wells, and the ones we were drilling, numbers 21 and 22, would be the last. Amy and Abby Saak, Sonny's wife, drove up to Odessa to try to find living quarters. Odessa was bursting at the seams, and a place to live was a real hairy problem. Amy finally bought a small house on East 17th Street. It wasn't half bad, small but livable. Poor Abby finally rented a junky two-room deal behind a cheap hotel. It was pretty awful for three people, and Freda, the daughter, was now twelve. But you were lucky to get a place to sleep in Odessa in 1947. They came back to Big Lake in triumph, and we made plans to move just as soon as we finished the well we were drilling.

Joe Jones, our pusher, fell afoul of management. Rumor had it that he would be let go, and it caused lots of talk in the company. We finished our well and moved out, but Joe stayed with the rig that was left. It was about ten days behind us and I never knew just what happened, but Joe never came back to Odessa. He retired and went back to Oklahoma. I, for one, did not miss him. We just didn't like each other.

Chapter Eleven

Back to Odessa, Still Drilling

Three of my roughnecks moved to Odessa—the Harris brothers, Wash and Pat, and J. N. Clark—but Prestige Kane stayed in Big Lake. He owned his little home there, and his wife was expecting a baby. I hated to lose him. He was my derrickman, but I put Wash Harris to working derricks and found out that he was a real natural born "attic hand."

Our rig moved into the Andector field just northeast of Goldsmith, Texas, on a Phillips Petroleum Company location. It was only 25 miles from Odessa, and the road was paved, a real luxury ride after Big Lake's dusty dirt roads.

I got some good news, too. I was up for a pushing job at last. Dick Hodges and Skinny Hunter had finally agreed, the company recognized seniority, and my hands knew they would work for someone on my rig. I would supervise, and I would take over when the next rig came in from Oklahoma. I sure was happy to have those three guys with me. They were extraordinary roughnecks, ornery, but smart and quick. I needed one more man, and he came out of nowhere that summer of 1947. A strange boy, quiet, willing, and badly in need of a job, since he had not a cent of money. I needed a hand, and since it was probably a short-time job, I had asked one of my roughnecks to find me a temporary hand. Pat Harris found this kid on the sidewalk in front of a cheap little diner, hired him, and we took him out to work that afternoon.

We were working 4 miles north of the village of Goldsmith. Goldsmith is 20 miles northwest of Odessa, where we all lived, and we always stopped on the way to the job each afternoon at a drug store in Goldsmith, drank cokes, coffee, or a soda, and exchanged gossip with the owner. It was a pleasant little routine, and we all enjoyed the pause. We took turns driving to work, and if a man did not own a car, he paid the driver "transportation." It was never a large amount; usually from twenty-five to fifty cents, depending on the length of the drive.

This boy had nothing, no gloves, no work clothing, and no work shoes. All the clothes he had he was wearing: a shabby pair of black oxfords, a cheap pair of slacks, and a dirty white shirt. When he got into the car, we each knew just how badly off he was, since at some time in our lives we had been in the same shape, flat broke.

We stopped for coffee at Goldsmith as usual. I bought the boy two sandwiches and a slab of apple pie, and an apple, since we would be working until midnight. A growling belly makes for a poor, inattentive hand. We all carried lunches and felt that he also needed one. I was driving that day, and the boy was in the back seat with J. N. Clark and Pat Harris. They said later that he ate those two sandwiches and the pie before we got out of town, wolfed 'em down in big bites, so they knew he was very hungry.

We got to the job, and by that time the boys in the crew had adopted the kid. They all had extra work clothes in the change house and outfitted him pretty well. He looked almost like a roughneck, but he was greener than a gourd. He had never been on a drilling rig floor before and sure as hell didn't know what to do, but he learned. Boy, did he learn! Those three outlaws who worked for me took full charge of that young man. By the time we came off tour at midnight, he could handle his tongs pretty well, remembered to always grab his slip, and had acquired a nickname. He didn't move too swiftly, so naturally they called him "Lightning."

Lightning was a strange lad. He would never look you squarely in the eye, never talk about where he came from, nor how he was raised. He never mentioned that he had a family or hometown, and if questioned along that line, would get wild-eyed and nervous. And he would either dummy up, or get up and move about, so we really never did learn much about him. This in itself was rare. Usually, roughnecks gave their life histories to other roughnecks. Lightning didn't; as far as we knew, he was born full grown, about ten days before we hired him.

He had been working for me for three or four days. I had loaned him ten dollars "eating money," and had earned his trust as a result. I was not just his boss, I was a "good boss," and he tried his best to please me. I asked him that evening as night fell to change three or four burned-out light bulbs. These were strung around the first girt of the derrick, about 10 feet above the derrick floor. He looked at me as though he was about to cry and said, "Stud, I can't do it. I just can't. They never would let me climb, and I'm afraid." It wasn't a big deal, so I called to Pat Harris and he changed the bulbs. And I didn't even ask who "they" were who would not let him climb.

We got a payday a few days later, and Lightning really blossomed. He paid me, bought some work clothes, moved out of the "fleabag hotel" to a fairly decent little third-rate rooming house. He perked up, joked with the boys a bit, and it was clear that he had begun to be a member of the oil-field trash fraternity. But he remained a bit of a mystery. He never talked about himself and was very reticent about his background, so we naturally wondered about him.

We still stopped at Goldsmith Drug Store for coffee each day. Lightning never stayed at the counter to chew the fat with the owner, as the rest of us did. He would get up and roam aimlessly around the drug store as we finished our coffee.

One day, Pat Harris came out to the brake to me and said, "Driller, Lightning is stealing little things at the drug store. He tries to give them to us, little things like combs, candy bars, handkerchiefs, and the like. He is going to get caught and be in trouble, and I think you should talk to him. He will listen to you."

I asked the boy about it, and he got very upset. He didn't deny the stealing, but did deny any desire to keep any of the stuff. He had a wild look in his eye and said, "I don't want that stuff. I try to give it to the boys. I don't know why I do things like that. Please don't fire me." I said, "Lad, I'm not going to fire you. I know you wouldn't steal from me, and the man who runs that drug store is a personal friend of mine. Stealing from him is just the same as stealing from me, so stop it, now!" He promised and kept his promise, and things settled back to normal again.

We made a couple more paydays and Lightning began to come out of his shell. He was proud of his job and had made a better than average hand. He could not climb, and we never got him to go as high as the first girt, but he wasn't afraid of anything else. So we could not understand why he refused to climb.

After he had been working with us for about three months, one afternoon I was driving and stopped to pick up Lightning to go to work. The rest of the crew was in the car. Just as he came out the door of the rooming house, two deputy U. S. marshals got out of a parked car and arrested him. I was surprised and angry, so I questioned these two men. I told them I was the boy's boss and knew he had been working steadily for about three months and caused no trouble, and they told me that he had escaped from the hospital for the criminally insane in Abilene, Texas, and they had a warrant for him. There wasn't much I could do, and Lightning looked stricken and was as pale as death. He asked me to please bring his drag-up check to the county jail and give it to him personally. I said I would and, angry and upset, went on to work. The kid had six days' pay coming, and I wrote him a time order, got his check, and went up to the jail the next morning. The sheriff let me see him, but before they took me upstairs, the sheriff gave me his background. Lightning was an epileptic and a kleptomaniac and had been committed by his mother after he beat up his stepfather. He had had an epileptic fit that night when they put him in his cell. The sheriff said that he had to go back to Abilene to finish his term, and I couldn't do anything to help him.

They took me up to see the boy. He saw me coming down the corridor and began to cry. He told me that the three months he had worked for me were the happiest days of his life, that he would always remember me and the crew, and with a pitiful bit of bragging, said he hadn't had a single seizure while he worked for me. I shook hands, cried, too, gave him his money, told him he had been a good lad, and left him clinging to the bars.

I never saw or heard of him after that day, but always thought he might have been saved under different circumstances. But we finally learned why he couldn't climb. Epileptics are constantly warned to never climb, and Lightning obeyed the warnings.

We missed Lightning and grieved over him, too, but he was out of our lives forever. We all felt that given a few more months with us, he might have made it. Alas, we never heard of him again.

Our rig was drilling for Phillips Petroleum Company. I knew the lease superintendent, George Mossman, and we got along fine. Mr. Mossman neither smoked nor drank, was religious, and a good man to work for. I was destined to cross his path many times in the years to come.

We were setting three strings of casing in each well, roughly 500 feet of 12^1/$_2$-inch surface pipe, then approximately 5,000 feet of 8^5/$_8$-inch casing for a "salt string." We had to drill through thick salt beds, using brine as a drilling medium to keep from leaching out big cavities in the salt.

Then, when we ran the 8^5/$_8$-inch casing, we calipered the hole for size, calculated how much cement it would take to fill, and cemented back the casing to the surface. This was done to prevent corrosion of the pipe. Sometimes we used huge amounts of cement. Then we would reduce the size of the hole to 7^7/$_8$-inch and drill to the pay zone at approximately 10,000 feet, then run 5^1/$_2$-inch casing as a production string. Phillips called the shots as to hole size and the weights and grades of casing. Their representative, or, in roughneck talk, the "company man," supervised the running and cementing of each string of pipe. He was very important to the rig crews and the tool pusher. He could be, and sometimes was, a "real bastard" who had to be pleased, *somehow,* but generally he was a regular fellow, and easy to deal with, *if* you did *your* job properly. A sorry, slovenly crew on a rig could make a company man's job much harder. We adjusted to each other pretty well as a rule. Hell, we had to. We all had to earn a living. Of course, the rig crews had to do most of the "getting along." A consistent bunch of complaints from company people could cause big repercussions, such as *you* getting fired. So, it behooved you to do your work as well as you knew how, and to create just as few waves as possible. There was often some friction, but never very much. We all practiced tolerance and tried to get the job done as easily as possible. We were lucky to have gotten George. He was one of the really good "company men."

We drilled two wells in the Andector with no problems. The promised rig was still in Oklahoma, so I was, in essence, marking time. Amy got on a deal, and swapped the little house for a trailer house, just in case we had to move. It was our first time to live in a trailer house, and when you start adjusting to living space 8 feet wide by 30 feet long, you have to adjust everything, including your thinking, because it is a very condensed form of living.

Trailer houses, or mobile homes, as they are called today, changed the oil fields completely. For the first time, wives and families moved with the men. It was a welcome but radical change; family life even in a trailer house beat living in a bowl and pitcher hotel. And dads got reacquainted with their kids. The old tale about the driller coming home from a long time away, who walked up to his gate and saw his eight-year-old daughter in the yard, only to have her jump up and run in the house yelling, "Mama, here's that man again," died away.

The kids adjusted fine and, even though they changed schools often, did as well as ever. The smart ones learned, and the dumb ones did not, just like the long-time-in-one-place pupils. Amy and I had no kids, so we had always been together. Still, the trailer helped us, too. We never had to rent and clean up another dingy apartment, and God knows, we had cleaned up many a one.

The trailer came in handy. The company got a contract to drill two wells in the old Dollarhide field about 12 miles east of Jal, New Mexico. We all moved to Kermit, Texas, and I was glad we had the trailer. We rented a place to park, rigged up, and were "at home" in half a day, a pretty good deal.

The wells we were to drill were for the Pacific Western Company, a wholly owned subsidiary of the Skelly Oil Company. They were projected to 11,000 feet and, though they were on the extreme west edge of the field, presented no problems. Our company man lived south of Kermit in a Skelly camp. We reported to him by phone and rarely saw him. He was strictly a production man and was not too familiar with drilling procedures. So, since it was a footage contract, we drilled it our way. In other words, we hurried. I had my usual, old crew: Clark, the Harris brothers, and one new hand. He was a good one, and we prided ourselves on speed. We pulled out of the hole one night to change bits. We were 10,000 feet deep, had 103 stands of drill pipe and eight stands of drill collars, each stand 93 feet long. We were back on bottom in four and one-half hours, drilling. The same trip today would take at least eight hours, as speed has gone from the oil fields. We were fast, and careful, too. Our safety record was perfect, and we looked out for each other. That was the best and smartest crew I ever had. They were wild, tough, and ornery, on and off the job, but they worked just like they lived, hard!

We punched that first well down in good time, drilled a few feet into the pay zone, the Ellenburger limestone. Skelly decided to drill-stem test the zone since we were on the extreme edge of the field. And taking a DST takes a bit of doing.

To take a routine DST, you first pull your drill pipe and bit out of the hole. Then you make up a special tool, furnished by a service company that does work of this nature. On this job we used the Halliburton Company. This tool has two packers made of rubber and steel that can be collapsed to seal the well bore. Below the packers is enough pipe to span the interval to be tested, with perforations in some of the pipes, to permit oil or gas to enter the tool. This tool can be opened and closed by manipulation of the drill pipe string, and is run in the hole in the closed position, which means that the inside of the drill pipe is empty.

We made up the Halliburton test tool and went in the hole, tagged bottom, then collapsed the packers and opened the tool.

At the surface we had installed a manifold with pressure gauges and chokes to be able to control the flow, if any, when the tool was opened. There is a small-sized high-pressure valve leading off one side of the manifold. A small rubber hose is attached to the valve with the loose end stuck down in a 5-gallon bucket of water. When the test tool is opened, if anything—salt water, oil, or gas—enters the empty drill pipe, you get bubbles in the bucket, so the hose is called a "bubble hose." If the flow is weak or strong, you have a good indication of the strength of the formation you have penetrated.

On this test, we got a fair blow immediately, gradually increasing to a good sustained blow where it leveled off. The choke in the bubble hose is $1/8$ inch in diameter, a small hole, and steady blow, not too strong, usually means salt water. Still, you can never be sure until you pull the tool, or get a flow at the surface, so a lot of learned guessing usually takes place among people at the scene, and most of it is wrong!

Generally, the operating company, on this job, Skelly, has an experienced geologist and a drilling foreman on the job, since the test is their

Gerald Lynch in Odessa, 1984

At his mother's farm, on vacation from Illinois in 1940.

(*Top*) Gerald Lynch on his first drilling job, Canton, Texas, 1929. (*Bottom*) Drilling with King and Stegall rig, south of Kilgore, ca. 1936–1937. Gerald Lynch is at left.

The Blanche Blewett No. 1 making a trip to change bits, 8 miles southwest of Canton, 1929. Gerald Lynch is at the brake.

(*Top left*) At his mother's farm in 1929: "I had just made driller—all 123 pounds of me." (*Bottom left*) Tool house and A-frame of jackknife derrick. (*Above*) Mr. Bailey (*left*) and Gerald Lynch (*right*) at a Safety Dinner in Lovington, New Mexico, 1954.

Standard derrick of the type used in the 1950s and 1960s. These have since been phased out.

Modern jackknife derrick.

responsibility. We were not lucky. Our man was a production foreman with very limited drilling experience, but a stubborn, opinionated man. The contractor's rep was our drilling superintendent, Dick Hodges, who certainly knew what he was doing. He had run many a test.

So we watched the test. The flow was steady, not too strong but fair. Our company man had orders to leave the tool open three hours if it didn't flow. He was about sixty years old, and didn't want anything bad to mess up his retirement, so he went strictly by the book. At the end of the three-hour period, he told the Halliburton man we would pull the tool, and just as the tool man broke a union on the line, lo and behold, oil came to the surface. A real big surprise. The company man yelled to put the line back together. We did and turned the flow through a line to a tank battery. It was getting late in the afternoon, and we figured an hour's flow would satisfy our man. We were wrong. He left that damned tool open three solid hours, put 210 barrels of oil into the tank, and then, late in the afternoon, let us shut the tool in, to get a shut-in pressure reading on the bottom hole pressure chart that had been run in the hole in the test tool.

Now, as a general rule, when a test flows and the drill pipe is full of live oil, you drop a steel bar about 4 feet long and open a circulating sub, positioned 60 to 90 feet above the packers in the drill string. Then, by closing the blowout preventer and pumping down the outside of your drill pipe, you can reverse out all the oil in the drill pipe, leaving mud inside the pipe. This eliminates the fire hazard—a very present danger, as live oil is just as volatile as gasoline. I got ready to drop the opening bar when the company man stopped me. He then informed me that we were not going to reverse out the oil. I asked him why the hell *not,* and didn't he know how dangerous it was to pull drill pipe filled with live oil, since every time you broke off a stand, the oil in the stand spilled out all over the floor, ran down into the cellar and all around the rig? He said it wasn't all that bad, and he wouldn't reverse out in any case, and we had a lively argument. Dick Hodges finally ended it by telling me to pull a few stands to see how it went. He was just being diplomatic and hoped that that stupid man would see how dangerous a position he was putting us in, so I pulled a stand, wrapped the mud box round the break, broke the joint, picked up the stand, and oil went everywhere. Then the gas trapped in the drill pipe with the oil belched and sprayed us, and the rig floor, again.

I had a bellyful, so I told the men on the floor to take the water hose and wash the floor, and the light bulbs around the first girt. Those were naked 100-watt bulbs strung around the rig floor and up the derrick leg behind the driller's station. The time was close to when we had to turn the rig lights on, and if a light bulb blew when oil was spraying, we were dead men. While they washed up, I went down the stairs from the dog house and talked to the powers that be, who were safe and comfortable in the company man's car, about 100 feet from the rig. I told them that we needed to either reverse out, or shut down until daylight, since the rig lights were not vapor proof and one defective bulb could kill us.

That stupid old bastard wouldn't budge from his position. It didn't look dangerous to him, so I said, "Listen, it's damned easy to be brave when you are not in danger. I'll pull this test out, but you two sons-of-bitches are not going to sit in the car while we do it. You come up on the floor and stand by *me* while we work. Surely you won't mind since it isn't, to hear you tell it, at all dangerous. Then, if we have a fire, we will all die together."

I'll give 'em credit. They got out of the car, followed me up to the derrick floor, and stood at my shoulder. Then I told them, "As long as you stand here with me, we will pull pipe. When you leave, we will shut down, so here we go."

I kicked the clutch in and started out, pulled a stand, and told Clark to stand by the master light switch, just in case. Of course, it was useless, but I wanted to make that old devil uneasy, and I did succeed in doing that very thing.

We broke that stand off and when the oil hit those naked bulbs and began smoking, our brave company man broke and ran, through the tool house and down the stairs. I shut down, called Wash Harris to come down out of the derrick, and to watch that oily ladder. We broke out the water hose, turned on the cellar jet, and began to clean up. It took two hours to get rid of that oil.

A car started up and left. Dick Hodges came up on the derrick floor, grinning. He said, "I think you made a true believer out of our company man. He has gone home, and he needed to go. He shit his pants." We laughed, but it wasn't funny. Idiots like him have caused many mens' deaths. We did gain something. He pulled in his horns from then on, and we got along fine. We completed the well, drilled another one, then moved the rig back to the south Fullerton field, about 17 miles west of Andrews, Texas. It was the month of January 1948, and the winter was *cold,* a forerunner of 1949, which was *really* cold.

We had trouble on that south Fullerton well, lots of trouble. It was scheduled to go to the Ellenburger, but we lost circulation in the Devonian formation. I was drilling morning tour, when I suddenly lost all the weight off the bit. I was running 25,000 pounds weight on the bit, and suddenly, I had nothing. I slacked off 23 feet before the bit took weight again, so I had drilled into a sizable cavity or crevice. Wash Harris came running up from the pits, yelling that we had lost returns and were pumping all the mud in the slush pits away. I pulled up to put the bit about 35 feet off bottom to avoid sticking the drill pipe, an ever present danger, then sent a man up to the Phillips camp about 10 miles north. He told the lease foreman, who immediately called the company mud engineer. We began to mix mud and lost-circulation material consisting of cellophane flakes, mica flakes, cottonseed hulls, cane fiber, and everything else on hand. But when we went off tour at 8:00 A.M., we had not gotten circulation back, and since we had a potential pay zone open, it began to present a real hazard. As the fluid level fell, the pressure on the formation grew less, so a blowout became a real possibility.

Drilling wells are controlled by the weight of your drilling fluids or by closing the blowout preventers (BOP). You cannot drill when the BOP is closed, so your key to well control is your drilling fluid. Drilling mud is made up of bentonitic powder or gels, weight material, commonly barite (the hands call it "bar," although I don't know how it came to be called that). You use gels for viscosity in order to improve the lifting power of your fluids. Samples come up larger and the geologists are happy, but your drilling slows down and the contractor is unhappy: a no-win deal for a driller. The zone we feared was the Clearfork at approximately 6,500 feet. It was being produced in the south Fullerton. In fact, a producing well, offsetting the one we were drilling, was a Clearfork well.

Our mud when we drilled into the Devonian at 9,600 feet weighed 9.3 pounds per gallon, which made the hydrostatic pressure of our mud column on the Clearfork slightly more than 3,000 pounds per square inch, a good safety margin, as the zone was not a highly pressured formation. However, when we lost returns, the hydrostatic pressure fell drastically. We didn't, and couldn't, know where the fluid level was, so everyone was a bit edgy, with good reason. We had a tiger by the tail.

We went off tour that morning, and I went home to bed, nervous and tired. Sonny Saak was drilling days, and he and Abby came over to our house that evening about 6 o'clock. I was awake and eating breakfast, not unusual when you are working midnight to 8:00 A.M. Sonny said that he had not regained circulation either, but had made a trip, stood the drill collars back in the derrick, laid down the bit and gone back in the hole open-ended. He said, too, that Leroy Pope, the mud engineer for Phillips, had just about decided on using Halliburton Cementing Company to mix up a conglomeration of drilling mud, lost-circulation material, and cement, pump it in the hole, and pray that it would set up and seal off. Both Sonny and I were doubtful about that scheme, but agreed that it *could* work.

It was bitter cold that night when we left to go to work. The heater in the car we were in was not working properly, and we were looking forward to getting to the rig, hoping that we had regained circulation and could get back to drilling.

We had turned off the highway onto a lease road and were about a quarter of a mile from the rig when a big ball of fire mushroomed out around the substructure and up in the air above the derrick floor. Our first thoughts were that everyone on the derrick floor was surely dead. We speeded up and got to the rig in less than a minute. There was a hell of an oil fire burning in the 10-foot-high substructure. Our derrick had a double floor, 2-by-12's crisscrossed one above the other. This had saved the men on the floor. The first burst of fire did not come up through the doubled floor, but went out around the sides. The men had run through the tool house, a 25-foot-long steel building, sitting on its own 10-foot substructure, and with one door end sitting on the derrick floor. The other door had a stairway going to the ground. Everyone made it out. There was only one injury, a broken leg. The guy fell down the stairway.

There was a Halliburton pump truck about 70 feet away from the rig. They had been pumping down that conglomerate plug of Pope's, when the well blew out and caught fire. That pump truck driver never missed a beat, he just kept pumping, and was still going at it when the rotary hose burned in two and mud began spraying everywhere. He didn't know it at the time, but he saved the day, and kept the well from getting completely away from us. He probably had more guts than brains, but our need at that time *was* guts, not brains.

We hit the ground running, Clark and I, to start the motor on the stand-by rig pump, while the other three men checked the crew we were relieving and tried to rescue our work clothes. No luck—that first blast had taken care of that. The change house with the men's clothes lockers was directly beneath the tool house, and the fire swept through there and burned up everything: work clothes, boots, and even the dress clothes of the evening tour crew, with their wallets, money, and hats.

We fired up the stand-by pump. We had about 750 barrels of mud mixed in our steel mud pits, and by turning the mixing guns on the pits toward the rig motors, we began to spray liquid mud on the motors in an effort to at least save them. Most of the fire was under the derrick floor, and the substructure began to buckle. The driller had set the pipe on the slips to pump the plug down, and the weight of the drilling string was on the slips in the rotary table, so, as the substructure turned cherry red from heat, the beams the rotary table sat on began to give way.

The whole thing looked like a cross section of hell, and was damn near as hot. The head of oil had subsided, but the well was still gassing and burning. The drill collars, twenty-four of them, were standing in the derrick, three to the stand, eight stands. They were sitting on 8-by-8-inch sills laid over that section of the derrick floor. Those sills were what we stood pipe on when we pulled out of the hole and were commonly called "the pipe rack." They were afire, as was the derrick floor. So we, Wash Harris, Clark, and I, grabbed the Halliburton fire hose attached to the cement truck and went in under the pipe rack to try to put the fire out before the sills burned through and dropped those drill collar stands 10 feet to the ground. They were very heavy, weighing 7,500 pounds each, and if they dropped out of the finger bars in the upper derrick and fell against the derrick, they would tear out the side of the derrick and fall to the ground. Not a pleasant prospect, especially if you were close to them.

It was eerie and scary in under those drill collars. There was a fairly strong breeze out of the north, the moon was shining, smoke from the fire was swirling about, and you could see up through the floor where it had burned through in spots. You couldn't keep from looking up at those drill collars towering above you, and I got the distinct impression several times that the damned things were weaving about and were about to fall. It scared me pretty badly, and the other two fellows told me later that they, too, had the same sensation when they looked upward.

The blaze began to die down, and we turned our hose toward the top of the BOP where the fire was concentrated and, lo and behold, we knocked the blaze out. The well was still gassing, but had lessened considerably. Lawrence Gentles, the evening tour driller, had stayed with his crew, and they rigged our rig hose to the stand-by pump and came in under the floor to help. Together we got that damn fire under control, and, fortunately, the well died down.

It was 2:30 A.M., 4° above zero, with a stiff breeze out of the north. We were wet, in our street clothes, and suddenly realized that we were freezing to death. The excitement and fire had kept us stimulated and very busy, and suddenly it had died down, and we began to suffer from a let-down and the cold. It wasn't a fun thing to experience.

Wash Harris was 6 feet 3 inches tall with a size 12 foot. He had worn his house shoes to work, and they were in rags. He was barefooted, and I really worried about him; he was plenty tough but not *that* tough. The tool pusher's shack, about 100 feet from the rig, was usually locked. Dick Hodges had been on the job when the fire started. He was drilling superintendent and troubleshooter. Blackie Gaines was the Phillips company representative, and he had gone to inform management that we had a problem. Dick had driven off as soon as we knocked the big blaze out, and no one knew where he had gone. I took a hammer up to his shack to knock off the lock and found the shack open and a good fire lit in the heater. We hustled old Wash in there, tore those ragged house shoes off, wrapped a blanket around his feet, and then crowded around that lovely fire. We were a dreadful-looking bunch of people— covered with mud, soot from the fire, and wetter than drowned rats. Steam began to rise from our clothing, and that shack began to look like a hogpen. Lawrence and his crew went home in their wet, filthy work clothes. That was all they had to wear because their street clothes had burned. Actually, what they did was fire up their car, turn the heater on full blast, pull off their clothes, and go home in their under- wear. There were a bunch of worried and then greatly surprised wives that night. I don't know what the guys told 'em, but they were three hours late and almost naked when they did get home.

Lawrence and his crew had hardly gotten out of sight when one of the Halliburton men came up and told us we still had fires. The 10-by-10 sills the derrick sat on were burning in between the sills. There were two sills, side by side, on each of the four sides of the derrick. I went down to look and, of course, he had told the truth. We did have smoldering fires between the sills and some in the pipe rack and derrick floor. They were not bad, but they had to be put out, especially if the well made another head. I put the stand-by pump on the fill-up line and began to pump mud into the hole, hoping against hope that Leroy's plug had worked. Imagine my surprise when the hole filled up and ran over in the cellar. The Lord was on our side, Leroy was a hero, and I heaved a sigh of relief that could have been heard in Andrews, 16 miles away.

Our ordeal had lessened, but was not over. We hunted around the pump parts house and found an old poleax, and, of course, it was dull. We began to chop on one of those 10-by-10-inch sills right in the middle, and eventually cut it in two, then pried the sills apart enough to get to the fires. It was cold, but the ax warmed us up. By the time Pat Harris and I chopped through four of those sills, we were panting like a lizard on a steam line, as warm as toast and bone tired.

We fought those little "piss willie" fires the rest of the night. Dick Hodges got back about three o'clock. That old man had waked up a man in Andrews who owned a clothing store. He brought us coveralls, shoes, sweatshirts, wool socks, flannel shirts, and dry gloves. And even though he was a teetotaler and dead set against drinking, he brought back a fifth of Old Grandad 100-proof bourbon whiskey. It went down very well and produced a warm glow in the belly, but we almost had to choke Wash Harris loose from the bottle. He said it saved his life.

We had 1,500 barrels water storage and managed, at long last, to rid ourselves of any semblance of fire. We used water liberally, and managed to build some enormous icicles as we struggled through the remainder of the night. Dick had called a rig building contractor while he was in Andrews, and a crew showed up at eight o'clock with two 100-ton hydraulic jacks and a set of drill pipe clamps. Sonny and his crew were on the job and trucks were on their way to start clearing off the location. We, my crew and I, stayed to help the rig builders jack up and lay down three joints of drill pipe. It took two and a half hours, but we finished at 10:30 A.M. and went home, tired, let down, and sleepy. It had been one hell of a night, and just the thought that it was over was overwhelming. I explained to Amy what had happened, ate breakfast, fell in bed, and slept twelve solid hours. When I woke up, I told Amy that my rig was on the way from Oklahoma, and as soon as we finished this well, I was going to start pushing tools. She wasn't too thrilled and said I had swapped my bed for a car, and from that day on, I would be a slave to that damned rig. She turned out to be correct, but at that time I couldn't see things that way. I really wanted that promotion.

We scuttled that burned derrick and rig. Ralph Lowe Drilling Company had bought a new National "75," just exactly like our burned one. Somehow, S-H-K made a quickie deal and actually bought it while it was on railroad cars on a siding in Odessa. Five days after the fire, we fired up that new rig.

Phillips Petroleum had decided to complete that well at the depth we had already reached in the Devonian. So we ran and cemented casing then and there and moved away. I had served my time as a driller, and my life was changed forever.

Scott Harris and I both started pushing tools at about the same time. He took over a National "75" about a week before *my* National "50" got in from Oklahoma. All of the major oil companies were demanding that tool pushers be more handy to them, and instead of looking after three or four rigs, get down to a maximum of two. Scott was the older brother to my two hands, Wash and Pat. He was a smart, knowledgeable driller and made a pretty fair pusher. I had recommended J. N. Clark as driller material, and Scotty took him and put him to drilling. He was a cocky little devil, but made a good driller. He had one bad fault; he couldn't get along with his hands, and his temper got him whipped a few times, but he was Scotty's problem child, not mine.

Chapter Twelve

Pushing Tools: Starting,
Then Becoming the Loner

Pushing tools was not wholly new to me. I had filled in at vacations and in emergencies for a couple of years, so I knew the score. I was eager to get going with my first well with my new rig, and it was a fairly new rig. It was about two years old and in excellent shape. It had a jackknife derrick, the very first one for S-H-K. They were a conservative bunch of people and had clung to the standard derricks. In fact, they still had two rigs on standards when I left them years later. My rig brought the number of S-H-K rigs in West Texas to six, five of them running for Phillips Petroleum and one for Texaco. They had two pushers on the payroll when Scott and I went to pushing, "Big" Jim Little and "Cajun" Boudroux. Dick Hodges was drilling super, and Skinny Hunter, one of the owners, was the big boss. So Scotty and I doubled the supervisory force. Even then there were not enough of us to really go around, for the oil companies were getting more demanding. We managed for awhile—Scott, Cajun, and I had one rig each, while Dick and Jim split the other four between themselves.

My three drillers were Sonny Saak, Glen Little, and Bill King. Sonny came with me by choice and was a godsend. He was an excellent driller. Glen was a new driller, Jim's brother, and the company assigned him to me. I hired Bill King. He had gone bust as a contractor, and since I knew him to be an able, smart driller, I was glad to hire him. I had drilled for him years ago and he had been forced to fire me. Bill and Sonny were a big help, and I got off on the right foot with my company and with Phillips Petroleum Company.

Our first well, a 6,500-foot Clearfork well, was on the east side of the TXL field, 23 miles west of Odessa. When the trucks from Oklahoma arrived, we began to sort things out and try to fit them together. It is a big chore to rig up a rig you have never seen before, and it took us five days to get the thing together and working. The National "50" was a small rig in those days, rated to about 8,500 feet. It was under-rated, as many 10,000-foot wells were drilled with those little rigs later on. They were good, solid pieces of machinery.

We got the rig going and started drilling. Our drilling prognosis called for 300 feet of 13 3/8-inch casing, then an 11-inch-diameter hole to 1,800 feet, and 8 5/8-inch casing run to that point, and a 7 7/8-inch hole to total depth, with a production string of casing of 5 1/2-inch OD. It was a good, solid program, except for one very bad part. It specified an 11-inch hole out from under the surface pipe, and that little item caused a world of trouble for us, for two other drilling contractors, and for Phillips Petroleum Company.

Now the reason for the trouble was a formation known throughout the Permian Basin as "the Red Beds." This was a red, clayey shale, easy to drill through but containing two characteristics that caused trouble at times. It absorbed water and would swell, and if you took too long to drill through and case it, it would slough in on you, stick your drill pipe or casing, and cause very expensive fishing and washover jobs, both to be avoided like the plague.

When I saw that prognosis, I protested to the lease foreman and asked permission to drill a 12 1/4-inch hole from under the surface pipe. I got a cold, stern, bitter "no." He told me that he had questioned that provision at a meeting and had been told in no uncertain terms that it was an engineered thing and could not be changed.

It was the same as Holy Writ, and the staff engineer who got it approved was sure it would save Phillips many dollars and enhance his reputation, and probably get him a promotion. So we were stuck with it and, sure enough, had trouble on our very first well. We drilled to 1,800 feet, pulled the bit up above the Red Bed, then ran it back to bottom with no problem. Then came out of the hole, laid down twelve 8-inch drill collars, rigged up and began to run 8 5/8-inch casing, and it stopped 200 feet above casing point. We rigged the rig pump onto the casing and tried to pump to bottom. No luck! We worried with it for an hour, got afraid we would stick the casing, and pulled out of the hole and stood the casing back in the derrick. Picked up a bit, ran back to bottom, circulated for three hours, then did it all over again. By the time we got that damn casing run and cemented, we had spent thirty hours' rig time, a hell of a lot of money, and had worn my patience to a frazzle.

I was determined to do something about that deal, but the big question was, what? I talked to my rivals, the men who looked after the other rigs, who had the same problem, Jake Lawless of Lawless Drilling Company and the pusher for Trinity Drilling Company. Both of them were having the same troubles I had, but we couldn't come up with a solution. It seemed that we were faced with an impasse. All of us were drilling for Phillips, and none of us could change the prognosis—it was a very frustrating deal.

The solution came to me. It was odd and really an accident. It happened like this: the Smith Bit Company, based in California, was trying to get a foothold in the Permian Basin. They did not yet have an organization, but had set up a consigned stock with two local men; these two fellows were really hustling business, but without too much success, since California tools were not popular in West Texas. One of these partners, Jack Lebus, was calling on me, even though I had not bought a single bit from him. He was a good-looking, pleasant, smart Cajun, as persistent as a head cold.

We had drilled out of our $8^5/8$-inch casing and were drilling ahead when one day Jack stopped by the rig. He was again trying to get me to run just one of his bits, saying that a trial would convince me. I was doubtful and was about to fluff him off, again, when I suddenly remembered from my days in California during World War II that people ran odd-sized bits out there, since they ran some odd-sized casings. So I asked Jack, "That prune-picking outfit you represent wouldn't have an $11^1/4$-inch or $11^1/2$-inch bit, would they?" He said, "As a matter of fact, they do make an $11^1/4$-inch bit, but I don't stock them. I could order you one, though, and have it in about a week." I ordered one for my next well, got it, ran it, then ran casing. That $8^5/8$-inch casing went to bottom like a dropped rock. We cemented it, and for the very first time since that absurd program started, someone got the $8^5/8$-inch to go the first time. I felt like a genius, a lucky one.

Halliburton Oil Well Cementing Company's trucks were barely off the location when Jake Lawless was over to demand just what the hell I had done. I played dumb, but Jake was a sharp guy. He saw that dull Smith bit sitting on the floor and wanted to know when I started running Smith bits. I told him that was my first one, but it had done a good job and I planned to run another one. Jake squatted down and gave that bit a good looking over, from every angle. Now visually it is hard to tell an 11-inch from an $11^1/4$-inch bit. Jake knew I had done something, but couldn't tell what and again asked me what the secret was.

Jake and his brother had just started contracting. The rig was their first. Mutt Lawless had his trailer parked next to mine. Jake was an ex-Phillips tool pusher and I liked both men. So I made Jake swear on his mother's name that he would keep the secret and told him what I had done. He immediately ordered himself an $11^1/4$-inch Smith, and his 11-inch-hole troubles vanished. We never told another soul, threatened Jack Lebus if *he* ever told, and ran quite a few of those bits. Being oversized, they did a good job, and I certainly felt as though I had done a good thing for my company and myself.

One quarter of an inch isn't very much. Still, it made all the difference in the world to us. Neither Jake nor I ever told the Trinity pusher. We didn't know him well enough to trust him, and decided to keep our secret to ourselves. And the good part was that we never again had to pull our casing, not even one time.

On our second well there in the TXL field, we skidded the derrick with the rotary table and draw works still bolted to the substructure. The water tanks, three of them, the tool house, change house, mud house, light plant house, and three steel mud pits were moved with trucks. Also, the drill pipe, drill collars, pipe racks, and catwalk. The skidding of the derrick was actually done by rig builders who specialized in that sort of thing. They jacked up the thing with hydraulic jacks, then set it on Caterpillar-type tracks and towed it to the new location and very carefully spotted the rotary table over the pre-dug cellar at the new location, then set the derrick down.

A drilling rig has a large number of parts: pumps, tanks, mud hoppers, shale shakers, BOP's, line pipe, and a myriad of pipe connections, that have to be joined together in order to make a smoothly operating rig. It had always been done haphazardly following a general pattern, but each rig-up was a little different from the previous job. The tanks were set a little closer or farther from the rig, a little closer to each other, the stand-by pump in a slightly different place, and then the gas, water, and mud lines, and the manifold that joined the water tanks together had to be changed a little bit. Nothing from the prior rig-up fitted; they all had to be changed. It was a costly, time-consuming, irritating job, but for thirty years that I knew of, it had been done by guess and by gosh, mostly by gosh.

Everyone got in a hurry on a rig-up job. There were three drillers, and they each had different ideas on how to do things. The tool pusher was usually on the move, yelling at the truck drivers, the rig builders, or running to the supply house in town to get something, so unless he was an exceptional organizer, everyone else went his uncoordinated way. Often mass confusion resulted, and as a consequence, it usually took four or five days to move a rig, rig up, and spud in a new well. I remember one time Cajun Boudroux, who was a fussbudget, took eight big days to rig up. The time wasted in argument and lost motion was astounding and costly.

I had always been appalled by the waste of time, money, and effort to move and rig up a drilling rig. So, when we skidded and didn't spud in until noon of the fourth day, I resolved to do something to speed up the process.

Rigging up was done with all three crews working the daylight tour. It was customary that the day you were sure you would spud in, only two crews would come to work in the morning. The morning tour crew would go home shortly after noon, then come back out at midnight. The evening tour crew would come to work at their regular time. This was called "breaking tour."

The day that we broke tour, I talked to the daylight and morning tour drillers at noon, and then had another talk with the daylight and evening tour drillers when the evening tour crew relieved at 3:30 P.M. I told them that we had a good rig-up job, but that we spent too much time accomplishing it. It came as a surprise, since we had made better than average time.

We decided to make a rig-up "blueprint." So, for the next several days, in our spare time, we very carefully measured out where each piece of equipment went, then made a sketch on an 18-by-12-inch piece of white cardboard. This sketch was carefully drawn, with exact measurements written and everything marked down. The center line of the hole was the starting point, and the thing entailed a great deal of work, but we finally finished, and it looked good, on paper.

The next question was: would it work? We finished that well, and since we did not complete a well, but moved the drilling rig off the hole just as soon as we ran and cemented the production string of casing, we soon found out the answer.

We finished cementing the casing about 2:00 P.M. one afternoon, then started "tearing down." The morning tour crew came out at midnight to finish up the rigging down, and by morning the rig was ready to move. I had arranged for the rig builders and the trucks to be on the job at 8:00 A.M. The evening tour crew came back out at 9:00 A.M.— went to the new location and began measuring and driving stakes, according to the plan. The daylight crew supervised the loading out, and saw to it that the trucks moved everything in the proper sequence, and it was amazing! Everything went into its proper place. The day crew was on the new location by noon, and both crews began to tie things together. The rig builders sat the derrick down by 2:00 P.M., and by 5:00 P.M. when we went home, we were so far along that I told the evening tour bunch to come out at their regular time, 3:30 P.M. the next day. The next morning, the day and morning tour crews put the finishing touches to the job, and we spudded the surface hole at 2:00 P.M. We had moved, rigged up, and spudded in just a little more than a day and one-half. To my knowledge, it was the very first time a drilling rig had been moved and rigged up according to a pre-set plan, and was I proud? You *bet* I was. So were the crews. We felt that we had achieved a solid improvement in the oil-field procedure.

I went into the office that afternoon to check over some invoices and found both Dick Hodges and Skinny Hunter there. Skinny asked me,

"Mate, do you think you will be ready to spud sometime tomorrow?" I grinned at him and answered, "Skinny, we are drilling." Dick did a double take and blurted out, "You are lying." So I said, "If you guys think that, jump in your cars and run out and see. It's only 25 miles; you can be there in half an hour. Me, I'm going home and sleep awhile. I'll be running surface pipe sometime after midnight."

I left and went home. They *did* go out to the rig, and sure enough, we were drilling. I'm pretty sure that they thought we had somehow pulled a shenanigan, but they didn't quiz the driller on tour, who happened to be Bill King. But Bill told me later that they were really looking the rig over and gave it a good eyeballing, looking for things left undone, but evidently did not find anything to really complain about, as we had the thing pretty well rigged up and it looked good.

We had set an attention-getting precedent, one that affected the company. Dick Hodges came out to the rig the next day, closely followed by Skinny Hunter. They hemmed me up and demanded to know how we did the quick rig-up. I told them we had made a "little sketch" of our last location and tried to rig up the exact same way on this well, and that it had worked out pretty well. They immediately demanded to see the "little sketch," and when Sonny Saak, who was on tour, showed it to them, both men studied it carefully. They actually took a steel tape line and checked a few measurements, distances between tanks, manifold measurements, and so forth, then got in their cars and left, without comment.

We had made quite an impact, I learned later. Skinny and Dick were old-timers, and they were both very smart men. Each realized that cutting rig-up time was "money in the pocket"—quickly made money, since contractors were usually paid per foot of hole drilled, and the sooner you started "turning to the right," the quicker you began to make money.

Skinny brought up the "little sketch" at our next tool pushers' meeting. He told the other pushers how many days we had cut off our rig-up time and that he wanted the idea used on all the rigs. He didn't exactly put an "or else" on the suggestion, but everyone got the idea. Scotty thought it was okay; Jim Little went along very reluctantly; Cajun Boudroux was loud in denunciation of the whole scheme and intimated that I was a troublemaker. All in all, I don't think I would have won a popularity contest in the company—but I was cocky and didn't care. The idea *was* adopted, and as far as I know, it was a first. I was proud that we had done it, and gave my drillers credit for lots of help.

Later, on the same well, I decided to bury the mud line from the stand-by pump to the stand pipe manifold. The mud line was about 30 feet long and was made of 4-inch drill pipe. It had a high-pressure vibrator hose at each end and generally lay on top of the ground. It was slippery when wet and a stumbling block all of the time, so I told the driller to have it buried, then went somewhere for an hour and a few minutes. When I got back to the rig, two obviously disgruntled roughnecks were digging a ditch beside the mud line. The ground was sandy and they were making good progress, and as I went by them, I said, "That looks like it shovels pretty good." They both stopped digging, rested one foot on their shovels, and gave me a look of complete disgust. Then one of them said, "Pusher, you know damn good and well that there is no such thing as good shoveling," paused a second, then added, "or bad whiskey."

I took the rebuke gracefully, grinned, and went on. Roughnecks were a different breed of cat anyhow, prone to saying odd things. Most of them were young, wild, don't-give-a-damn types. They were migratory in habit, got "full of quit" quite often, and rarely stayed on any job for six months. The character of the hands was just beginning to change. Now some of the young married men were looking for stability, and I resolved to make a job on "my" rig as attractive as possible in order to keep good hands. I must have succeeded, as many years later, when I finally quit S-H-K Drilling Company, I had roughnecks who had been working for me for nine years.

We did all right in drilling our Little Clearfork wells. Our usual company man for Phillips was a fellow named Millhollan—he was big, 6 feet and 3 or 4 inches tall. Everyone called him "Man," and the name fitted. He was what Phillips called a "sub foreman," recently raised from pumper. He was easygoing, learning his way, was great to work with, and we really liked him. He made lease foreman later and transferred to New Mexico, where we worked with him later on. He was one of the good ones.

We drilled a well, then skidded the rig about every twenty-five days for five wells. Then the sixth location fell on the north side of the Odessa-Kermit highway. We still were going to skid, but it took a little doing to do so, since I had to cross two fences and a highway. We were moving in on the Slator Ranch, which lay north of the road and had a four-strand barbed wire fence that we had to cross.

I got a permit from the state highway department to cross the road. The company got verbal permission from Mr. Slator to remove, then replace a section of fence. I notified the rig builders and truck contractor, and it looked like we were all set. Little did we know! The moving crews showed up early—everything got underway, so I went to town to the National Supply Company to get some needed rig parts. I was gone about two hours and fully expected the rig to be in place or nearly so on the new location when I got back.

It was still on the south side of the road and wasn't moving. I drove up and saw the rig builders sitting around on the substructure doing nothing. I asked the pusher for McCain Rig Builders what in the hell he thought he was doing.

He jerked his thumb across the road and said, "I'm waiting for you." I looked across the highway and saw that the fence was still up—and also that three men on horseback, one with a .30-.30 carbine rifle across the saddle, were sitting there. I walked across the road and asked the man with the rifle what was going on, and then was informed that nobody was going to cut that fence, that he was the ranch manager, and that was that. I told him that we had permission in writing to remove and replace that damned fence, and it looked like he was bucking his boss. He wasn't the least bit impressed, just repeated that his boss owned the place but that he ran it, and what he said went. There wasn't much I could say. You can't usually win an argument with a .30-.30 carbine, and he had us stopped cold. The rig builders didn't care, and my day was slipping fast.

Then it dawned on me that he had two cowboys with him, which was exactly two more than he needed—that he wanted to do the fence work and be paid for it. So I asked him, as a favor, what he would charge me to take the fence down, then replace it when we were through. His eyes lit up like a Christmas tree, and he figured he could do that, and it would only cost me one hundred bucks.

I said, "Friend, you've got a deal. The job is yours, and since you are doing it, it should be done right." He signaled his hands; they tore down a 200-foot section of fence in nothing flat, and we moved across the highway through the gap and onto the location. They replaced the fence, I wrote him a check for a hundred bucks, and we parted on the best of terms. A hundred dollars was about one week's wages for a ranch foreman in 1948, and a little extra cash saved a lot of hurt feelings. I learned a valuable lesson, too; always bring the ranch foreman into damage negotiations. He might be your door opener. That knowledge helped me many times later in my career. Somehow I always managed to be friends with the landowners and their foremen.

We drilled that well and one more north of the highway, with no problems; then the company got big-hearted; they gave me another, bigger rig to go with my little National "50." It was a Bethlehem "450" rig which had a standard derrick and was rated to 11,000 feet. I transferred Sonny and Glen Little to the Bethlehem, and left Bill King on the "50." He preferred the little National anyway. I acquired three new drillers, and embarked on a very frantic two months. We were unfamiliar with the rig; it had been neglected, was an orphan, and looked it.

We spent five days getting rigged up, and for once, the office didn't say a word. They knew what shape that rig was in and had bought out or fired the tool pusher who had been supposedly looking after it. He had spent more time parading about in his "swage nipple" breeches and "muzzle loading" boots than tending to his job, so they "bumped" him back to driller. He never forgave me, who had nothing whatsoever to do with his demotion, and I sure as hell didn't need another rig to worry with, but he quit soon afterwards, and things settled down. All I got out of the deal was another rig and an ulcer, neither of which I needed.

I didn't know that I had an ulcer. I had been having little troubles on both rigs. They were running about 10 miles apart and were 25–30 miles away from Odessa. I was on the go day and night, eating most of my meals at odd times in little oil-field cafes. I began to have some distress soon after eating, and the doctor I was seeing was treating me for gall bladder trouble and had me on a greaseless diet, which was a joke. There is no such thing as a greaseless diet in the oil patch. Hell, we lived on grease, stale grease at that, and were used to it.

Anyway, the combination of overwork, odd eating hours, and worry began to get me down, and nothing helped. I felt lousy, and I'm afraid I took some of it out on my crews. They told me later that I was hell on wheels for about two months that late summer. My cure came about in a very odd way. One morning I left the office and started out the Kermit Highway to the National "50" rig. I was fuming, as usual. The hole was running crooked on that rig; I had inherited a driller that I wanted to get rid of; the Bethlehem rig was costing a great deal to upgrade; and I just hadn't been pushing tools long enough to really be able to cope with all the problems.

About 15 miles out of town, a terrific pain struck me in the center of my chest. I felt like an iron band was squeezing the breath out of me. I pulled off the road into the barrow ditch; I just knew that I was having a heart attack. Scared? You bet I was. It was a brand new experience for me. Sickness and I had been strangers up until now, and it scared the devil out of me. But the pain subsided gradually, and I began to think about living again, when a strange thought struck me. What if I had *died* sitting there in that ditch? And the answer was, some other guy would be doing my job, the very next day, and it was a sobering thought. The realization made me review my whole concept of my importance, and it wasn't all that great a deal. I thought it all out and firmly resolved that from that minute on for the rest of my life, I would do the best I could with the tools I had to work with, and never, never again would I worry myself sick over that damned job. That philosophy has stood me in good stead for many years. I drove up out of that roadside ditch and went on to the rig. Then that afternoon I fired the driller who had been my bane, went to the "450" and talked over our problems with Sonny Saak, then went home and slept all night. My pains went away and I felt fine. One year later in a routine physical examination, the doctor said my X-ray showed a quarter-sized scar on my duodenum, but my ulcer was gone, never to return. I cured it with lots of black coffee and greasy steaks. So what I was eating didn't bother me. It was what was eating me that almost did me in.

We finally got the Bethlehem rig fixed to suit us and moved it to the location just off the Caprock about 6 miles west of Notrees, Texas, which is 26 miles west of Odessa. We made a blueprint to rig up by on our next location; then I made every roughneck on that rig mad at me.

Let me explain. The rigs we had in those days had mostly gas-burning motors. Natural gas was usually available within a mile or two of most locations, and we used 2-inch line pipe to pipe the gas to the rig. Then we also used 2-inch line pipe for water lines. They ran to various places around the drilling rig. Gas and water were two absolute essentials. They had to be present before you could even start up a rig. The pipes were normally screwed together around the rig with many ells, tees, and nipples to go around corners and fit pipes into close spaces. This usually involved a lot of cutting and threading pipe, which was time consuming and, therefore, costly. I had the bright idea that while drilling the well, the hands could cut and thread random lengths of 2-inch pipe; then I would buy a large number of hammer-up unions. We would make the unions up on the pipes with a female half union on one end and a male half union on the other end. Then, instead of tying up a crew of five men laying lines, two men with hammers could do the job. There was a whole lot of bitching and a great deal of talk about a "hard-ass" tool pusher who hated to see men idle, but they did it, and on the very next rig-up, guess who bragged about how quickly they laid the lines? They did, because I was gone, but that is another story.

I've said it many times, so once again won't hurt. Things change slowly in the oil fields. For many years, too many tool pushers had looked after two, three, or more rigs. Cursorily, they would go by each rig every day, some days. In fact, they left most of the thinking up to the drillers, who were at best a mixed lot. Consequently, the companies who used the contractors' services began to think that they were not getting their money's worth. Of course, they were not, so they began to put a great deal of pressure on contractors to put a pusher full time on each rig. The contractors didn't like it, of course, but after losing a few contracts, they began to like it very much indeed. In fact, they loved it and began to expedite the idea. So "one rig, one pusher" slowly became an accepted fact.

I took my vacation late that year. Amy's health had not improved, and we made an appointment at the Mayo Clinic in Rochester, Minnesota. We went up there by car in late July and spent twenty-one days, as she went through the whole works. We had some time off from the clinic routine and drove around the countryside. It was different and beautiful. I had never been in that part of the country before and found it very interesting. Amy's results from this prolonged stay were that they couldn't find anything organically wrong with her. She could be, and probably was, allergic to a large number of substances, and her psychiatric tests showed that she had a "deep anxiety complex." The doctors told her to try to find a competent allergist and to try not to worry too much. That day, the company called and said I was urgently needed, so we drove to Omaha, Nebraska, from Rochester, spent the night, and then left early the next morning and drove through to Odessa. We stopped twice to eat and several times for gas. We got into Odessa at 2:00 A.M. after driving nineteen solid hours. I was dead beat and fell into bed and asleep instantly. Then at 6:30 A.M., the phone woke me. It was Dick Hodges, and he told me that a man had been electrocuted on one of our rigs. The location was in the Andector field, just north of Goldsmith, and he wanted me to take an insurance investigator and a deputy sheriff to the rig and try to find out what had happened and caused the accident. I told him that I was dead tired and asked, "Why me?" The rig had a tool pusher, and the accident was his problem, not mine. Dick said that the pusher for that rig had kind of come unraveled, and that I was temporarily the man in charge, to get up and go, and that he would explain it all to me later. I got up and went, picked up the insurance man, the deputy followed us in his car, and we went out to the rig.

The dead man had been a member of the morning tour crew. They had made a trip to change bits about 3:00 A.M. They were only 3,000 feet deep, and the round trip out and back in had taken an hour. The Yates sand had headed and blown a great deal of drilling fluid out of the hole on the trip in the hole. The fluid was brine, and that particular man got drenched; his clothing was soaked through, and since it was a cool morning, he ran out to the light-plant house to warm up a bit. They missed him later, and when they looked in the light-plant house, he was lying on the steel floor face down, and he was dead.

They called in on the radio, an ambulance was sent out to the rig, the boy was taken to the hospital, but he was dead on arrival. The radio answering service alerted Dick and Skinny Hunter. They, in turn, called me, the insurance claims man, and the sheriff.

When we drove up on the location that morning, the morning tour crew was still there. They had been told to stay until we arrived, since we needed as much information as we could get from them. I had hardly set foot to ground when one of the morning tour hands blurted out, "If you are going into the light-plant house, don't step in, jump in, because it is hot!" That insurance claims man's ears pricked up like a bird dog's. He asked, "What do you mean, hot?" The man said, "If you step into that house, it will shock you, but if you jump in with both feet, it's okay." We looked at each other, and each man knew the answer: a shorted steel building, a brine-saturated man, cold and in a hurry, spelled death. He stepped into the house, and the shock was intensified enough to kill him instantly.

S-H-K Drilling Company had excellent light plants. Each rig had one. These were war surplus bought from equipment made available after World War II. They were housed in an all-steel skid-mounted building, designed for the housing of generators, summer and winter. Each light plant was an eight-cylinder LeRoi gas-fueled motor with a 30-kilowatt generator on a direct drive. There were two of these on each rig. They were back to back in the light-plant house, and the radiators on the motors faced the doors, one at each end of the building, so whichever motor was running got good ventilation. There was a panel board mounted between the generators with an automatic switch, so if a light plant went out suddenly, the other one started immediately. This panel board was wired for 220 volts and also 110 volts. Heavily insulated wires ran from the circuit breakers all over the layout. It was an elaborate system, and we were all very proud of it, as it was far in advance of most drilling-rig light plants.

We always set the metal skids on the ground when rigging up and never set them on sills or boards. This grounded the light plants effectively and rendered them safe, in case of a short in the system. We had never had an accident, so this was our first, with that electrical system. But on this job, the light-plant house was sitting on two 3-by-12-inch boards about 10 feet long, one under each end, so it was not grounded, and the awful part was that the crews knew this, but nothing had been done about the short, or lack of grounding. The tool pusher was told, but he was a tightwad with the company's money and trying to make a name for himself as a conservative, "careful with a dollar" pusher. He put off calling an electrician, nobody took the boards out from under the house, and it cost an innocent boy his life.

S-H-K didn't try to gloss it over. They took their lumps. The insurance company paid the compensation for accidental death; the sum in those days was $16,000, not much by today's standards. The dead boy had left a wife and infant daughter, and S-H-K settled out of court with her. Dick Hodges told me it was a good, fair settlement, but I never was told the exact amount.

I was sore about the whole thing, and when I gave my report to the company, I left the bark on it. It was rough, but damn fool carelessness like that should never be condoned. They bumped the pusher back to drilling and he never forgave me. But he had to blame someone and couldn't very well blame management, if he wanted to keep working. The company put Sonny Saak out as a pusher on the Bethlehem rig and Louis Jones on the National "50." I wound up with another run-down rig and three resentful crews. The rig was one I was familiar with. It was the National "75" that had replaced the burned draw works. Since I had helped rig it up the first time, it was familiar to me. Therefore, even though the crews missed their pusher, who had been lax, they adjusted to me pretty well, since I kept them too busy to do much bellyaching. The company had wholeheartedly adopted the "one rig, one pusher" deal and I never had to see after two rigs again, thanks to Phillips Petroleum Company. So I gave those young men my full attention and gained their grudging admiration and undying hatred.

Still, we shaped that old rig up pretty swiftly, just a general tightening up. Two of the drillers were well known to me: Red "Boog" Reed was an old friend, not brilliant by any means, but a solid driller; and the other man, Lawrence Gentles, was an excellent driller but didn't like the oil fields. He was a religious man and didn't enjoy the rowdy habits and earthy language of his fellow workers, but he did a good day's work nevertheless. He was a pleasure to work with—a bit prissy, but a solid driller.

"Boog" Reed was a stubborn man, raised on a farm in Oklahoma, who went into the Marine Corps at a young age, served again through World War II, and was just as tough as he was hard headed. He and I got along fine, but I led him, since I couldn't drive him. Still, he was a better than ordinary driller.

We drilled field wells all that winter, inside locations where everything was known. No problems with the wells, just the day-to-day ailments of a hard-driven drilling rig. Still, we had some funny moments. You really never can let your guard down while drilling a well. If you do, you will probably regret it. "Boog" Reed had this happen to him one day. He was drilling surface hole. This was a 15-inch diameter hole, pretty big. He was drilling in "Red Bed" about 600 feet deep. "Red Bed" clay has a tendency to ball up, and it has stuck drill pipe while drilling because the rotary would slow down and stop. Sometimes it got pretty hairy, but usually it was just a big annoyance. This time, I was standing in the dog house, and Boog was standing at the door talking to me. He had taken a lot of pains to adjust the brake, and it was feeding off very well without him standing there with his hand on it all the time. This was an old trick of drillers everywhere; they devised all kinds of ingenious contraptions to keep from standing at the brake in all kinds of weather. Some of them were very clever, and all drillers had a system that they swore would work better than all other systems.

Boog was standing at the dog house door about 7 or 8 feet from the brake talking to me when all of a sudden the rotary slowed down and the kelly joint started up out of the hole. He ran to the brake, yelling at the top of his voice, "Whoa, you son of a bitch, WHOA! Whoa, God-dammit, whoa!" He kicked the high hoist clutch in and the pump clutch out all in the same motion. The high clutch jerked the swivel and traveling block up to keep the block from falling over sideways and cutting the drilling line. The pump stopped pumping the balled-up bit out of the hole, and the rescue was complete. The day was saved! Boog glared at me as though it was all my fault; he was still scared, since it could have been a real disaster. I just grinned at him and said, "Booger, your rig don't mind worth a damn." He finally laughed and said, "You never get all of the 'country' out of your blood. Whoa! was all I could think to say."

We drilled three wells to the Ellenburger lime in the Andector field that winter; then in early spring when the wind began to really blow, we moved the rig to Crane County into the sandhills. The spring winds in West Texas are unreal in their strength and intensity, and when you are working in sand-dune country, they are a real cross to bear. I have seen all the paint and chrome finish blasted off a car in two or three hours. And trying to operate a drilling rig under those conditions is not child's play, but somehow we managed. We would cover our cars with tarps, tried to make trips to change bits when the wind died down a bit, and generally made the best of things. The wells we drilled in the dune country were only 8,000 feet deep. We popped two of them down pretty quickly, and then I got moved to another rig, again!

Cajun Boudroux was hired in Louisiana right after World War II by Skinny Hunter, who was just back out of the Sea Bees. The company had bought a new rig, a Bethlehem "950." It was the biggest, best-equipped rig that S-H-K Drilling Company owned. They drilled several wells in Louisiana and did well. Cajun was from that part of the country, so he was on familiar ground. Then they moved the rig to Chickasha, Oklahoma—a different deal altogether. Cajun wasn't any too fond of "hard-rock" drilling; he persisted in trying to drill Louisiana style and did a mediocre job. They finally finished the well at Chickasha and moved the rig to Odessa. Cajun came with it but turned out to be a fish out of water. He simply couldn't or wouldn't adjust to drilling in the Permian Basin, scorned any suggestions any of us made, and kept saying we didn't really know how to drill.

He drilled one 11,000-foot well on the south end of the TXL field west of Odessa, did very poorly on the footage part of the contract, which cost S-H-K, and did even worse on the day-work part, which cost Phillips Petroleum Company. Phillips complained about his slowness to S-H-K. On his second well, he did even worse. He took eight days to rig up, took twice as long to finish the footage contract, then rode the day-work portion again. The Phillips lease superintendent got very unhappy with Boudroux and warned him that he had to do better "or else." The third well went just as poorly as the other two had gone, and when they finally finished, Phillips informed S-H-K that if they intended to drill any more wells for Phillips, Mr. Boudroux would have to be removed as pusher. It didn't leave S-H-K much choice. Word came down from our office in Tulsa to let Cajun go, so they did. Skinny hated to do it. He was really fond of Cajun, but we had five rigs running for Phillips, business is business, and we danced to Phillips' tune.

They called me into the office one morning. I couldn't imagine what they wanted to talk to me about, as I never was prone to listen to company gossip and did not know that Cajun was in real trouble. I never dreamed that I had been picked to replace him, but that was exactly what happened. I was certainly surprised.

Dick, Skinny, and I had about a two-hour-long discussion that morning. I wasn't at all anxious to take over Cajun's rig and crews. The rig was the largest and newest rig that the company owned, but it was moving to Kermit to drill a number of wells in the Keystone field, which was in the walking dunes, a sand-dune desert. The number of wells contracted for was what had shot Cajun out of the saddle. S-H-K couldn't stand to lose six wells. The three drillers were barely known to me. They had worked for Cajun for years, and were bound to be resentful of me, a new pusher, with the reputation of a "whop-down driver." To make matters worse, I had bought a house in Odessa, was in the final stages of the purchase, but had not taken possession just yet. That little house was the realization of a long-time dream of Amy's and mine, and we were looking forward to living in a house again, especially one that we owned.

We still owned a trailer home, an 8-by-45-foot "Detroiter," and didn't have any kids in school, so I was elected by management to move to Kermit. We had a lively talk about that, as I had just been offered a tool pushing job by another drilling company. Both Dick and Skinny knew this, so they "sweet-talked" me, told me that I would have much more of a free hand, that the company would hire a mover to move the trailer house, and that I would not have to move into a trailer park, but could rent a vacant lot or space and have all necessary utilities installed at the company's expense. I would not have to attend tool pushers' meetings each week, and could call in my reports each day. There had been questions raised by Phillips Petroleum personnel about Cajun's drillers' competence, and on my evaluation of them, they would stay or go. They said that I had a very good reputation with the Phillips people and they spoke highly of me. Lots more of this, and though I knew most of the talk was bull, I was flattered, I must admit. Still, I stalled them and told them I would give them a final answer the next morning. I knew that if I didn't move to Kermit after all that palaver, I would have to quit and take the offered job from the rival contractor. Both the company and I had reached the point of no return.

I talked it over with Amy that afternoon and night, and it was a big decision for us to make. On one hand were our years with S-H-K; on the other, a start with a new company. We finally decided that we would take the transfer, stay with S-H-K, lease the new house, keep the trailer, and move to Kermit. The free hand on the job was the big advantage. Amy had lived in Kermit before and liked the town. I also liked to live there, as it was a very nice little city. So we agreed that getting away from company gossip, backbiting, over-supervision, and many other things compensated for the lost opportunity to live in our new house.

We took the deal, the company hired a mover, and we went to Kermit, then *bought* a lot where a house had once stood. The house had since been moved, but the utilities were still in place, gas, electricity, and sewer. We moved onto the lot, got hooked up, and I got a telephone installed. We were settled into a new style of life. Our lot was in a residential part of town and we had the only trailer house in the block. The neighbors wondered about a trailer moving in, I am sure, but Kermit was an oil-field town, so nobody thought much about it. We were accepted.

Dick Hodges had supervised the tearing down and moving of the rig while I was getting moved and settled. So as soon as I got free of house movers and rigging up the trailer, I went out to the new location and officially took over the rig and got acquainted with my new drillers.

I had met all three men when they were working for Cajun, but we were barely known to each other. They had worked for Cajun for several years and were pretty sure I was going to be very difficult to work for, and I, in turn, felt that they were going to be difficult to work with, and, as usual, we were all wrong. They were used to Cajun's slow, deliberate ways, and the fact that he made all the decisions about drilling—when a bit was dull, when the mud needed working, and all the day-to-day decisions that a driller has to make. And, as a matter of fact, they had resented it deeply, but couldn't do anything about it since Cajun was pretty autocratic.

I was a different breed of cat, and let them know it at our get-acquainted meeting that day. I told them that I expected drillers who worked for me to be able to make their own decisions—that we would have things that we would discuss before doing, but that the day-to-day problems were theirs to solve. They liked the idea, and we at least got started on the right foot. Cajun had never cottoned to my rig-up blueprints and, in fact, had made light of them. He got away with not using the method, even though Skinny made the other pushers adopt it. So on our first rig-up, Cajun's drillers and I set up the rig in the old way, but we deliberately took our time. We set up carefully, used it for a model, and it took four days. The rig was designated no. 6, since it was the last one bought. Our derrick was a standard as opposed to a jackknife and remained "as was" as long as I worked for S-H-K Drilling Company.

The drillers that I inherited with Rig 6 were destined to remain with both me and the rig for several years, and one of them, Jack Bailey, stayed with me the whole nine years, except for a short tool-pushing stint of about four months. Mr. Bailey was a "one-er"; they made him, then broke the mold. He was 6 feet 3 inches tall, with a hawklike nose, coal-black hair, and dark eyes, and had a sense of humor like a cigar-store Indian: none. He called every man "Mister," very formally. In all the years that he worked for me, he always called me "Mr. Lynch." He even called his roughnecks "Mister," so naturally, we called him "Mr. Bailey." I still think of him after thirty-four years as Mr. Bailey. He was moody, temperamental, a hard worker, and an excellent driller. I came to understand Mr. Bailey, finally, and we had a good working relationship for many years.

Jack Evans was altogether different from Mr. Bailey. Jack was a native of Wetumka, Oklahoma, but he had moved to Louisiana as soon as he grew up and entered the oil fields. He had married a girl from Buras, Louisiana, and had become a native for all intents and purposes. He was a loner, not particularly friendly, and turned out to be far and away the best driller that ever worked for me.

The third man, Jim Davidson, was the only one of the three who had not come from Louisiana with Cajun. He had gone to drilling with Cajun when the rig came down from Oklahoma, and had been working for him about one and a half years. He was a good, competent driller, but he had a drinking problem. He was a pleasant, easygoing type, and we had no problems at first. They came later.

We rigged up on our first well. We made good time, and I found that I had an excellent rig and three fine crews, and it was a very nice surprise. The job I had dreaded to take turned out to be a pleasure. The time was early fall in 1949. I had fenced our lot where the trailer was sitting. Amy and I had acquired a dachshund pup from my stepfather. We named him Fritz and he became my assistant tool pusher. He went with me everywhere and loved Rig 6. He thought that it belonged to him.

Cajun had lived at the rig. The house that the company had made for him was the most elaborate one I had ever seen on a rig up to that time. It was skid mounted, wooden structured, 32 feet long and 7 feet 6 inches wide. It had two three-quarter beds, a refrigerator, a gas range for cooking, and a gas panel-ray heater. It was double walled and floored and had a window-fan-type air conditioner in one window. It had a dinette-type table with four straight chairs and an easy chair. It was a hell of a lot better than the 16-by-7-foot-wide shacks I had used up until that time, so naturally, it caused a furor in the company: me, the nonconformist loner, who was not popular with management, having by far the best accommodations on the job—a fancy dog house with all the trimmings—while the older pushers made do with much less. I thought, "What the hell. I don't blame them, and since I've got nothing to lose, I'll help them agitate." I did, too, and surprised everybody, but we must have done something right. S-H-K was known not to pamper their pushers, but they did begin to replace those Mickey Mouse tool pushers' shacks with much more livable houses.

We all liked Kermit. It was a friendly little town, pretty much oil-patch oriented. The old-timers liked the money we brought into the town, and we enjoyed being treated like valuable citizens. The natives warned us we were in for a bad winter, that all the signs pointed that way. I, for one, took their warnings seriously. On one of my infrequent trips to Odessa, I bought several "hot wires" and wrapped my water and sewer lines. Trailer houses are very vulnerable to freezes. Those lead hot wires wrapped around lines and connected to an electric line will keep them from freezing. As things turned out later, it was a damned good thing that I took the precaution. We had a real tough winter in 1949.

Our company man was Blackie Gaines, an old-time acquaintance. He was the company rep up in the south Fullerton field when the rig burned down. He was an excellent well man, smart, outspoken as all get-out, and a real pleasure to work for. We felt lucky to have Blackie as boss again. He really was easy to work for, since all you had to do for Blackie was do your work and cause him as little trouble as possible. He, in turn, caused you as little trouble as he could, but woe be unto the people who tried to take advantage of the little man. He was a tough cookie.

We were drilling Ellenburger wells at about 11,000 feet. The area was not a troublesome spot in which to drill. No real problems, like loss of circulation, crooked hole, high-pressured zones, or heaving shales, that made a tool pusher's life miserable. I settled into a pleasant routine. My drillers were not just competent, they were good. We had a few problems, as I'll tell later, but generally things went well for me. In those days, it generally took seventy to eighty days to drill an 11,000-foot well. We moved onto our first location in the middle of September; the weather was just like summer, and that continued on through October. We were about 9,000 feet deep and things were going fine when all of a sudden management threw me a curve. They pulled Jack Bailey, put him to pushing tools on a rig down southeast of Midland, and left me short-handed. I had a young man working for Jack Evans named Johnny Martin. We had been grooming him as a driller, but I was unsure of him. But I put him to drilling in Mr. Bailey's slot, and he did a capable job. Since he was a green driller, I rode herd on him closer than the other drillers. Lack of experience can get a young driller in big trouble in a hurry, and I had enough problems, without adding any new ones. However, the boy was ready. He made a fair driller.

Chapter Thirteen

Kermit and New Mexico: The Exodus from Odessa

I missed Mr. Bailey, but his departure opened my eyes to many things that I had not been aware of—mainly that I was a guinea pig, and would be constantly moved, have drillers taken away, and be expected to keep my rig operating smoothly, in spite of anything management might do to me. But I welcomed the challenge. I needed to avoid too much supervision, as it was something that I resisted, usually to my detriment.

The company had put Jack Bailey out to pushing once before, but his abruptness and abrasiveness had worked against him and he was put back to drilling. I did not know it at the time he went to work for me, but he resented me, since he thought he should have been the man who succeeded Boudroux. When he got put to pushing this second time, he told me that he was finally getting the job that he deserved, and we parted on not too friendly terms. He also told me that he thought he should have had my job. It didn't bother me. I had never "buddied up" with my drillers, but tried very hard to keep our relationship businesslike and fair. I never cultivated friendships with my crews, as I could not be sure I wouldn't have to fire somebody any day. It's tough to fire someone that you really like, so I stayed a bit aloof, and it paid good dividends.

After Mr. Bailey left, we kept on drilling, and "bottomed out" the last week in November. We moved the rig, set surface pipe, and were drilling the intermediate hole when the weather turned cold, and I do mean cold. The winter of 1949 was a dilly; it was one of the coldest winters I ever experienced in West Texas. The Siberian elm trees on the courthouse square in Kermit split from the freeze. I stepped outside one cold night and could hear them cracking, eight blocks away.

Getting anything done was an effort, and keeping a drilling rig operating in extremely cold weather takes a lot of doing. Water lines, mud lines, engines, pumps, stand pipe, and Kelly hose are all subject to freezing. It took lots of effort, especially while tripping to change bits, to keep something from freezing up. We kept the pumps running through bypasses to the pits, drained the stand pipe and rotary hose, and worried a bit, too, but we were lucky. We had no freeze-ups. This is a dreaded thing. If a pump goes down and needs to be worked on, it has to be drained. If the motors die for any reason, everything has to be drained. If you don't do this draining immediately and a mud pump bursts, you have just blown away $20,000. It has happened that a progressive freeze started and mud lines, hoses, pumps, and everything with water in it froze solid. It's a bad thing and a hell of a frantic job to thaw out. But we kept going okay, had no problems, bottomed out our intermediate hole at 5,500 feet, and prepared to run pipe.

The casing that we ran was 8⅝-inch outside diameter (OD). We had a guide shoe on the bottom joint and a float collar on top of that same bottom joint. So when we cemented the casing, we left the bottom joint full of cement, since the Halliburton plug stopped at the float collar. It was customary to tack-weld the collars top and bottom on the bottom three joints of casing. This was done to prevent "backing off" a joint or two or three of pipe while "drilling out." The drill collars were usually six inches in diameter, and when weight was applied to them while drilling, they would "buckle" slightly and thus drag against the inside of the casing as you turned the bit to the right or clockwise. The torque applied to the bottom joints of casing would sometimes unscrew them, and they would go downhole, sometimes only a few feet, sometimes a hundred feet or more, and become a real problem.

We did not tack the bottom collars. The night was brutally cold, about 10°. The welder was late and Blackie got impatient, so we went ahead and ran and cemented the casing. The job apparently went well; we had no noticeable fluid loss while cementing, and the cement circulated, which meant cement outside the casing from the guide shoe to the surface, so it looked like a good, solid job.

We waited six hours, then we cut off the 8⅝-inch casing and nippled up the blowout preventer stack, which took about fourteen hours. We then tested the BOP and took off drilling. The morning tour started drilling. They drilled the float, the cement in the bottom joint, the shoe, and started drilling formation. Jack Evans was drilling days, and he finished dulling the bit and pulled out of the hole. By the way, S-H-K rotated tours each thirty days; drillers rotated from mornings to days, to evenings, a constant annoyance.

The new driller who had taken Mr. Bailey's place was a young man named Johnny Martin. He was a smart, experienced roughneck, and I up-rated him to driller when Mr. Bailey left so suddenly. He was working out very well, doing a fair job, and what happened was not due to any fault of his.

As I said, Jack Evans left Johnny out of the hole. He screwed on a new tricone bit and started in the hole with it; he was not expecting anything unusual and was dropping the drill pipe at a fairly fast clip. Just below the bottom of the $8^5/8$-inch casing, he hit something with a hell of a jar. The bit stopped, and Johnny showered down on the brake in time to keep the traveling block from capsizing. He knew that he had hit an unusually wide amhydrite ledge or the casing had parted. So he picked up the drill pipe and bit, turned it one-quarter round, and slacked off again; the bit bumped something, then fell through into the clear. He went on to bottom cautiously, but couldn't drill. The rotary would stop, and the bit would hang up, snap, and pop. He fooled with the thing about ten minutes, then pulled out of the hole. One cone was off the bit and was, of course, on bottom. Johnny shut down, went to a phone about half a mile away, and called me, then told me what had happened and what his status was: out of the hole and waiting on orders.

We had orders to inform Phillips Petroleum Company if we had trouble, so I hunted up Blackie. He just happened to be at home. I told him the story as Johnny had given it to me and added that I was pretty sure that we had one or more joints of pipe off the bottom of the casing string and it seemed that they had gone downhole about 90 feet. Blackie said that he didn't think that was the trouble, that Martin, being a green driller, had hit a ledge and knocked the cone off, and that we just had a fishing job. I argued a bit, but he was obdurate, so I gave up, went by a fishing tool company, and rented a "globe basket" to recover the cone, screwed it onto the bottom drill collar, and started in the hole after my "fish," the cone, cautiously! Sure enough, we set down on something at the same depth Martin had lost the cone. We worked the basket through it, finally, with difficulty, went on to bottom, and recovered the cone. While they were coming out of the hole with the fish, I went to Phillips' field office and told Blackie that it was definite that we had metal down the hole, and I had trouble getting the basket into it. He would have none of that story, then told me that there was not any pipe loose, and to quit bothering him, and get back to drilling. It was an impasse; in a footage drilling contract, the contractor is responsible for twist-offs and things that happen downhole, but trouble with casing and abnormal pressures, or lost circulation, are on the operator, in this case, Phillips Petroleum Company. Loose casing is definitely in this category, but it is hard to correct and very expensive, so Blackie wasn't about to admit that the casing was parted. Some staff engineer might want to try to repair the casing, a tedious, often fruitless, task. Besides, they might blame him!

I, too, had a problem. I felt sure that we could finish drilling the well, by using great care on bit trips. But my company was in some danger of costly fishing trips if we didn't make Phillips admit liability. It would have been easy to prove, but I would have made an enemy, Blackie, and I really liked Blackie, so I called the office and talked it over with Skinny Hunter. I explained my predicament and told him I was confident that the drillers and I could handle the job. He consented for me to go ahead, with the provision that if the loose pipe caused real hairy trouble, we would "holler long and loud" and let Phillips take over the problem.

That is what we did; we just went ahead. When going in the hole with a new bit, we would slow down at the top of the loose casing, creep down, set about 1,000 pounds on the bit, turn it with the tongs, it would fall into the loose pipe, and we would go on to bottom and start drilling.

The first bit trip after we recovered the cone was made by Jack Evans, and he wrote on the daily drilling report that he "went in the hole, set down on loose casing, turned bit into it, and went to bottom." The next morning when Blackie picked up the report, he read that bit and hit the ceiling. He scratched through that sentence with a pen, then told Evans, "I've told you guys for the last time, that damned 'thing' isn't loose pipe, so don't let me catch you putting that loose pipe story on the report again." Jack said, "Yes sir, and I'll tell the other drillers." So, to the end of that well, on each bit trip the driller would write on the report, "Went in hole, hit 'thing' at 5,560 feet, turned into it, and went to bottom." Blackie accepted that and we finished the well with no trouble.

Jack Evans finally had the last laugh though. When we finished the hole and ran electric logs, the logs plainly showed three joints of pipe, in one piece, 90 feet down the hole. He told Blackie and Blackie just laughed and said, "Well, not admitting it worked; you all finished the hole okay, didn't you?" He was a funny, iron-headed, tough little man, Mr. Gaines, but we drilled six more wells for him and got along with him just fine.

We ran 5¹/₂-inch casing on that well. It went to bottom okay, the cement job also went well, and we were off the hook. Even though we had a minimum of trouble, finishing up was a real relief and everyone breathed easier, especially *me*.

Our next location was in the "walking dunes," very large dunes of clean, light tan, almost white sand. They run in a belt from a point about 25 miles northeast of Kermit, then curve south 5 miles east of Kermit and continue south just east of Monahans onward to a point just west of Crane. This makes them over 60 miles long, and they vary in width from 5 to 10 miles. They are a very impressive sight; some are over 70 feet high. The hardpan underlying them is a hard, reddish clay-sand mixture and very firm. The West Texas winds keep a continuous trickle of sand moving up and over the top of the dunes, and they constantly change shape and size as the winds shift direction and strength. The dunes are constantly moving ever so slightly and sometimes move very rapidly in high winds and sandstorms; hence the name "walking dunes." There is a state park 5 miles east of Monahans in the dunes just off Interstate 20 today. Kids love the dunes; they pull off their shoes and run like crazy through the clean sand, sand ski on their bottoms, and sometimes on real sand skis. Mothers don't mind 'cause they can shake the kids clean before they let them back in the car. The dunes, all 60 miles of them, have been a great playground for arrowhead hunters, picnickers, and kids for many years.

But they present some real problems to drillers of oil wells. Building a location is a problem, building a road to the location is a problem, and keeping both road and location free of drifting sand is a *real* problem. Roads had to be built with a rounded crown, locations built much the same, then hard surfaced with caliche, watered till set up, and they would then let the sand blow across them and down the other side, with occasional buildups that would have to be bladed away.

Then, since the rig sat on a semi-dune which would not hold water, we had to use a rat hole machine, actually a huge Auger, drill a 30-inch-diameter hole to a depth of 40 feet, then set and cement a so-called 26-inch-diameter "conductor pipe," in order to "spud in" in the hardpan. After surface was set and cemented at 200 feet down, things smoothed out, but the ever-present blow sand stayed with you, and keeping a rig clean and sand out of your gear boxes was a day-to-day chore, never ending, always present.

It was customary in those days to "shine up" a rig with a mixture of one-fourth motor oil and three-fourths diesel oil or kerosene. Since all drilling rigs were painted with a good grade of steel enamel paint, it worked well and made a rig look shiny. The roughnecks went over the rigs each day with brushes and wiping rags. All our rigs were painted "National Blue," and we tried valiantly to keep them clean and shined, to make them pretty to the eye.

However, it didn't work worth a damn in the dunes; when the wind rose and the sand flew, that mixture was just sticky enough to let the sand stick, and our rig began to look as though it had been stuccoed. We did not like it, any of us, from me down to the newest roughneck, but it was an accepted custom. We argued it pro and con, and the upshot was that one day I went into a Kermit supermarket and bought ten giant-sized boxes of Tide. We used Tide, long-handled brushes, and wiping rags, and gave Rig 6 a thorough cleaning. The results tickled us; the rig wasn't shiny, but it sure as hell was clean. And, for the record, it never was shiny again, but it stayed clean and everyone remarked on the change, and even Dick Hodges and Skinny Hunter approved. They started using detergents on all the rigs, and about a year later, the supply houses began to stock a detergent called "Rig Wash" in 20-gallon drums. The practice spread, and the old oily mixture faded from the scene.

Our job went well; we had few troubles and the bitter winter of 1949 faded into spring. Everyone welcomed spring, sandstorms and all, because that had been one tough winter. We started our third well, and things looked pretty good for all of us.

Mr. Bailey got laid off from his tool pushing job. It hit him very hard; he was an excellent driller, but a poor communicator. He did not stand stress well, and would never admit the possibility of being wrong, so he stayed in hot water. Then he had a particularly nasty fishing job and got caught between Skinny and a professional fisherman. Skinny sided with the fisherman and fired Bailey, telling him that he would have to ask the other tool pushers for a drilling job. Jack needed the job; he had a wife, two kids in high school, and one in grammar school, so he swallowed his pride and asked all five pushers who lived in Odessa for a drilling job, but no one would take him. So, as a last resort, he came to Kermit to ask me for his job back. It is bound to have been a bitter pill for him, but he took it like a man, said he was sorry for his remarks when he left me, and could he please have his job back. It put me in a bind, since Johnny Martin had made me a pretty good driller and didn't deserve to be laid off. I called Dick Hodges; he talked to Sonny Saak, who had a driller who wasn't keeping up; Sonny took Martin off my hands; and I gave Mr. Bailey his drilling job back. Even though Mr. Bailey resented me to the day he died, he was a good driller, and I valued him. We made a team.

We moved farther out in the dunes on our next location and didn't drill a water well. Instead we took a bulldozer and scooped out a 6-foot-deep trench about 50 feet long into the bottom of a place between two big dunes that had blown clean down to hardpan. Before the dozer got through, water was seeping into that trench, fast. The dozer operator spooked and got the hell out of that hole, barely in time! It filled to the top with clear, cold water and we had ample water with which to drill. The high school kids from Kermit found the pond and used it as a swimming pool all that summer of 1949. We used it to drill two wells, then moved about 2 miles south and abandoned the thing. It filled with sand that winter and vanished forever, but it sure worked

wonders for us, and I learned how the scrubby willow trees that grow
spottily throughout the dunes survive. Their roots go down to water. It
was altogether an amazing thing to find water so near the surface, in
the middle of a shifting, sandy desert.

I hunted arrowheads a lot that summer, Fritz the dachshund and I.
There were at that time a great many to be found because in times past
Indians had camped in the dunes—because of the availability of water,
I suppose; also, the surrounding countryside had many shin oaks growing. They are only shin high, but the acorns are full sized. I've been
told by Indian-lore buffs that the old-time Indians always camped near
the shinnery each fall, gathered the acorns, parboiled them to remove
the tannic acid and make them edible, then used the water they boiled
the acorns in to tan hides. It was a very useful arrangement. Anyway,
they left many traces of their passage, metates, manos, needles, awls,
arrowheads, even beads and an occasional Comanche spear or lance
head. Amy, whose health had taken a turn for the better, sometimes
joined us, usually in the mornings before the sun got too hot, or late in
the afternoons, just before sundown. She loved to hunt artifacts and
found many more than I ever found. I just did not have an "eye" for
arrowheads, but Fritz and I walked many miles in the dunes while
waiting for a crew to pull out of the hole or go in the hole, often three or
four hours at a time. The sand wasn't easy walking, but it surely did
wonders for your leg muscles. Both Fritz and I stayed lean and trim
that year. He, being a true dachschund, didn't show too much interest
in arrowheads, but the "Sand Hills," as the locals called them, had a
fairly large population of jerboas or kangaroo rats. They were pretty
little creatures with pinkish and white fur, and really did look and act
like tiny kangaroos. They were nocturnal, moving around mostly at
night, but often came out early in the evening at sundown, or stayed
out a little after dawn in the morning. Fritz was certain that they were
delicious and tried mightily to catch and eat one. He never did catch a
single one, but had a lovely time chasing them, being sure that some
day one would fail to get away. It never happened; they had large furred
feet and hopped about 2 feet at a time, while poor Fritzie had to plow
through the heavy sand. But we had some fine days in the dunes.

The two years that we spent in Kermit were good years, but they
went fast. The job settled into a fairly pleasant routine. The drillers
and I became accustomed to each other. The wells that we were
drilling presented few problems, and the rig was making money. Our
two company men, Blackie and his sub-foreman, Joe Upton, were
knowledgeable, pleasant to deal with, and we had the world by the tail
and a downhill pull, we thought; it felt good. I even played golf with
Blackie, a novel treat.

Amy perked up, and since we had made friends with the young couple who lived next door, she had someone to visit and run around with. The two young folk were named Harbin, Darwin and Pat. He worked for Gulf Oil as a pumper, but hated his job. She was an R.N., a fine nurse, but had taken leave of absence to have a baby. So she and Amy spent lots of time together, pleasantly. Kermit in the '40's was a very nice place to live. We loved the town.

Due to the natural cussedness of roughnecks, and a certain attrition that all jobs are subject to, we had lost some hands who came to Kermit with us and replaced them with local men—most of them good, experienced hands, young, married, and pretty steady men. Three of them were made into drillers later, and one of them, John Dennis, was drilling for me years later when I quit S-H-K.

Jim Davidson had hired two young men who were buddies, and this was a practice that I frowned on. I would not let a driller work brothers in the same crew, nor father and son, because if you lost one, either by firing him or him quitting, you always lost the other one. Then half your crew was gone and that crippled you until they could be replaced. But these two boys were both married and were also exceptional hands, so I looked the other way, for once, pretending that I didn't know they were close friends. Jimmie was working derricks, while Bob was the motorman. The derrickman on a drilling rig takes care of the drilling mud, catches samples, and looks after the pumps when not making trips. It is a responsible job and pays more money than a floor hand, which it should, and a good derrickman is a highly prized hand.

Jimmie's work began to suffer. He had always been a top hand, alert, willing, and smart. Then, overnight it seemed, he changed to a slovenly, inattentive man, doing sloppy work, leaving things he should have done to his relief man, and gazing off into space when he should have been working. I noticed the change and mentioned it to Davidson, who said that he thought he would straighten out in a few days and that he would talk to him. However, he didn't perk up, it went on for two weeks, and I got a bellyful of Jimmie. I drove up to the rig one day and looked at the mud pump as I went up the back stairs, and it was filthy. Evidently the crew had gone through the valves and had gotten mud all over the pump. Jimmie had not cleaned things up, and it was the last straw as far as I was concerned, so I brought things to a head.

I went up on the floor, called Jim Davidson into the dog house, and told him that I had put up with Jimmie just as long as I was going to, and to replace him immediately. Bob was splicing a rope, sitting on a bench in the dog house. He laid his work down when he heard what I told Jim and came up to where we were standing and said to me, "Pusher, please don't fire Jimmie. He really needs this job. His wife is expecting a baby this month. Jimmie has been screwing that little blonde waitress in so and so's cafe. His trouble right now is that he's got his love and pussy confused. I think he is beginning to wake up, and just as soon as he realizes that the fucking he's getting ain't worth the fucking he's *getting,* he's gonna be all right. Let me talk to him and I guarantee you he will straighten up."

I gave Bob and Jim a long look and said, "Well, he has been a good peart hand, so I'm giving you two days; then if he don't improve, he's gone."

I left the rig and don't know what Jim and Bob said to that boy, but it worked. He made a hand and earned his money from that day on to the end of his stint on Rig 6. I don't know how his love life went, although it must have made a change.

We finished our last well in the sandhills, moved down close to Phillips' little field office, and started what turned out to be our last well in Kermit, although we didn't know it at that time. The Phillips Petroleum Company's Talvez no. 8 was to stick in my memory for many years. It was a landmark in my life.

For one thing, it was my last contact with Blackie Gaines, of whom I had grown very fond. He was a tough, combative little rooster, just about sixty-one years old and four years from retirement, but afraid of nothing, certainly not management. He knew without doubt that he had it made and could make it to retirement on one foot, so to speak. Once Blackie and I were having lunch in Mac's Cafe. It was the best eatery in Kermit. Just about the time we ordered, the door opened and "Tex" Mallow, the district manager, came in with a young engineer in tow. We hollered at them, and they came over and sat with us. Tex began to bitch at Blackie in a mild sort of way about something he had done. Blackie, who had known Tex for many years and who had, in fact, been Tex's sub-foreman many years previously when Tex held the same position now held by Blackie, wasn't impressed at all. He looked Tex squarely in the eye and said, "Tex, quit bucking for promotion. You came up through the ranks just like I did, and you have out-stripped me. You are the district superintendent now and I'm working for you, but face it, friend, you are just as far up as you will ever go. You will retire as a district superintendent, just as I will retire as a lease foreman, so cool it, will you?"

Tex looked at Blackie for a long minute. "Why do you say that, Blackie? That I'm as far up as I will ever go?" Blackie said, "It has nothing to do with your ability, but Phillips Petroleum is an Okie outfit, and you didn't come across Red River with a red blanket wrapped around your ass."

Tex just grinned and said, "You are probably right, and that 'Tex' nickname doesn't help any either."

Blackie was right. Tex did retire as a district "super," but Blackie did not live to see it. He died with a massive heart attack three years after that incident. I know, because I attended his funeral. He was a great little guy who played strictly by the rules. He showed no fear and no favor. My crews and I thought he was great, one of the real good ones.

The office called me one morning and told me to come to Odessa. I went and got some unwelcome news. Rig 6 was going to move to New Mexico very soon. We were only a few days away from total depth, and Phillips Petroleum had a rather large lease that was going to expire in just a few days if a well wasn't "spudded in" and drilling by a certain date. It was west of Lovington, New Mexico. They told me that I had to be through in five days and be moved to 35 miles west of Lovington inside of eight days. It was a tall order with absolutely no margin for error. They said Phillips had started to build the road to the location and would be finished with the location "pad" the next day. I was to go to the new location right then and give the pit and reserve pit dimensions to the dirt contractor. The rig builders would start the derrick in two days. It usually took three days to build a standard derrick, and the pad had to be ready the next day.

I called Amy and told her what I was going to do, and that I might be late getting home. The new location was 140 miles away, and I had to find the thing, give the dimensions, and come home. She certainly wasn't thrilled with the prospect of a move, but took it pretty well.

I took off for New Mexico, went through Lovington, turned west, had 10 miles of blacktop pavement, then turned northwest on 22 miles of the worst, roughest, meanest caliche road that I have ever had the misfortune to drive over. It was sharp, triangular, blue caliche, as hard as steel and just as sharp. We found out just how tough it really was later, when we had a flat each trip into the rig.

This location I was hunting was on the Stevens Ranch. They told me that Mr. Jim Stevens was a millionaire about seventy years old, spent as much time as he could on the ranch, but had extensive property and business interests in Roswell. No one seemed to know too much about the man himself, but I was supposed to look him up and, if possible, establish good relations with him. The well we were going to drill was a 13,000-foot-deep wildcat, so we were going to be on his ranch for a fairly long time; therefore, good relations with the rancher were to be desired.

I had pretty good written directions and lots of experience in finding new well sites, so I found the south boundary of the ranch about 30 miles out of Lovington, turned through a cattle guard and began to drive west looking for ranch headquarters. I could see the unfinished derrick about 4 miles north of where I was, so I knew that I was on the right road. Then I saw a windmill about 100 yards off the road; there was a man there and he was horseback, so I rode over to ask him where the ranch house was, stopped the car, and got out. He got off the horse as I drove up, and stood waiting. The horse was old; so was the man. The saddle had seen years of wear; so had the man's clothes; and he wore a Stetson hat that was so battered, creased, and greasy, it had to be twenty years old.

We shook hands, and I told him who I was and why I was on the ranch and, presuming that he was one of the hands, asked him if he knew where I could find Mr. Stevens. The old man gave me a slow grin and said, "I'm Jim Stevens, so you are talking to the right man, but this windmill is down and I've got to have a half-inch bolt and nut about 2 inches long, and don't have one with me, so we will have to visit later. I'm going home to get a bolt."

I always carried a tool kit in my company car and was almost positive that I had the right-sized bolt in the kit, so I said, "Maybe I can help you; I think I have a bolt." We looked, and sure enough, I did have one. I helped the old man get the windmill to running; he thanked me and told me that when I came back from the well site he would be home and to stop by; we would drink a cup of coffee and get better acquainted. I looked at the old paint horse he was riding, and the old man laughed and said, "Yep, he is old, too, but we will be home by the time you drive to that derrick and back. It's only 3 miles, and he singlefoots along pretty peart."

I went on to the location and talked to the rig-builder pusher and the dirt contractor, gave the dirt contractor the slush pit and reserve pit dimensions, got assured by both men that they would be through the next day, then went back to the ranch house to meet Mrs. Stevens and drink the promised coffee.

Mrs. Stevens was a nice, soft-spoken, skinny little lady. She made me welcome and poured her husband and me coffee, out of about a 2-gallon ranch coffee pot. This was boiled coffee, old style. When she poured mine, the lid was off the pot and I saw that the pot had 6 inches of grounds in the bottom, and some of these grounds had been boiled at least ten times, as they were almost white. That was absolutely the worst coffee that I ever drank, before then or since, but I drank it with a smile. They were good, likable people and were nice to me and my people while we drilled on their ranch. More about that later, but at first, I gave most of the credit for that friendly atmosphere to the half-inch bolt.

I wound up my visit with the Stevens and headed back to Kermit. I blew out a tire on the way into town and had to buy a new one. That sharp caliche chopped the flat up pretty badly. It looked bad as to being able to keep men on that job. Drilling crews had always furnished their own transportation up until that time. It had always been that way, but I knew that drillers and roughnecks couldn't afford to buy a tire or two each week, just to get to work, and it looked like trouble ahead.

This was in August of 1950. The weather was hot, and the days were long. As we grew nearer to finishing up, both Phillips Petroleum and S-H-K grew increasingly antsy. The deadline for that lease to expire was fast approaching and it had begun to look like a very close squeak. Believe me, it was *extremely* close; we barely made it.

We bottomed out about noon August 29, 1950, circulated the hole three hours, came out of the hole laying down drill pipe, then rigged up the casing crew and began to run casing. The daylight crew went off tour and headed for Lovington. The company had hired professional movers to move their trailer houses, and the wives, kids, and trailer houses were already in Lovington. The evening tour crew finished running casing and we cemented it at about 11:00 P.M., when the plug hit bottom, and the cement job was complete. The crew began to tear the rig down; the morning tour crew had come out early and they, too, were rigging down. The moving trucks began arriving at 1:00 A.M. and began to load out the rig. By 9:00 A.M. the morning of the 30th, the last load left the location for Lovington, where the daylight crew was on location to start putting it together again.

The other two crews moved that day, and let it be forever to our credit, everyone moved. We didn't lose a single man.

The daylight crew and I, the truck drivers and swampers, and a roustabout crew I hired got a lot done that day, had everything spotted and began to think we might make it.

On the morning of the 31st, all three crews came out and we finished rigging up, half-assed. We had to be spudded by midnight or lose the lease. The State of New Mexico had a man on location (it was a state lease), to see that we didn't fudge, and we made it, by the skin of our teeth. We spudded the 17½-inch surface hole at 11:00 P.M., and at midnight were 100 feet deep. The state man went to Roswell, and just as soon as he was out of sight we shut down, left a watchman to keep the lights burning, and all went to town, pooped! We had run and cemented casing, torn down and moved a rig 150 miles, rigged it up on a standard derrick, and spudded in three days. But it wore us to a frazzle. I was forty-two years old, in perfect health and as hard as nails, but it tired me out completely. I'm sure that Phillips remembered all about it, because they pulled the same stunt on me again four years later. Someone forgot about a lease expiration and everybody got into a flap over the oversight, then ran around like a bunch of stomped-on red ants, wanting somebody, *anybody,* to *do something.* The awful truth was, *somebody* usually did.

Anyhow, we were started in New Mexico, but had many handicaps to overcome. Amy had not come up with me, so I had checked into the Llano Hotel in Lovington. It was an old hotel but had an excellent coffee shop and, most important to a tool pusher, two telephone booths in the lobby. Phones were at a premium in Lovington at that time, and if you put your name on a waiting list for a phone, it might be three or four months before you got one. And a phone, or access to one, was an absolute must for a tool pusher. All the major supply houses were in Hobbs, and many things you needed had to come out of Odessa. Odessa was then, as now, a major oil-field supply center. Lovington was the county seat of Lea County, New Mexico, a slow farm and ranch town of about 7,000 people. It was not in any way geared to the pace of the oil patch, and couldn't have cared less. We could like it or lump it as far as they were concerned, so we made do as best we could with what was available, and it sure wasn't much.

Each morning at report time, from 6:00 A.M. to 7:30 A.M., there would be fifteen or twenty tool pushers gathered in the lobby of the Llano Hotel waiting to use the phones. It took a while, since two phones were all we had, but most of the guys were good natured about the long waits, and since we all knew each other, if you had trouble or an emergency, they would give you a break and let you go ahead of someone. But it had better be a real case, because if you faked trouble, they would pay you back with a vengeance. It was an honor system with real teeth, as a couple of smart-asses found out. Those two clowns did an awful lot of waiting, while their counterparts carefully monopolized the phone.

Housing, too, was a real problem. There were about twenty drilling rigs running out of Lovington, and it had never had a large transient population. Nearly all the local people owned their dwellings, and rental houses were almost nonexistent. Fortunately, our people all had trailer houses, so we didn't have to cope with that problem. Some other rigs had a real problem. The labor pool in Lovington was small because they had no place to live.

Sonny Saak and Abby had been living in Lovington a little over six months when we moved Rig 6 to Lea County. His rig was running 9 miles northeast of town, and they had a rented house. He was rapidly nearing casing point and knew that he was going to move to a location between Kermit and Monahans when he finished the well. I said in the beginning, it's a crazy business. Sonny went from Lovington to Kermit about two weeks after I arrived from Kermit. Since he had rented a house when he came up and had waited out a phone, the company decided, in order to keep the phone, which was in S-H-K's name, that when Sonny moved out, I would move into his house, even though I had a perfectly good trailer house in Kermit on my own lot. Out of necessity, they would pay the rent on the house, not because they were big-hearted, but in order to be able to get in touch with me. In the meantime, I would stay in the hotel.

At that time in the late '40's and early '50's, people moving from Texas into New Mexico had another problem. Southeast New Mexico has been known for many years as "Little Texas," for in the early days, most of the oil-field hands came into New Mexico from Texas. New Mexico is ruled by men from Santa Fe, and the politicians made it just as tough on newcomers as they possibly could. The main highways coming into the state had check points called "Ports of Entry" just inside the border, usually 5 miles or less, and trucks from other states had to stop, be weighed, and have their gas tank contents measured; permits had to be bought and New Mexico tax paid on gasoline in their tanks. Sometimes loaded trucks would be held up at the ports for hours. On passenger cars, if you were moving to New Mexico to work they demanded that you buy a New Mexico license plate almost immediately. Since they cost about four times as much as Texas plates, and six or seven times as much as California plates, and many roughnecks came into town running on "short money," they resented having to do this, so they stalled, and the New Mexico state police got nasty with them and it made a bad situation. All that is in the past, it couldn't happen today, but it was a real bad thing in the year of our Lord 1950.

On my fourth day in Lovington, I went to the rig about 4:00 A.M. and came back to town about 7:00 A.M. to phone in my report. It was late summer and broad daylight when I came driving into town. I had ruined a tire on the way in and was in a very bad humor. On the edge of town a state cop pulled me over, and I couldn't imagine why, since my car was new and I was driving very sedately. I got out of the car as he came up and asked him, "What is the matter, officer?" and he asked, "Are you working in New Mexico?"

"Yes I am, I'm pushing tools on a rig that just moved up from Texas, and I'm staying at the Llano Hotel."

"I know where you are staying. I have been checking licenses in the hotel parking lot every morning, and you have been there four days."

"So what? Is staying at the Llano a crime?"

"No, but I want a New Mexico license on this car tomorrow."

I gave him a hard look, but he was serious. So, I said, "Sorry, friend, that is one thing you are not going to get. This car doesn't belong to me, and I can't possibly put a license on it today, or tomorrow."

He said, "Then I'll just have to confiscate it." That really burned me up. I reached in and yanked the keys out of that damned Ford, dropped them in his hand, and told him, "It's all yours, friend. I don't own a bolt in it. This car belongs to Schoenfeld-Hunter-Kitch Drilling Company, and the title is in Tulsa, Oklahoma. I couldn't buy a license if I wanted to, and I don't want to, but I *do* want your name and badge number. I'll walk to town and call my company and tell them who is responsible for their car."

It must not have been the answer he expected, and I have always thought that he had exceeded his authority. He looked at me oddly, and said, "Mr. Lynch, I don't want your car."

I was still angry, so I said, "Well, you said you did, and you've got it. You told me you were going to confiscate it, so there it is; take it and be happy, and take good care of it; it is a new car."

We finally compromised. He didn't really want my car, and I wasn't anxious to get into a row with the New Mexico state cops. I promised to get a license just as soon as I could get the car title from Tulsa, and he decided I could keep the car and work until that was accomplished, so we parted, not friends, but at least aware of each other. I got the license about two weeks later, and the cop and I would give each other a small "two-finger" wave when we met on the highway. But the worst was over, and I got along fine for many years with the New Mexico state cops, who were just doing as I was, following orders.

Chapter Fourteen

The Tulk Field

The road to the rig was another matter. The men began blowing out tires on their personal cars, and it got so bad that they were threatening to quit en masse, go back to Texas, and to hell with S-H-K Drilling Company. I told Skinny this, and he said that I could start buying replacement tires and charging them to the company, just to pacify the men. I established credit at a Phillips service station in Lovington. Phillips Petroleum Company was selling Lee tires in all their stations at that time. These tires were insured against "hazards of the road," unconditionally, and we began to give that Phillips tire adjuster a real workout.

But it simply was not enough. Some rigs just south and west of us were having a real turnover in personnel. They were losing people faster than they could hire them. The turnover was terrific, and one contractor had finally begun to furnish transportation for the crews. The road was just as tough on cars as it was on tires, and I duly reported this to the office, but was met with much skepticism. They simply didn't believe it was that bad a situation. Dick Hodges had quit the company, and I had lost my "ear" in the office. Dick would have taken my word for it; Skinny did not, but in the long run, everything worked in my favor, and I came out smelling like a rose.

The three partners came up to Lovington in Skinny's new Oldsmobile and drove to the rig over that miserable road. I had persisted in my complaints, finally telling Skinny that if my men began to leave the company, I, too, would quit my job. I simply did not intend to put up with new hands coming and going every day.

So they came up to see for themselves—Bill Schoenfeld, Bill Kitch, and Skinny. As soon as they arrived, they told me that the road was bad, but not as bad as I had made it out to be. They also said that my pitch for two company-owned crew cars was to be talked over, and I would get a decision fairly soon.

Bill Kitch and Skinny did talk to the driller and one roughneck and got a solid earful, as the men had a gutful of that damned road. The partners soon left for town, not noticing the big bulge on the side of one of Skinny's shiny new tires.

I started to town about an hour after they had left the rig. I had bought another wheel and tire and was carrying two spares, because I had learned on that road that one spare was not enough. About 10 miles from the rig, I came up to the big blue Oldsmobile with two flats and one spare. It was early September and hot as hell; all three partners were beginning to suffer, as they had no drinking water. I gave them a drink from my gallon jug, loaded them in the Ford, and took them and the two flats to town, in perfect silence. I bought two new tires, had them mounted, took Skinny back to his car, helped him install the new tires, then followed him to town. They left for Odessa without further talk, and two days later, I got word to buy two Chevrolets from a local dealer, then keep them running and shod at company expense. I did just that, the hands loved it, and our labor troubles ended. We never lost a man while we drilled that 13,500-foot wildcat and four 12,000-footers out there. But while we drilled those five wells—and it took a year—I either got an adjustment on or bought ninety-one tires. Lee Tires took a beating. They hadn't counted on a road like that one.

We had drilled a water well for the rig supply. You had to get a permit from the State Water Engineer for a "temporary" water well. These permits were tightly controlled, and you had to sign an affidavit that you would plug the well when you were through with it. New Mexico did not allow landowners to drill wells into the Ogallala aquifer without permission, and it was almost impossible to get permission. The oil-field permits were usually handled by the water-well drilling contractors. I used Abbott Brothers out of Hobbs for many years and never had a bit of trouble. They knew the score, and the state engineer trusted them.

Our water well produced, along with the water, huge quantities of sand. When a well was first put to producing and pumping, in that order, you had to leave it running constantly, until it quit making sand, since if you shut it down, the sand would settle. Your pump and shaft would sand up solidly and you would lose your water well and your pump. Sometimes, even if you left it running, it would be touch-and-go and keep you a bit edgy until it quit making sand, so we kept a very wary eye on that water well for several days, even leaving a man with it at night.

We drilled our water well about 300 feet north of the rig on the bank of a small ravine. This ravine was about 60 feet wide and 10 feet deep. I had a bulldozer build a dam across the thing about 100 feet down from the pump and well, and we turned the water and sand into the pond thus formed.

This kept sand out of our lines and water tanks. The sand was heavy and settled out quickly in the pond. We set a centrifugal pump on the bank of the pond with the suction barely in the water and had good, clear, sand-free water to start our oil well with, and the dam made a reservoir of several thousand barrels.

The summer of 1950 had been very dry in Southeast New Mexico, no rain to speak of, and the fall rains had not happened yet, so the vegetation was burned and dry. Stock water was just about nonexistent, all the ponds were bone dry, and ranchers were completely dependent on windmill water. The cattle were having to walk a long way to drink, and with the sparse, dry grass, it walked 'em bone-skinny pretty rapidly. It was a bad time for the ranch people, and by mere happenchance, we got the opportunity to further cement our good relations with Mr. Jim Stevens.

Our rig was on a small knoll, and just east of us about a quarter-mile was a very large "playa," or dry lake; it covered at least 50 acres. The center of this depression was 100 feet wide, 200 feet long, and 6 feet deep. This was a catch basin for surface water, bladed out by a bulldozer, and the heavy black soil held water like a jug. You wouldn't get a big enough rain to fill a whole playa once in three years, but usually the catch basin would catch water and provide drinking water for cattle over a large section of pasture.

This fall, however, it was dry as a bone. Mr. Jim came over to the rig on the morning of our third day; we were getting ready to spud and didn't pay him too much attention. While he looked the entire lash-up over, he paid particular attention to our dammed-up ravine reservoir and the little water-well pump putting water into it, at about three barrels per minute. Before he left, he asked me how long I was going to let that water-well pump run. I told him that as soon as the well quit making sand, we would shut the pump down, then run it only as needed to keep our water tanks full. He then told me that he had noticed an 8-foot length of 6-inch pipe buried in the dam about a foot from the top. So, I said, "Yes, that is in case the well keeps on making sand for another day or two and the reservoir gets full. It will keep the overflow from washing the dam away."

The old man grinned at me and asked, "Boy, could I talk you into running that pump for a few more days? I'll plow a furrow down to my tank, we can get some water caught in it, and my cows won't have to walk 5 miles for a drink. This pasture has about 7 sections of land in it, and 2 miles would be as far as any cow would have to walk. I can put some mother cows in here, and it would surely help my sore back."

I grinned right back at him, then said, "Mr. Jim, if you want it to, I think that my water well may make sand indefinitely, so I'll have to run the pump day and night for awhile, but you will have to promise not to tell the New Mexico water board on me."

He laughed, promised to keep mum, and left.

I was busy, but did remember to tell the drillers not to shut the water well in, as I wanted it to run for a day or two.

The next morning at the crack of dawn, Jim Stevens, two of his hands, a four-wheel-drive Jeep, and a big gang plow showed up. They hitched the plow to the Jeep, one hand drove the Jeep, one rode the beam on the plow, and Mr. Jim handled the plow handles. He was over seventy years old, 6 feet 2 inches tall, and was made up mostly of rawhide and tough, stringy muscle. They plowed a furrow from just under the dam to the upper end of the catch basin in the playa, not on a straight line, but following the contours of the slope. The old man handled that plow like a master. He made three passes at that furrow, and by that time Mr. Bailey's roughnecks, who admired the old man's spunk, had taken shovels and gone down to help shovel clods out of his ditch. They neither knew nor cared that he was worth several million dollars; he was much man, and that was enough for them.

The pump ran; the catch basin filled, then overflowed into the playa. The drillers and I got caught up in the spirit of the thing, and by the time we finished that well after four months, we had water 5 feet deep over that whole damned playa. And best of all, we had earned the undying gratitude of Jim Stevens, and our relations with him stayed good. We drilled three more wells on the ranch with never a cross word. We skidded the derrick each time with no damage charge from Mr. Stevens, though he gave hell to Texaco and three other drilling contractors. He may have been as tight as the skin on a dead horse's belly, but he never showed that side to us. We liked him fine, and he liked us.

Our well was a wildcat, under Phillips Exploration people. The mud engineers were Phillips hands, as were the geologists. The lease foreman supervised casing jobs and that was about all, as the "rock hounds" called most of the shots. We had a "footage" contract to 9,000 feet; then we went on "day work." "Day work" is just that; your rig, crews, and pusher are leased to the operator. He pays a daily fee for all this, and also assumes all risks, troubles, and expense. It is a no-loss deal for a drilling contractor, but since the accusation of "riding" day work is always in the back of your mind, things go forward as well as if you were on footage all the way, or at least you hope that they do go well.

Things went well with us. We whipped that little booger down to the Abo shale in about fifty days. We were "clear-watering" the thing and it drilled fairly rapidly. It would be slow by today's standards; we didn't have the bits or know-how then that we have since acquired, but did a pretty fair job.

Carmen Stafford of McVey and Stafford had a rig running just southwest of me about 3 miles away. I liked Carmen and thought him very smart about drilling in Lea County, so I visited his rig often, especially when I thought he might be there. I enjoyed talking to him, and learned a lot about Lea County formations. He really was smart, one of the finest drillers I have ever known. He studied ways to do things better; I did, too; so he and I had many things in common, and he was very observant. I was visiting him one day as they were rigging up their second rig. He and I were watching a crew laying a 2-inch water line from the light-plant house to the rig floor. The men were young, but one of them, a good-looking lad of about twenty, got up from a stooping position very slowly, as though he had a bad back or had aged suddenly. We watched them for awhile and finally Carmen said, "There's something the matter with that kid. He's acting like he's eighty years old. I'm gonna find out what's ailing him."

We walked over where they were working and Carmen asked him, "Kid, what in the hell is the matter with you? Have you got the clap?"

The boy straightened up, slowly, then put both hands on the small of his back and answered, "Yes sir, I do; doesn't everybody?" I laughed with Carmen and we left him to his sorrow. I guess other people's troubles are always funny.

The Abo shale in parts of Lea County is a rather peculiar formation. There is a diagonal line across Lea County from northeast to southwest. On the east side of the line—and bear in mind that it meanders and is not a straight line—you have to "mud up" to drill it, or it will slough on you, giving you worlds of trouble. On the west side, you can drill it with clear water, a fast rate of penetration, and no trouble. Carmen Stafford and I worked on the line for awhile and thought that we had it clearly defined; we were quite positive we were on the west side and planned to "clear-water" the Abo.

Imagine my surprise when I got to the job one day and found the crew "mudding up" and the rate of penetration down from 15 feet per hour to 4 feet per hour. I jumped Jack Evans about it, and he showed me an order signed by a Phillips geologist saying "mud up at a certain depth." I didn't like it a bit, but there was nothing I could do; we were on day work, and they had the say. I started back to town, and about 10 miles from the rig I met a Phillips car with the Phillips 66 logo on the side. I had an S-H-K decal on the top center of my windshield, and the driver of the Phillips car waved me to a stop. The driver was an open-faced, smiling man, with sandy red hair and very blue eyes. He asked me, "Are you the pusher on the Phillips wildcat?" I admitted that I was; then he asked, "How are you getting along? Is it drilling pretty good?"

My temper flared a bit, and I told him, "It isn't drilling worth a damn. Some pinheaded geologist named Hanagan gave orders to mud up. We did it, and our rate of penetration went to hell. We could have drilled that damn Abo with clear water, but he didn't ask anybody about it."

He looked at me oddly and then said, "I guess I am the guilty party. My name is Hugh Hanagan, and I'm the guy who signed that order." HELLO!! Mr. Hanagan—I was speechless, but didn't take back my words. We both survived the deal. After thirty-three years, Hugh still delights in telling about our first encounter, and we have been good friends through all these years. He was wrong that time, but he was a real brainy little guy and hasn't been wrong many times since. He is now a millionaire, but still the same tough little shanty Irishman he always was, one of the real good ones who made it big. I still think of him fondly. He is a *man*.

We drilled ahead, taking numerous drill stem tests, and got salt water in the Devonian. Plugged back to the Pennsylvanian, at 12,000 feet, and made a pretty good well. Skidded the rig 3 miles due south and got ready to drill another well. The winter was nearly over; we had spudded in late August and finished in late December. In fact, we were waiting on orders on Christmas Day.

Amy had come up. We were still in the rented house, and Amy's sister Ruth, whose husband was drilling for Sonny, was living in our trailer. It wasn't too bad an arrangement. I had puttied the windows in October, and Amy brought up a bunch of household plunder in a two-wheeled trailer she had borrowed. The house was a one-bedroom, four-room house, but it had a garage and a fenced back yard. Fritzie loved that yard. And the crowning glory of the house was that it had a telephone. It made all the difference in the world, and I forever deserted the line waiting for a phone in the lobby of the Llano Hotel. We, all of us, had entered into a new way of life. The office was far away; I had much more control of my job than the average pusher, more freedom to make my own decisions, even though I had to live with the results of those same decisions. There was no one to pass the buck to; it was all mine.

We made some extensive changes in Rig 6. We lengthened the upper dog house to 36 feet long and made a "change house" for the rough-necks with fifteen individual lockers in it. The change house sat on the ground, and the upper dog house sat on top of the change house. Both places were painted white inside and kept clean. The upper dog house had been 28 feet long originally, but since we were so far away from supply houses and the road spooked salesmen, we had begun to have trouble getting repairs done. Jack Evans had made a study of air valves and relays; our rig was air operated, and we had hell getting parts and especially repairmen from Odessa. It made a bad situation, since a defective valve could shut you down, with disastrous results if you were on bottom and couldn't pull your pipe off bottom. Jack proposed to lengthen the dog house and put in a drill press, bench grinder, and all the tools, parts, O rings, and everything it took to repair valves and relays. He would teach the hands how to do the work, and we could free ourselves from waiting forever on repairmen. I took him up on the deal, stuck my neck way out, and added 8 feet to the upper house. We did the job while moving between locations, and the company squeaked a bit about the cost, but it paid off, big!, and the grumbling died away. Evans was an exceptional man. He had more curiosity than a cat; he had to know how everything worked and why it worked, and he constantly amazed me. I went along with many of his ideas, and added a few of my own, and we made a "brag rig" out of no. 6.

The drillers and roughnecks all bragged about the rig and the good conditions they worked under. Our labor turnover was the envy of every tool pusher I knew. We rarely lost a man, but it didn't "just happen." We all worked at it, and I can say after all the years since that it was a "happy rig."

We solved our own problems and, in roughneck talk, "killed our own snakes." In the nine years that I pushed tools on Rig 6, we only had one fishing job that lasted more than twenty-four hours, an almost incredible record. I have always prided myself on my ability to "fish," oil-field style. One of the things you must have to be a good oil-field "fisherman" is the ability to visualize or "see" downhole. I have always had this talent, and Jack Evans also had much of this gift. We had our share of fishing jobs, dropped pipe, twist-offs, back-offs, stuck pipe, and occasional lost cones, but always managed to clean them up in a hurry. As a consequence, the rig made money, *lots* of it, and that is the *only* way to make management happy. You can upgrade your rig and do many things, as long as you make money. Start losing money and you are a spendthrift and a detriment to the human race. We somehow managed to stay ahead of any losses.

One bad thing happened on our third well in what had become known as the Tulk field. I had to fire Jim Davidson. I certainly hated to have to do it, but he left me no choice.

When I first began to push tools, I made an ironclad rule: no drinking on the job, no bringing out a drunk hand to sleep off too much drink, and no failing to show up on the job because you were drunk, and there were no exceptions. Any driller who violated those rules was fired instantly. I had seen too much down through the years, of drunks and the problems they caused, and swore that I wouldn't put up with any drinkers who brought their problems to the job. So far, I had only had to discharge one driller. That was back when I was looking after two rigs and a driller brought out a drunk hand and was letting him sober up on the job. I showed up unexpectedly at 3:00 A.M. one morning, found out about the deception, waited until tour changing time, then fired driller and crew. Once was enough—the men knew that I wasn't kidding, and I didn't again have to prove that I meant business.

Jim had always been a drinker. He knew that I was aware of it, and had been careful to drink on his own time. And though he had come to work suffering from hangovers many times, I knew that he always managed to be sober when he came to work. He suffered, I am sure, but did it in silence. He was a good, solid driller—not an innovator, but a good, steady man, dependable, and a good man to stay out of trouble. I valued him.

He did not show up for work one day. We "rotated" tours, a much hated system. A driller would work one month daylights, one month evening tour, and one month morning tour. It was supposed to even things up and do away with the "head driller" concept. I'm not sure that it did, but management had decided, so we had to go along with the deal. Jim was on evening tour. He was relieving Jack Evans, when his crew came to work one day without him. I was at the rig and asked the men what had happened. They were evasive, said they had gone by Jim's house and his car was gone, and his wife must have been away, too, as no one answered the door. They waited a bit, then came on to work, thinking maybe Jim would drive out later in his own car.

Evans doubled over and stayed with Jim's crew. His own crew would go by his home and tell his wife not to look for him. I went to Lovington to look for Jim. I went by his trailer house; no one there, of course, but a neighbor told me that she thought Jim was in jail. She didn't know where his wife and ten-year-old daughter were, but I knew that they were not at home.

I went to the county jail; sure enough, he was there, charged with D.W.I., and his wife was also in jail. She was charged with drunkenness and using abusive language to the arresting officer, and they intended to keep both of them in jail, which left the little daughter stranded. I got Amy, who knew the kid on sight, and we started out to find the child. We found her sitting on the steps of the trailer, locked out. She had been visiting another little girl, had stayed late, and got home to find the trailer locked and her parents gone. She was crying, so we took her home with us to spend the night. Amy called her grandmother in

Odessa, and she promised to come get the child the next day. She wasn't any trouble to us, just ate her supper, went to bed early, and we heard her crying after she was in bed.

I let Jim go, but I really hated to do it. He knew the rule, and he had come to work several times so hung over he was sick, and I had warned him that booze would get him fired. He had become an alcoholic, though, and was sure he could handle both job and drink, and went the way they usually do, down.

After I fired him, he got a job drilling on a rig near Odessa, and he lasted two months and got the sack again. I never saw him again but heard that he was picking fruit in California and drinking steadily. I've often wondered what happened to his little daughter.

I put a roughneck to drilling in his place. Ben had been working motors for Jack Evans for three years, and he was ready for a drilling job. He took Jim's crew over and fitted right in. It made things better for all of us, to elevate a good roughneck to drilling. It made the men feel that they, too, might get stepped up some day and gave them something to look forward to.

We had made friends with Hugh Hanagan, the Phillips field geologist. He was a good man at his job, and a likable cuss to boot. He helped change my view toward "rock hounds," whom I had always regarded as pests. He was regular people, and I began to learn a good bit about the geologic structure of the Permian Basin. This knowledge of "lithology" stood me in good stead later, and helped me immensely in bit selection and formation changes to look for. Hugh started me to studying this lore, and Jim "Pappy" Vaughn, an older geologist, finished my education and put me miles ahead of my rivals. Really, it is amazing how a little cooperation can change your attitude toward people.

We lost Hugh. He was young, single, and ambitious. He transferred to Alaska, told us all goodbye, and left. We got another young geologist named Larry Gnagy. We were lucky again, too; Larry turned out to be a fine geologist and friend.

It was on our third well in the Tulk field that we had a very peculiar occurrence. Parker Drilling Company had a district office in Lovington. The district manager was named LaDet, pronounced Laday. He was smart, a good manager, and a thoroughly nice man. I used to stop and visit him occasionally at his office, about 1 1/2 miles south of Lovington, just to exchange gossip, a few lies, and lots of good feelings. We enjoyed each other.

Parker moved a rig into the Tulk field. They were drilling for Texaco. The rig and the crews came to Lovington from Louisiana. The rig was a National "100," and the crews were born and bred Cajuns. The

tool pusher was named Louis Hebert—pronounced "Louie A-Bear."
He was short, dark, excitable, smart, and a good driller.

The first signs we had of the Cajun crews were one morning while
driving to our rig. I passed a car with five small men in it, each wearing
a shiny hard hat, not the usual soiled, grimy ones that you saw in the
patch. This was unusual, since "hard hats" were *never* worn to and
from the job. They were always left at the rig. Those guys were different; they wore their hats to and from the job, and if you were smart, you
accepted this custom. They didn't think it funny and were pretty
damned touchy about people who thought their customs odd. They
were not men that you laughed at lightly. They took themselves seriously, and expected you to take them the same way. I knew what they
were, stopped by their rig, and met their pusher.

We visited, Louis Hebert and I. I liked Cajuns from my early days in
Louisiana, and he, in turn, wanted to learn all that he could about
drilling in the Permian Basin. His boss, A. C. LaDet, had given me a
good send-off with Louis, and we got along fine.

Parker's location was about 2 miles south of the well that we were
drilling. The road to our rig passed about 200 yards north of their
location, and their rig was clearly visible from the road, day or night.

One morning about one o'clock, I was going to my rig. I do not
remember exactly why I was making the trip, but do remember the trip
was not particularly urgent. When I drove past Louis' rig, I noticed
that the traveling blocks were not hanging in the derrick, and that the
derrick had a curiously empty look in the artificial lights. I turned
around, drove back to the lease road, drove down to the rig, and saw
that they had a real disaster on their hands. The blocks were certainly
not hanging in the derrick; there were no wire lines to be seen and the
rig was quiet. This was not normal.

I got out of the car and went up into the tool house. As I climbed the
steps, I saw three men up in the derrick at about the sixth girt above the
floor. They were obviously inspecting for damage.

Louis was sitting on the steel bench in the tool house with his head in
his hands. He didn't even look up when he heard my footsteps on the
steel floor. I looked out on the floor. The traveling blocks were lying
across the top of the draw works, the drum was turning slowly, and at
each revolution, a 10-foot-long length of wire line reached out and
whacked the floor. I knew then what had happened. Someone had run
into the crown block, cut the drilling line, and dropped the whole
string of drill pipe, creating a tough fishing job, as well as a lot of
expensive rig repair.

I said, "Louis, what in the hell happened to you?" He looked up at
me and said, "Friend, when I see him, he is dead man. I'll stick my

knife in his navel and run all the way around him. He'll fall in two pieces!"

I said, "Who in hell are you talking about?" Louis said, "My morning tour driller, that's who. He run into crown, drop blocks, drop pipe, run down steps, get in car and leave. When I wake up and come up on floor, he is gone. I'll kill him dead when I see him!"

Suddenly, he jumped up, ran out on the floor, looked up in the derrick, and called out, "How many men I got in tower? Three? Half of you come down, NOW!"

I knew I wasn't needed, so I left, but to this day, I don't know how Louis got *half* of the three hands out of the derrick, but I wouldn't say that he didn't do it. I *do* know that the morning tour driller never picked up his "drag-up" check. He was afraid of either Louis or A. C. LaDet, probably both of them. They knew their business, cleaned up the fishing job, repaired the rig, and drilled their well. I have often wondered if Louis ever saw that morning tour driller again. I doubt it, especially if the other guy saw Louis first.

That third well in the Tulk field was a dry hole, and the fourth promised to be our last. If it turned out dry, we were through. Luckily, we made a fair well.

Amy and I had long since moved our trailer to Lovington, rented a vacant lot, put in utilities, and fenced the lot. It was in an old, settled part of town and the trailer house sitting in the midst of all those permanent dwellings caused a real furor, and a few indignant meetings. Some folks even went down to City Hall, but found out there were no ordinances against trailer houses, and the panic died away. Amy and I, in our ignorance, just thought the neighbors were stand-offish. We didn't pay them much attention, though *they* certainly watched *us*.

Our neighbor to the north told us all about it later. He was a retired newspaper owner and editor, and he, too, thought the flap was funny. His name was Logan Beal. He sponsored me in the Masons later, and we became friends. He was of Scotch descent and had a wry sense of humor that I really enjoyed.

We were into our second winter in Lovington, the winter of 1951. Mr. Bailey's kids were about through high school. Charles was a senior and Nancy a junior. They liked the Lovington schools and didn't want to move. None of us did, even with that miserable road that we had to travel, and it certainly was not getting any better. But our days in the Tulk were coming to an end. We finished our fifth well in April of 1952 and got word to move to Andrews, Texas, possibly for just one well.

As usual, nobody wanted to move; we were all happy in Lovington. Everybody wanted to stay, so I proposed to my drillers that, as it was only 60 miles to our new location, we stay in Lovington, drive the crew cars back and forth, and see if the one-well rumor was true, because we just might be working in New Mexico again soon.

Now we all had good reason to want to stay in Lovington. Bailey and Evans had kids in school, as did many of the roughnecks. Amy and I were very pleased with where we were living, and I was active in the Masons. I was sure I could keep the two crew cars at least for one more well. Lovington was a pleasant place to live and trade, and best of all for me, we were far away from the office.

However, due to the true cussedness of all drillers and roughnecks, the proposal met with stiff resistance from the people I was trying to help. They were sure I was trying to impose my will upon them, for some obscure reason. So, they demanded to be allowed to move to Andrews. Mr. Bailey was particularly noisy about it, so I told 'em to move, and then to keep their damned mouths shut to me if it turned out badly.

So they moved. The company took the crew cars away and sold them; the hands bitched to each other, but said nary a word to me. I had made an issue out of it, and they were stuck with the results.

We finally ended up drilling eight wells near Andrews before we moved the rig back to New Mexico, so the men were right after all, but they walked softly around me for some time. I was sore at all of them.

And we all lost something; I never again interceded for the men; when we had to move I told them where we were going, that they could come with me, or stay and hunt another job, that their desires meant nothing to me, and it was "root hog or die" on the job.

Chapter Fifteen

Andrews and the Maguetex

The company had replaced Dick Hodges as drilling superintendent with a young man named Jack Haberlein. He was a graduate of the University of Oklahoma, a petroleum engineer, and was married to the only daughter of the Vice President of Operations of Phillips Petroleum Company, a Mr. Fitzgerald. Jack was a big, good-looking, blond boy, and a thoroughly nice person. He had roughnecked for a couple of years, then moved into the office in Odessa as engineer; then when Dick left he was made drilling superintendent under Skinny Hunter. He didn't make waves, didn't flaunt his position, and turned out to be a real help. I liked him a lot, and he, in turn, seemed to like me, and we both gained from our association. He helped me when I wanted to beef up my rig, and I taught him a great deal about pushing tools.

We moved the rig to a location 12 miles east of Andrews, just off the Lamesa highway. There were already three rigs running in that field. It was called the Maguetex field; I've always wondered where they got those field names, but no matter. I had been agitating for a new and more powerful mud pump, had enlisted Jack Haberlein as a helper, and we made bold predictions about how much a high-pressure pump would improve our drilling time. "Jet" bits were coming into general use, and pump pressures were rising. As usual in the oil fields, they rose slightly faster than a glacier moved; tool pushers distrusted high pump pressure, and contractors feared their old pumps would fall apart, so there was resistance. But Jack and I had persisted and had prevailed. I was getting a new pump at last. We would rig it up on our first well east of Andrews. I had done my homework on hydraulics, and both Jack and I were certain we were going to do great things.

The three rigs already in the area we were moving to belonged to Big Chief Drilling Company, Trinity Drilling Company, and our own company, S-H-K. They were all on their second well and had averaged about 108 days, drilling their first wells to 13,000 feet. I felt sure that I could beat their time with our new big pump and a paper Pappy Vaughn had brought me which told me where formations changed in that area. The paper enabled me to pick bits for the different formations, and that not only cut down my drilling time, but saved a fairly large number of bits per well—no small item at that time, or now either. It makes a difference.

I had consulted with Bethlehem engineers about my new pump. They assured me that the pump could handle pressures up to 2,500 pounds per square inch. I proposed to run about 2,200 PSI in the pump and speed up my drilling. Not too surprisingly, Skinny objected. He said that I was going to scuttle my new pump and he didn't want me to damage it, but I clung to my position and he finally said, "Go ahead, but if you bust the water end on that pump or mess up the gear end, you have had it. I'll let you go." It didn't worry me. I could get another job inside a week, and we both knew it.

We spudded in, set surface and intermediate casing, and reached 10,000 feet deep in thirty-two days; went on day work at that point and finished that well in seventy-eight days, thirty full days ahead of schedule. It astonished everyone, including me, and that 2,200-pound pressure paid big dividends for a while, until Phillips cut the footage price a dollar per foot. But, as the lion said after he ate the midget, "It was good—while it lasted."

Everyone moved to Andrews. I was staying at a small motel, and in what spare time I had, which wasn't much, I looked for a private place to move my trailer house and set up on, and I finally found one. As usual, it had no utilities and I had to get them all put in—water, gas, electric service, sewer, and telephone. The lady I rented the lot from was delighted and figured on renting that space many times. I am sure that she did; private trailer spaces were greatly prized. We moved in and stayed for two years. That one well turned into eight, and one of them went well below 14,000 feet.

Things were still changing in the oil fields. Weight indicators had been in use for years, muds were increasingly sophisticated, mud engineers had gained in importance, bits had been constantly evolving, and the new jets were drilling holes faster and cheaper than ever. Geolograph and other companies had recorders in every dog house. They recorded with pens and ink, rates of penetration, weight on bit, shutdown time, and trip time, even how much torque was being applied to turn the bit. In the beginning they were called "tattletales" and were hated, but were accepted everywhere now because they helped keep you out of trouble.

Casing was being run by "professional casers" who came to your rig on call, brought their air or hydraulically operated tongs, and speeded up running casing to an astonishing degree.

A year or two before we moved to Andrews, a man named Leo Bell invented a gizmo that he called an "automatic driller." Its main component parts were a Bourdon tube and a sensor. Drillers gave it a bad name, many of the more stupid ones, thinking it would replace them, but Leo merely wanted to keep an even weight applied to the bit at all times while drilling. It also freed the driller from constantly "feeding off" the brake. I rented one; it was offered as a rental tool and the rent was modest, $250 a month. Mr. Bailey didn't completely trust it, Jack Evans and Ben loved it, and it did improve our foot-per-hour drilling time. Everyone in S-H-K said I had lost my feeble mind, but success is very hard to argue with, and I was out-drilling my competitors very badly. I can't take all the credit, as my drillers were exceptional men. We were all proud to be the best and strove to always beat the rival companies.

Sonny Saak had quit his pushing job and gone back to Stroud, Oklahoma. He and Abby had kept their home there for many years, wouldn't buy a trailer house, and always talked about "going home." They went to Stroud at every opportunity and finally went to stay. I missed them, for we had been close friends many, many years. It was a wrench to lose them.

We had installed a radio system on all the rigs about two years earlier. I had used it between the rig and my car and home in New Mexico, but was out of range of the base station in Odessa. When we moved to Andrews, just 35 miles from Odessa, we were back in range, of course, and the radio became a real help to me. I could always reach help in an emergency. It was also a source of company gossip, because airing your troubles let everybody on an S-H-K rig listen in, avidly!

One night in January of 1953, we were fishing. We had had a twist-off, had gone in the hole with an overshot fishing tool, caught our fish, and were coming out of the hole with it. I, of course, was at the rig waiting for Ben to get out of the hole so that I could lay down the fish, check the bit for damage, and do all the little things that a tool pusher is supposed to do. The night was clear, moonlit, and cold. I was wishing I could finish up and go home to bed. It was 2:00 A.M. and I was getting a little weary.

Suddenly, the radio in my dog house blared. "Rig 2 calling Odessa." The Rig 2 driller got the answering service and told them that he had trouble and needed to talk to his tool pusher. In just a few minutes, John, the tool pusher, came on the air. He was talking from his car, and it hadn't warmed up yet, because his teeth were chattering. He asked what the trouble was, and the driller told him that he was stuck, 30 feet off bottom. He had pulled up to "make a connection," that is, to add another joint of drill pipe to the string. He had pulled into a tight place, and the bit had stopped moving. He couldn't go up or down, but still had circulation, and he wanted to know how John wanted to handle the deal.

Stuck drill pipe can be a really bad problem. There are many things that can cause drill pipe to stick, too many things to enumerate here, but one of the primary rules of working stuck drill pipe is "don't pull on it too hard." Try to jar it downward to knock it loose if you are off bottom, figure your displacement, and spot oil, either lease crude or diesel, if you have circulation around your bit, and try to lubricate it loose, and a few other "do's." But, the main *don't* was, *don't* pull on drill pipe hard. You are about to learn why NOT to pull on pipe.

S-H-K Drilling Company had a hard and fast rule: when stuck, try everything, except to simply try to pull the pipe loose. It rarely worked and might get you fired. This had been set up years before by both Skinny Hunter and Dick Hodges. It was an excellent rule, had saved thousands of dollars, and kept many tool pushers out of difficulty.

Therefore, I was shocked when John asked the driller how hard he had pulled on the pipe. He told him he had been pulling up to make a connection and had pulled 50,000 pounds over the weight of the drill string before he realized and reacted to the fact that he was stuck, and that he had been trying to work the pipe down ever since but had had no luck.

The string of drill pipe that was stuck was brand new, $5^1/_2$ inches in diameter, and of "D" grade: not the best drill pipe available, but a good, solid string. It was used in large-diameter holes and usually laid down and not used after the intermediate string of casing was set. So the driller had reacted in the proper manner; *he* was in the clear.

My surprise was even greater when I heard John tell him to pull up on the pipe and to go 80,000 pounds pull over the weight of the string, then tell him what happened. The man to his credit, protested, and was harshly overruled.

He came back on the air in a minute and told John that he had pulled 80,000 pounds over the weight and the pipe had not moved. John chewed on him a bit and told him to pull harder. Again, he argued, and again, he was overruled.

Ben and his crew came into the dog house at that time. We always made it a habit to take a short coffee break on trips, especially on cold days. They each poured themselves a cup and Ben said to me, "How are they coming along with their stuck pipe?"

"Not very well. John has him trying to pull it loose, and it isn't working."

"Doesn't he have a set of drill pipe stretch tables in his knowledge box?"

The driller answered that question by telling John over the air that he was getting close to the limits of the tensile strength of the pipe.

Now many people do not know that steel drill pipe will stretch when heavily pulled on, but it will always go back to its original length when the pull is relaxed. However, if you ever exceed the stretch limits of a string of pipe, it is forever ruined and can only be junked. So, we were amazed that John kept pulling on that damned pipe. He HAD to know that every rig that S-H-K owned was listening in and second-guessing every move he made that night.

We stood and listened to him browbeat his man to keep pulling a little harder each time. Finally the driller announced that he had gained 6 inches above the chalk mark he had put at the top of the rotary table to mark his stuck point. John asked, "Did it come loose?" He said, "No." John told him to pull again, just as much as he had pulled the last time. He then announced that he had gained a foot, but still wasn't loose.

Ben and I looked at each other and shook our heads, then stood and listened while the driller stretched that 4,800-foot string of 5½-inch pipe 34 feet, where it pulled in two.

I turned our radio down. Ben came on out of the hole and laid down our twist-off. I went home to bed, never dreaming that what happened that night would ever affect me. But it certainly did affect me; I lost my best driller, Jack Evans.

The phone woke me the next morning. It was Jack Haberlein. He asked me to come to the office for a business discussion. Jack and I were friends, so I asked him what was up. He said that he and Mr. Hunter wanted to talk to me and I had to come down, so I did. I drank a cup of coffee and went to the office.

Well, the subject that morning was: Jack Evans. I had touted Evans to both men, so they quizzed me about him, his personality, temperament, ability to handle men, and many other things. I told them he could handle a pushing job with no problems, and, for once, they took my word for something without a lot of palaver. Then they told me that they were going to put him in John's place and to tell him to come to the office; then they asked me what I was going to do about replacing Evans. It was a good question, but I had a good answer. John Wayne Dennis was ready to start drilling, and I told them I would just turn Evans' crew over to Dennis, and Mr. Evans was all theirs.

It worked out fine. Jack washed over the pipe left in the hole, recovered everything, and ran casing. He was an immediate success. John Dennis took over Jack's crew, and we never missed a beat. Mr. Bailey's nose was out of joint for a few days, but he knew the story and snapped right out of the dumps. I felt sorry for the pusher who had been fired. He deserved a better fate. He had been a steady, faithful hand for years. I still don't know why he pulled that string of pipe in two. He certainly knew better. Some-form of mental lapse, I felt sure.

Our third well east of Andrews was a semi-wildcat. That was the well that I lost Evans on, and it turned out to be a dry hole. We were 2 miles east of the field, and the dry hole put an end to expansion in that direction. Phillips moved my rig to a location $3^1/2$ miles southeast of Andrews, much closer to home for all of us, but it did not turn into a bed of roses. It was a troublesome area, crooked-hole country, with a dose of lost circulation thrown in, and, to top it off, a formation unfamiliar to me which almost ate my lunch. All in all, it made a mean job.

Phillips Petroleum Company had always pioneered in drilling-mud research. They had a full staff of chemists, mud engineers, research experts, and a full department in Bartlesville, Oklahoma, devoted to drilling-fluid problems. Those guys were good. They had patents on derivatives to add to mud systems, and since the company kept a staff of their own mud men in the field, we got many benefits in new mud programs not available to many contractors. One of the mud engineers, Leroy Pope, and I had been working together for several years, and my rig had been selected as a "guinea pig" rig a number of times. The "Boys from Bartlesville" would come down and "work out" a new experiment. My tool pusher's house at the rig would become a lab, and those guys cooked, froze, and played with their mud experiments until they nearly drove me wild. Still, I and my crews learned an awful lot from those fellows. I've been grateful for the opportunity they gave me ever since those days.

We were in a lost-circulation area, as I said, and, sure enough, we drilled into a bad loss zone on our first well. Now the operator has the responsibility of regaining circulation. After a set number of hours, usually twelve, the rig would go on day work, and we *did* go on day work. Phillips had been experimenting with dried chicken feathers as a means of plugging off lost returns. We hated them. Those that came back out of the hole stunk to high heaven, and the pits and everything around the rig smelled like wet chickens. But that is what we had the bad luck to contend with on this well. The fluid loss was heavy, and we weren't having any luck at all with the feathers; they simply were not working. We mixed them in the pits just as fast as we could, then pumped them into the hole, and they vanished. It got downright embarrassing, and Phillips kept sending us more feathers to mix. Finally, after three days, I was going into town to eat lunch when I met Leroy and he waved me down. I stopped, and he asked me, "How is it going and are you accomplishing anything?"

I looked him squarely in the eye and told him, "Yes, we are accomplishing something. We have put those damned chicken pluckers on overtime."

He said, "Well, let's give up on 'em. I'm going to the rig. I've got a load of lost-circulation material on its way. We will use whatever it takes to get back to drilling, and may the Lord preserve us from chicken feathers for the rest of our lives."

He had been just as sick of the damn things as we were, but had orders from above to use them, but that forever cured Phillips of the "chicken-feather blues." We regained returns the next day and drilled ahead.

This was crooked-hole country and the three rigs already drilling on offset wells were having lots of hell. I had attended a seminar sponsored by Hughes Tool Company on the pendulum effect on straight-hole drilling. It was conducted by one of their engineers and a mathematician named Lubinski. It involved the use of a short drill collar and roller-type stabilizers positioned in various places in your drill collar string, then varying your drilling weights out, and I resolved to try it on this well. The crooked section was from 8,500 feet to 10,000 feet, and I had time to plan my strategy. I got one of my 30-foot-long drill collars, cut it in two pieces and rethreaded it, got a three-point and a six-point stabilizer on location, then browbeat my drillers into learning Lubinski's formulas. The younger drillers went along, but I had a problem with Mr. Bailey. He really didn't approve of some of my newfangled ways, so I finally pulled rank on him, and he went along, with reluctance.

The method worked in that particular area. It was the answer to our problem. We drilled that section in a dead run and became the envy of our competitors. Of course, it would not work to the same degree in every field, but it helped every time we used it later on, and some variations of it were used for years. Learning is a never-ending task in the oil fields. There is simply too much to learn and too little time to learn it all. As John Wayne Dennis said to me once, "Every time I think I've got it all together, you change what it is."

One of the oldest, truest sayings in the oil fields is that oil wells are like people, individuals, no two exactly alike, and we had that proved to us again on our next well. We finished the first well and skidded the rig one location. The field spacing rule for that field was one well on 80 acres. We made great plans on how we would handle our problems, the ones we had so much trouble with on well no. 1. We drilled into the lost circulation zone with our drilling mud laden with lost-circulation material. We were loaded for bear and didn't lose a drop of mud. The zone had vanished. The crooked-hole section gave us no trouble either, though we prepared for it, too, with a straight-hole assembly that we did not need. Then we got caught in a brand new difficulty.

But I must now digress and attempt to explain two of the most useful devices that are used on drilling rigs, the rat hole and the mouse hole. They evolved years ago, have changed very little, and are still used on today's most modern drilling rigs. First, the rat hole. When the kelly joint was invented, the average length of a joint of drill pipe was 20 feet. The wooden derricks were 108 feet tall, and when you "made a trip" to change bits, you pulled the pipe in "fourbles" and stood it in the derrick. These fourbles were all about 80 feet in length; the other 28 feet of height in the derrick was "head room," necessary for the traveling block, big hook, elevator bails, and elevators to travel above the length of the stands of pipe, and not bump into the crown block on top of the derrick. If that happened, you had a real disaster on your hands.

The kelly joint was either hexagon-shaped or square. It was always longer than the drill pipe and in the beginning presented quite a problem to the drillers. When you made the original kelly "down," you had drilled 38 feet of a new hole. Now you had to add another joint of drill pipe to your string in order to drill deeper, so you pulled the kelly up out of the hole, broke it off, and picked up another joint of pipe. Except, what did you do with the kelly? It was too long and heavy to lay down, and you had to do something with it. The old-timers "hung it back." It was dangerous, time-consuming, tedious, and stupid, but that was accepted procedure for a time. That kelly had a large swivel with heavy bails on top of it. It was top-heavy, cumbersome, unwieldy, and a real pain in the neck. The cable you hung it on was fastened to the crown block, and it was one hell of a job for a derrickman to hang the kelly back, and it had to be done on each connection, by main strength and awkwardness.

Then some unknown hero decided to find a better way, and the rat hole was born. He simply moved over about 6 feet from the centerline of the well bore and dug an 8-inch OD, slightly slanted hole. He put in a joint of 6-inch OD casing with the bottom end closed except for a 2-inch drain hole, drilled the hole shallower than the length of the kelly, and never again had to hang the kelly.

Now, when he made a connection, he broke the kelly off, set it in the rat hole, got the hook loose from the swivel bail, picked up a fresh joint of pipe, made it up, let it down, then latched back onto the kelly, made it back up in the new joint, and went back to drilling. Not only did this speed things up, but the safety factor improved tremendously.

The mouse hole came later. The old wooden derrick floors were almost on the ground, the draw works were on one side of the derrick floor, and directly across from the draw works where the driller always stood was a 28-foot-high inverted V built into the side of the derrick. This was naturally called the "vee door"; a walkway called the "catwalk" extended away from the vee door, and on each side of the walk were racks that drill pipe was stored on. All pipe that was picked up on that well came in through the vee door. At first, a new joint was dragged in by the catline, laid in the vee door with the end on the derrick floor, and raised enough to be able to latch the elevators onto it; then when the joint was used in making a connection, another one took its place. This began to change in the 1930's as blowout preventers came into general use. In order to accommodate the BOP's under the derrick floor, substructures began to come into use, and they grew higher and higher as more sophisticated forms of BOP's came into use. Nowadays, they run from 15 feet tall to more than 30 feet tall. As they grew taller, it became much more difficult to latch onto a joint lying in the vee, as the angle of inclination got too steep. So again, some unknown genius said, "Let's drill a shallow rat hole right beside the rotary table and put a joint of pipe in it standing up; then we can just make the kelly up in it and be off and running." I am sure that objections were raised, but somehow reason prevailed, and soon everyone wondered why HE hadn't thought of it, since it was so simple and worked so well. Of course, I am guessing, but I expect it happened almost as I have described it.

So now you know more about rat and mouse holes than you really wanted to know, but I had to tell you so my troubles on the second well would make sense to you.

We were drilling below 9,000 feet. Dennis was on tour. He made a joint down and started to pull up to make a connection when he stuck the bit. He tried jarring downward with no luck, called me on the radio, then decided to try pumping loose, started the pump and got loose, shut the pump down, and in just a minute was stuck again. Then he pumped loose for the second time. He finally left the pump running as he picked up the pipe, got the kelly above the rotary table, then shut the pump down and made his connection. Everything worked just fine until he tried to pick up off the slips after the connection. He couldn't move the pipe until he started pumping again; then it moved freely. I came to the rig about that time. Dennis told me what he had been doing, and that he couldn't account for the problem, that it was beyond his experience. We went back to bottom, and the bit acted up a little; it would crow-hop, drag, then break loose and spin, acting just as though a chunk had broken off a cone and we had a piece of steel in the hole.

One of the oldest rules in drilling is, when a bit isn't acting just right, pull it. So that is what Dennis and I decided to do, but we had to leave the pump running to get off bottom. The pump pressure through the jets in the bit, and the upward velocity of the drilling fluid, kept whatever was binding us above the bit, and we could pick up the pipe, but when we shut the pump down, wham! Stuck again! We used the kelly and pump to pump off bottom, and had to pump out and break off in the mouse hole five joints of pipe, and lay them down, before the bit freed up enough to move without the pump, but it finally did free up and we came on out of the hole. To our great surprise, there was nothing wrong with the bit, so we had a puzzle on our hands. There was, and still is, a tool that has been in general use for years, to catch and hold small bits of steel in the hole from time to time—pieces of cone off bits, roller and ball bearings out of bits, tong dies, and other pieces of iron that somehow manage to get into the well bore. It is called a "junk basket" and is simple and effective to use. It screws into the bottom drill collar, and the bit screws into the bottom threads of the junk basket. This basket is skirted, has a receptacle, and can catch and retain pieces of steel up to $1^1/_2$ inches in diameter.

We picked up and ran a junk basket when we went back in the hole, hoping to catch a sample of whatever was giving us all the trouble. We had a couple of times we had to use the pump, but ran the bit around twelve to fourteen hours and dulled it, and when we pulled out of the hole and dumped the basket, we learned what had happened. There were eight or ten pieces of heavy, dark rusty red, egg-shaped nuggets in the basket about the size of pigeon eggs. We could not identify them, but knew they were what had been sticking us. We re-ran the basket, of course, and Pappy Vaughn, the geologist, told us what the chunks of material were, an obscure form of iron ore rarely ever seen in the Permian Basin, but always found in loose, egg-shaped form in an unconsolidated formation. We contended with them for a 500-foot interval and then they vanished. We sometimes drilled into some strange things. I cut a core once at about 4,000 feet deep. It was about $4^1/_2$ inches in diameter, and when we laid it down on the catwalk it parted, and where it broke in two was a perfect outline of an oak leaf, laid down millions of years before, but still recognizable as an oak leaf. Gives you a funny feeling sometimes, that you are disturbing things better left alone.

We finished our second well near Andrews and moved back to the Maguetex field. We moved north of the road and spudded in on what was to be the deepest well that I ever drilled while I was pushing tools. It went to 14,300 feet, gave us no trouble, defined the north edge of the field, and made, as I remember, a mediocre well.

The summer of 1954 was a stormy one. Jack Haberlein and I were standing on the porch of the upper dog house of Rig 6 one thundering, stormy afternoon when we saw a funnel swoop down out of a cloud, apparently just west of Andrews. I got in my car to run into town and warn Amy, who had a tremendous fear of tornadoes, but I need not have bothered. Amy always got acquainted with people who had storm cellars wherever we lived and went to 'em on stormy days. But I almost drove into that little tornado on my way to town. It just touched down for a minute on the southeast side of town, just south of the road. Amy and Fritz were safe in a neighbor's storm cellar, but I got the hell scared out of *me,* and that damned little twister skipped on east and missed the rig by about half a mile, scaring Mr. Bailey, who was an Okie from up in the Tornado Alley country. He, according to his hands, shut down the rig and got everyone down in the substructure, which was the safest place on a rig. The storm missed them, but Mr. Bailey was in a very nervous state when I got back to the rig. He was leery of tornadoes.

We moved to a "step-out" or semi-wildcat on our next well. It was roughly 5 miles southeast of the field proper, and would hold a large block of acreage if it should make a well. The Phillips geologists were not optimistic about it, but felt that they had to prove or disprove its value. We moved in November and were down to casing point on our intermediate hole on Christmas Eve. I had ordered a casing crew, and they were bringing the first set of big hydraulically operated casing tongs in the Permian Basin to run 5,500 feet of $9^5/8$-inch casing. Well, the casing crew got there, and they were drunk. I hit the ceiling, got on the radio and got in touch with the man who owned and operated the casing running company, and told him his people were drunk, and if he didn't get a sober crew out there pronto, to forget about ever running pipe for S-H-K again. We ran that damned casing all right. The owner, his two brothers, and one more man ran that pipe. It was the first, last, and only time that a casing tong operator/owner ran pipe in a $400 suit and alligator shoes. We finished up and cemented the casing string on Christmas Day at 2:00 A.M. It made for a weird holiday.

We drilled it to 13,600 feet, and it was a dry hole. We finished testing and plugged and abandoned the thing in April of 1954. As usual, we had to make a move, this time a long one. And to make matters worse, I lost a good driller. Ben quit. It was a combination of things that led to my loss of Ben. He and his wife Beryl were childless, both in their early thirties, and both wanted children very badly, but were not able to have any of their own. They had tried to get a baby through regular adoption agencies for about four years, but couldn't qualify under the insane rules. Both were good, moral people and he had been steadily employed for years, but . . . he was oil field, therefore, suspect, and finally got discouraged and gave up. Beryl was determined, though, and she was a stubborn, gutsy lady. She intended to get a baby, somehow, and did. A shyster lawyer in Andrews had heard about Beryl and approached her with a scheme a year before, when we were all living in Lovington, New Mexico. He told Ben and Beryl that he knew a girl who was single, pregnant, and broke. Her lover was serving a term in the pen for burglary in Santa Fe, and she would give them her baby when it was born, in exchange for her care and delivery, plus two thousand dollars, and the baby was due in six weeks. They went for the deal, hook, line, and sinker, and wouldn't listen to any warnings, especially mine.

It cost them $4,000, and they kept the baby ten months. Then the girl's boyfriend got out of jail, and they sued for custody of the baby, claiming that Ben and Beryl got the child through illegal means, and they got the baby. That paper the lawyer had given to Ben wasn't worth anything. It did look illegal, and the judge sided with the natural mother.

Beryl began to beg Ben to get out of the oil fields so she could legally adopt a baby. Just as we finished our well, Ben's uncle in Lampasas, Texas, died and left a 40-acre pecan orchard to Ben, so he quit and went to Lampasas to live. I missed him; he was a good, steady man. Incidentally, he and Beryl did adopt a baby, a Greek orphan, a boy, through some overseas agency. From all accounts, the baby turned their life around, and I'm sure *he* was a very fortunate young man. They may have been "oil field trash," but Ben and Beryl were as solid an All American pair as I have ever known. And the loser in the whole sorry deal was the first baby. The natural mother and her man went back to jail later, and the baby wound up with an alcoholic grandmother. Life takes funny twists at times.

We were finished in Andrews, and I never lived there again, but it had been a good two years, and the oil fields had run true to form: get settled, make a few friends, then pull up stakes and move.

Chapter Sixteen

Back to New Mexico:
Wildcat at Clovis

The company had taken a contract to drill a wildcat well in an area known as the Plainview Basin. The location was 23 miles northeast of Clovis, New Mexico, over 200 miles northwest, mostly north, of Andrews. It was for a subsidiary of a Louisiana gas company. I went to Clovis and met the company man, Mr. Wardlaw, found the location, gave the rig and pit dimensions to the dirt contractor, and found a place in a private yard to park the house trailer. Then I went back to Andrews, called the rig builders, and told Mr. Bailey and John Dennis to go to Clovis and find themselves trailer spaces and get ready to move. Then I called the office and told them I needed a good driller to take Ben's place. I knew that they had a rig down and it would be no problem. I wound up with Johnny Martin, whom I had "turned out" some years back, and I was glad to get a man whom I knew, and who was familiar with our way of doing our work.

As usual, no one wanted to move; only this time, it was some of the old longtime roughnecks. I didn't quibble with 'em, just told them to move or go elsewhere, that I quit arranging transfers when we moved to Andrews. Surprisingly enough, all of them moved to Clovis, though there was a lot of grumbling.

The job went slowly. I had made arrangements with a local water-well driller to drill a water well at the location. It was not a good well. It made enough water to barely furnish the rig. Luckily, I had 2,000 barrels of storage, four 500-barrel water tanks. Then the weather conspired against us. I moved to Clovis on the third day of May; the rig builders started the derrick on the next day. When I woke up on the morning of the fifth, there was 4 inches of snow on the ground, a real freak storm. I didn't plan to go to the location that day, as I felt sure the rig builders wouldn't work, but it warmed up rapidly, and the snow began to vanish. So that afternoon about two o'clock, I drove out to the location, and found out that the rig builders had worked and that a man had fallen from the fifth girt, about 45 feet up and had been instantly killed; of course, his death stopped all work, and we didn't get the derrick finished for three more days. By then, all the hands had arrived and were anxious to get back to work. They had been off for ten days and had spent most of their money.

So our well got off to a bad start. We were a hundred miles from the nearest supply house at Tatum, New Mexico. There were no oil-field service companies any nearer than Hobbs, 140 miles away. If you had trouble, help was far away, so I had stocked our "parts house" heavily before the move. It saved us lots of shutdown time. Still, we would get caught short occasionally; then the five-hour lag between ordering something and getting it would really cost you.

To add to the difficulty, we were drilling in an area totally unfamiliar to any of us. Our company man had never worked west of Fort Worth before, and the two company geologists who had been sent out to call the shots were also unfamiliar with the Plainview Basin. It turned out to be a classic case of the "blind leading the blind." I called Pappy Vaughn with Phillips, and he sent me a paper with the formations that I would be drilling through listed, and some of the characteristics of these formations, so I at least had some information, and since this was a "day work" contract and the exploration department of the gas company was calling all the shots, I didn't have to worry about footage prices. It was a good thing that I didn't, since I sincerely believe that the cost per foot of that well was the highest of any well I drilled in my whole career.

Still, it had some lighter moments, one of which came early. We had come into Clovis, which was primarily a railroad and farming town, and our arrival attracted no attention. We rigged up, set and cemented 500 feet of 15-inch-diameter casing, and were drilling a 14-inch intermediate hole to approximately 3,300 feet, where we planned to set another string of casing. We had drilled some red beds, and our drilling fluid was fairly heavy with dissolved clays and very red in color. We had reached a depth of 1,200 feet, and had acquired some visitors, about six or seven local farmers, who had come to see this contraption that was drilling for oil. I was at the rig when they drove up in three pickups, introduced themselves, and asked permission to go up on the rig floor and look around. These were nice old boys, successful landowners, fairly well off moneywise, sharp in their thinking and trading, and tough as a wood hauler's ass, and anyone who has ever ridden a load of logs with the bark on 'em *knows* that is pretty tough.

I told them to come with me, and we went up into the tool house, then stood to one side while I tried to explain what we were doing and why we did it that way. They were attentive, curious, and friendly, and I was enjoying myself when Mr. Bailey, who was on tour, made the kelly down, then pulled up to make a connection.

When he broke the kelly off to make the connection, red mud flowed up through the drill pipe, which was sitting on the slips in the rotary. We paid no attention to this, since the fluid outside the drill pipe is heavier than the fluid inside the pipe because of cuttings and dissolved solids, and it usually does flow back until it reaches a balance.

These visitors noticed this, and I was explaining the reason to them, when, while spinning up the kelly in the joint in the mouse hole, Mr. Bailey broke the spinning chain. Then, since there was no reason to hurry, he shut down a moment to fix the chain. Suddenly, one of the visitors grabbed my arm and said, "Look, that is clear water coming back out of the pipe now." Without really thinking, I answered, "Well, the old man must have drilled into a water sand, but it shouldn't cause us any trouble." Mr. Bailey heard me and spoke up: "I thought that last 10 feet drilled pretty fast; I probably am in water sand."

You wouldn't believe the sensation that little exchange caused in our visitors; before you could say "Boo!" one of those farmers ran over where the water was bubbling out of the pipe, cupped his hands, caught some water, tasted it, and proclaimed loudly, "It's sweet water!" Two others demanded to know how deep we were and if the water was artesian and would it flow. They all wanted to know how thick the water sand was, and asked more questions in five minutes than I could have answered in two hours. An oil well was one thing, a pie-in-the-sky thing, that might or might not materialize. But WATER! That was something else, here, now, and maybe forever, and if true, a real blessing.

We finally calmed them down; Mr. Bailey made his connection and began drilling again. Sure enough, the next 20 feet he drilled went fast. It was a loose water sand. Then the drilling slowed down again, so we knew we had gone out of the sand. But we had drilled a total of 30 feet of sand. The derrickman caught a sample of cuttings, and sure enough we had a fine-grained, tan, unconsolidated sand zone. Honestly, I thought some of those men, all of them in their forties and fifties, would have a heart attack, they were so excited. We had forgotten just how important irrigation water was in a dry, dry country, and for their money, water beat the hell out of oil or gas. I spent the next hour answering questions. You can imagine the questions because the answers went like this: "No, I don't think it will flow.—No, I have no idea how many gallons per minute 30 feet of sand will give up.—Yes, we topped the sand at 1,190 feet and went out of it at 1,220 feet.—Yes, I do think it will produce water but have no idea how much.—Yes, it is costly to pump water from 1,200 feet in large volumes." And then finally, "Gentlemen, the only way you will ever know the answers to all these things is to drill a test well. Everything I am saying is supposition; it is just one man's opinion, and I could be wrong about it all."

They finally left, all three pickups of them, still talking and all highly elated. Mr. Bailey and I shook our heads in wonder, then went on with our rat killing. We had a well to drill, and did not own one foot of real estate in Curry County, New Mexico, and we really couldn't have cared less!

The next day I was in my shack on location doing a bit of sorely neglected paper work. The door opened and a total stranger asked, "Mr. Lynch?" I said, "Yes." He then informed me that he was from the local radio station and wanted to interview me. I must say, I was flattered, and I wondered how in the world he knew my name, since I had been in Clovis less than a month and had certainly not attracted much attention. He wasn't the least bit interested in me. He wanted to do an in-depth interview on that damned water sand. My ego deflated considerably, but I rehashed the whole thing with him, gave him the pros and cons as I saw them, and sent him on his way.

The next morning, Amy and I were driving to some place in town at 9 A.M. She had the car radio tuned to the local station when the announcer suddenly said the next program was an interview with the supervisor of the drilling rig northeast of town, who would answer questions about the possibility of water for irrigation in that area. And I got the shock of my life; all of my life I had imagined that my voice was a light, pleasant baritone, but the voice that came out of that damned radio was a coarse, deep, raspy bass. I almost jumped out of the car, but Amy assured me that it really was me, so another dream went glimmering. The water well came back to haunt me later, but for the time being, it was put to rest.

We drilled ahead, set our intermediate casing, and started for our objective, a granite wash, at approximately 8,500 feet. We also were told that we could expect granite proper, or other igneous rock, basalt, porphyry, or whatever at somewhere above 9,000 feet. So, we took off, fat, dumb, and happy. We had an excellent rig with the latest, most modern additions, our steel pits were equipped with the best guns, stirrers, and bypasses available at the time, and we just knew we were the greatest drillers of them all, the greatest tigers in the whole jungle . . . and promptly got into trouble, not altogether of our own making. The geologists and Mr. Wardlaw were not on the same wavelength. They had a boss; he had a peculiar name that I have forgotten, though he caused me lots of grief. His name seemed to strike fear in Mr. Wardlaw's heart, but not mine. We had an ironclad contract, and all I had to do was keep the rig operating efficiently. The other problems were the company personnel's concern; but they didn't know what the hell they were doing, and Mr. "Whosis" in Lafayette, Louisiana, had to make too many final decisions. It made a mean, bickering, backstabbing job, quite different from our jobs for Phillips, where everybody knew their job and did it.

Then, too, we were mudded up and had been right out from under the intermediate pipe. We took cores, cores, and cores. Those geologists were determined to check out everything, and did! and I began to have problems with my crews.

I had reacquired Johnny Martin on this job, was glad, and thought he would be happy. It did not work out that way. I had put him out drilling before, then had put Mr. Bailey back in his place. I had gotten Johnny switched to another rig so that he could continue to drill, and assumed that he was at least content with the deal. I was wrong; he resented being "bumped" and carried the resentment with him. Then when he came back to Rig 6, his dislike of Bailey colored his work. At first, I wasn't aware of this, but roughnecks talk and drillers' wives talk. Not much goes unnoticed on a rig crew. Johnny was a bachelor, big, strong, open-faced, and fairly handsome, but he was not popular with the men in the other crews. He was relieving Mr. Bailey on the job, and I began to hear rumors of friction between the two men. Oddly enough, my informant was Mr. Wardlaw, who had overheard some tool-house arguments at tour changing time. I took action, went to the rig while they were changing tour, and demanded to know what the hell was going on between them; they denied any trouble but were just evasive enough to set my teeth on edge. I told them to end it then and there or there would be some new faces on Rig 6—that I had all the problems I needed, and not to try to push me. They knew I meant it and pledged cooperation.

Mr. Wardlaw's wife was another problem. She had come out to Clovis about three weeks after we began the well. Amy met her, helped her find an apartment, since she didn't bring a car, and was nice to her. She was a tall, angular woman about forty-five years old. She and her husband had been married about five years; both were in their forties when they married. He, according to her, was an alcoholic, a reformed one. She was out in Clovis at Mr. "Whosis'" request to keep her husband on the straight and narrow, and while she hated West Texas, New Mexico, and especially Clovis, she would do her duty. She was a self-righteous prig and I didn't care for her at all, so poor Amy took the brunt of her whining, but, in fact, Amy found it amusing and would regale me with the lady's latest woes when I came home at night.

Curry County at that time was a dry county. The only bar near Clovis was about 8 miles west of town. I didn't drink, so I had never been there, but Johnny and his hands, or some of them, went there regularly. They were single and always on the lookout for girls. Mrs. Wardlaw's brother came out to visit her after she had been out for about six weeks. He was a tall, cadaverous character, about fifty years old. He was single and resembled his sister. They went out to this place one night. Mr. Wardlaw and I were at the rig pulling a core out of the hole. I never found out exactly what happened, but Johnny and Mrs. Wardlaw's brother got into some kind of hassle, mostly verbal, I think. At least no blows were exchanged. It was unpleasant at any rate, and they were all asked to leave.

I heard about the mess the next afternoon. I had gone back to the rig early, as we were running a core barrel again. It belonged to the operator. They did not have a core drilling specialist, and diamond core heads are expensive, so I was spending most of my time at the rig. When I got home, Amy was very angry. It seemed Mrs. Wardlaw had been to see her and told her that I was pretty dumb, didn't know what was going on at my rig; that my people were rude to all company people and she was going to complain to her company. Amy was not employed by S-H-K. She told Mrs. Wardlaw that, then added that since she felt as she did about me, to just stay away from our house and complain to whoever she damn well pleased, but to leave her, Amy, out of it as she was not interested. I agreed, then told Amy to give the lady a cold shoulder from that day forward, and that ended that.

We were coring salt. I had drilled lots of salt sections, but this was the first time I had ever cored one. Those geologists called the shots, and we cored 250 feet of solid salt. Contrary to what almost everybody thinks, subterranean salt is not pure white. This particular section was lovely—black, amber, rose, white, with streaks of blue, and glossy and crystalline in appearance. We still had lots of local visitors, and some of the ladies had taken pieces of cores home as souvenirs. One lady complained bitterly that her foot-long core had changed shape and size when she washed it to clean it. I explained that warm water would dissolve salt and she should have used brine. She was surprised. She had thought it was alabaster and didn't know it was salt. Subsurface things are still mysteries to most folks. She had never thought to taste the thing.

We finished coring, drilled ahead, were drilling at 8,200 feet, and thought we were almost finished. We went in the hole with a bit; dulled it; Johnny started out of the hole and got stuck. He pulled into a tight place at 5,800 feet and got solidly stuck, and we couldn't get it loose. We spotted oil, jarred downward, and got no results, so I called a service company, Dia-Log, ran a stretch survey, and found out exactly where we were stuck. It was right at the top of the drill collars. I had twenty-four of the things in my drilling string and I thought "key seat" immediately. In oil field talk "key seat" is big, ugly, hairy trouble, so in order to explain why it is trouble, I am going to explain what a "key seat" is, so bear with me. It isn't going to be an easy chore.

Key seats are caused by a combination of things that, by themselves, would not be bad, but taken together are a costly dose. So to begin: Drilled holes are never completely perpendicular. They tend to wander around, usually in a spiral, so the drill pipe rubs against the side of the well bore in many places. This rubbing action usually causes no problems. The usual limestones, shales, sandstones, clays, and anhydrites that you have drilled through resist abrasion very well. Occasionally, you get a streaky formation, a few feet of anhydrite, a few feet of shale, and a few feet of clayey shales, laid down like a layer cake, and taken in combination with other factors, these layer-cake formations can be real trouble. One of these other factors is the makeup of your drilling string. Let's start at the bottom and work our way up and you will get a better picture.

On this well we were drilling an 8 3/4-inch-diameter hole, so our bit was that size; then immediately above the bit we had ten 7-inch-diameter drill collars. These things are heavy. A 7-inch drill collar with a 2 1/4-inch bore through it weighs 117 1/2 pounds per foot, so a 30-foot drill collar weighs 3,525 pounds. We had ten of them, then immediately above them, fourteen 6 3/4-inch collars weighing 3,255 pounds each, for a total drill collar weight of over 80,000 pounds. On the top of the drill collars is a crossover joint never over 2 feet long to literally cross you over from drill collars to drill pipe, since many drill collars have different tooled joint threads than do the drill pipes. This crossover is 6 3/4 inches in diameter, and the drill pipe tool joint is 6 inches in diameter. So you go from 6 3/4 inches to 6 inches in a 3-foot distance, making a wedge-shaped connection with the small end of the wedge on top. This little "booger" is what you need to watch; it is your sticking point. From here up, you have drill pipes 4 1/2 inches in diameter, each joint 30 feet long, with a tool joint pin on the bottom of the pipe and a tool joint box on top. These make up a string, and it has a knot in each joint, the tool joints. So you have a 6-inch-diameter tool joint each 30 feet of drill pipe from the top of the drill collars to the bottom of the kelly. And we have completed the drill string.

We now have two ingredients of a first-class key seat (the layer-cake formation and the crossover joint almost an inch larger than the tool joints), but we still have two to go. Here is the next one. We had a crooked hole, not very crooked, well within the 3° maximum allowed, but still a bit crooked and right in the layer-cake formation at 5,800 feet deep. That is three ingredients, and we still have one to go. Hang in there . . . we are close to the end.

We had 80,000 pounds of drill collars hanging to the bottom of our drill pipe; we had been coring a salt section at 6,500 feet and using 10,000 pounds of weight to drill with a diamond core head for five days, so we had 70,000 pounds of excess weight hanging and, consequently, the drill string was in great tension and was as stiff as a bar of solid iron. Across the layer-cake section of hole, the drill pipe had worn a groove 4 1/2 inches in diameter as it lay against the crooked place and turned, turned, and turned. How deep it actually wore I'll never know, but it cut pretty deep, about $30,000 worth.

When Johnny was coming out of the hole, he was pulling pipe at a good clip. The pipe was, of course, dragging against the low side of the crooked hole, probably in the groove that we had worn. He had no reason to think anything was wrong, and when the pipe stuck suddenly, he had pulled over 250,000 pounds before he could get the clutch out of gear, and had planted the pipe pretty solidly. That little 3/4-inch wedge had done its job and, believe me, if there is anything that the oil fields ingrain into a man, it's humility. You simply cannot outguess downhole problems.

We had located the stuck point. Now we had to get it loose. I'll tell you how we did it. It may not be a classic example of problem solving, and it took a little time, but we did get loose.

I had called M & B Fishing Tool Company in Hobbs. A fisherman had come up and brought the necessary tools. He was Jack Krebs, a good, solid man, and we had known each other for many years. We discussed my problem, then decided to back the string off and go after the fish with a bumper sub, jars, and an overshot; with that assembly we could hit up or down with a great amount of force, and it greatly enhanced the possibility of jarring the stuck drill collars loose. We did that; we had Dia-Log back the pipe off one joint of drill pipe above the top of the drill collars. We hated to do that, since drill pipe is springy compared to drill collars, thus lessening our jarring action. Still—we were stuck at the very top of the collars, were sure that the collars were over to one side, and felt sure that we could not get over them with the overshot, so we left one full joint above them to act as a fishing neck. Our brainstorm worked fine. We went in the hole, latched onto our joint of pipe, and began jarring. We beat on that damned thing downward for two hours and never moved it, then began to strike upward with the hydraulic jars, hitting a 30,000-pound lick each time for two more hours. No movement. That one joint of drill pipe was elastic enough to defeat our efforts. We worked the jars and bumper sub for a solid eight hours, and jarred that joint of 16 1/2-pound 4 1/2-inch drill pipe in two. It parted about midway of the joint, and we came out of the hole with a nub, not a good deal.

What to do? Jarring certainly was not the answer, so we called the Dia-Log men into the discussion. They suggested going in the hole with the drill pipe only, open-ended, then going down inside the drill pipe by way of their wireline with a so-called "string shot," going down as far as we could, then dragging it back up the hole. The idea was to let the shot pull in on the low side of the hole, hoping to get behind the drill collars, exploding the string shot and literally blowing the drill collars loose and letting them fall to bottom, then retrieving them. It was not a foolproof method, but that is what we did and it *worked*. The collars came loose when we exploded the shot and fell to bottom, but not with a bang. The hole was full of 9.8-pound-to-the-gallon mud, the bit was full gauge, and the drill collars were 7 inches in diameter. The fluid rushing by as they went to bottom acted as a brake, and the piston effect of the bit further tended to slow the fall, so actually the collars and bit floated to bottom, at a good but not excessively fast rate.

We didn't know this had happened, of course, so we fired the shot, came out of the hole, picked up our overshot, bumper sub, and jars, and went in the hole, hunting our fish. We found it just where we wanted it to be, on bottom. We latched onto it and started out of the hole, approached our stuck point cautiously, and, sure enough, pulled into it, not very hard; stopped, banged down with our bumper sub, and knocked loose; stopped, laid down a joint of pipe, put the kelly on, started the pump, and rotated the pipe while pulling up the length of the kelly. We had our swage above our key seat and were in the clear. We set the kelly back after stopping the pump, then came on out of the hole. The pumping and rotation, or a combination of the two, had brought us up past our bad place. Best of all, all three cones were still on the bit. We felt lucky, picked up a new bit, and went back in the hole, but left the bumper sub in the string on top of the drill collars, because we still had the key seat. It certainly had not disappeared.

We had dealt with problems of this nature before, and since we were almost at total depth, decided that since we knew where the seat was located, we could pull up to it, put the kelly on, start the pump, then let the rotation and fluid movement keep us from sticking again. We, my drillers and I, agreed that it would work because we had done it many times before in years past. The bumper sub was insurance. If someone misjudged and pulled into the key seat, he could stop, strike down with the bumper sub, free the pipe, then install the kelly and work up past the bad place. We discussed this thoroughly, and agreed that we all understood the problem and would be careful. The end was near, and we all wanted to be through with an unpleasant job.

I went to town for some rest after almost four days of tension, worry, spasmodic meal times, and very little sleep. Fishing on a drilling rig is never a restful time for a pusher.

I took a bath, Amy cooked a good hot meal, we ate dinner, talked for awhile, and I went to bed to fall instantly to sleep. I slept ten hours, woke, and went out to my car to call the rig on the radio. I got Johnny Martin, and he told me that the geologists thought they had found traces of granite wash in the cuttings, that they wanted to run the core barrel, and that he was circulating to condition the mud, preparing to come out of the hole. I warned him about the key seat, and he assured me that he understood. He sounded impatient, but I let it go without comment, figuring that he, too, was tired of all the troubles we had encountered.

I went into the house, shaved and showered as Amy cooked breakfast, then started on the 23-mile drive to the rig, grumbling to myself about those two geologists and their cores. I drove up to the rig and found out that Johnny had ignored everything we had talked about, had yanked the drill collars up into the key seat, hard, and was stuck again.

On the drive back to town I reviewed what had happened, then decided to let Johnny go, to fire him for cause, although it wasn't an easy decision. When I told the office what had happened, they agreed that I needed another driller. Jack Evans' rig was down, and he volunteered to come up and drill for me until we finished the well. Of course, I was delighted. Jack was extraordinary, and I needed help.

We were back where we had been. I called the service people back, knew that it would be five or six hours before their arrival, went back to the rig, gave Johnny a time order and told him we wouldn't need him any more, then asked his roughnecks how many of them wanted to stay, as I had another driller coming up from Odessa. Surprisingly, they all stayed, so the problem of finding Evans a crew was solved. Johnny made a half-hearted apology for getting stuck, but even though I sensed that he really did regret what he had done, it didn't change my mind. He left the job that afternoon and I never saw him again. I later heard he signed up to go overseas to Venezuela. I wished him well. He was a capable driller, but not for me.

We went through the whole fishing procedure again: backed off, but didn't try to jar loose this time, just went back in the hole open-ended, ran a string shot, fired it, and came back out of the hole; picked up the overshot and jars, then went back hoping to find our fish on bottom again. We found it, but it had remained right where it was, stuck in the key seat. Our luck held: it was bad.

We tried again, with the same results. Nothing had changed except the expense; it went up and up. My ego deflated considerably. It was my first long-drawn-out fishing job, and I was getting damned tired of it. Mr. Bailey, too, was beginning to fray around the edges. He was edgy, short-tempered, and nervous, unusual for him. He generally took things in stride.

I was at the "knowledge box" in the tool house the second day. The knowledge box is a metal desk in one corner of the tool house. Report books, technical books, and other paperwork are kept in the box, while the top acts as a desk. I was doing some kind of paperwork, and Mr. Bailey was chewing out his derrickman for some minor lapses. The boy wasn't all that interested and showed it by his manner, when all at once, Mr. Bailey burst out, "Mr. Lamb, when I am talking to you, you quit looking off like a dog fucking, and pay attention, do you hear!?" It shocked me, as Jack Bailey used very little bad language. I said, "Mr. Bailey, what is the matter with you?" He answered, "I don't know, but I've been mad for three days." I told him, "Don't let it get you down; after all, it's *my* baby." Jack looked at me, then said, "Mr. Lynch, Johnny stuck that pipe to spite you, but he did it because you put me to work and bumped him six years ago. You know it and I know it, so a lot of what happened is my fault." I told him, "Mr. Bailey, I make my own decisions, and I have never regretted that one. Let's get this fishing job behind us now."

We went through the same dreary routine one more time. Wonder of wonders, this time it worked. We fired our string shot, made the trip, and found the fish on bottom; retrieved it, sent the service people home, and went to coring. We had slain the dragon, and the nightmare had ended. Incidentally, that last string shot blew that key seat to hell. We never felt it again to the end of the well. Sometimes clean living pays off.

Jack Evans had brought me some news from Odessa. S-H-K had been getting complaints from our clients. They said we were rude, uncooperative, and lots of other things in the same vein, and Skinny had sent me a message: that this was the first, last, and only well we would ever drill for these people, and to treat them as I damn well pleased, with no fear of repercussions.

We came out of the hole with our fish, and I had a meeting in my tool pusher's house with my company people. I told them that we, my people and I, had tried to get along with them, and that *they* had been a bunch of 22-carat horses' asses, no less. That I neither knew nor cared who had been whining to Mr. "Whosis" in Lafayette, but that I had read my copy of the contract and nowhere in it was there one word about furnishing them a place to stay while they were at the rig, nor was I supposed to keep my refrigerator stocked with cold cuts, cheese, bread, and other things to eat. That I had given them the use of my dog house, that they had slept in my beds, eaten my food, and made themselves at home, but had never swept the place, had the sheets laundered, washed a dish, nor showed the slightest appreciation. All they had done was be a damned nuisance to me, then had the guts to bellyache to their boss about *our* uncooperative attitude, and as far as I was concerned, the dance was over. That if I heard *one,* just one more complaint from them or their office in Lafayette, I would lock the shack and they could damn well finish the well sleeping in their cars and driving 46 miles to town and back to eat. That I could be, and would be, just what they had been complaining about—hard to get along with and mean to boot.

Those three fellows sat and looked at me like a trio of slack-jawed idiots. They had never seen me lose my temper before; I was angry and didn't mince my words. Of course, they all denied having complained to their office, so I told them that *one* of them had to be lying, but that I didn't care. The rule applied to all of them.

It certainly cleared the air! They became much nicer, more polite, and we got along okay to the end of the well. They even stopped sniping at each other. Sometimes it pays to get your Irish up; this was one of those times.

We topped the granite wash on the core we were cutting and also retrieved about 25 feet of hard, dark red shale, just on top of the wash. This shale was like no shale I had ever seen before. It was dense and heavy. One of our rock hounds said it was expected and usually lay above a layer of granite wash. He seemed to be pleased, even though the cored section of granite wash showed no signs at all.

Our diamond core heads were 7 inches in diameter and cut a 4^1/$_2$-inch-diameter core. We cut a 50-foot-long core each trip in the hole, then went in the hole with a bit to ream the hole out to gauge, 8^3/$_4$ inches. Reaming is slow, tedious, and can be trouble. You are just cutting about a ^{7}/$_8$-inch ledge, and a tri-cone bit can be wedged into a smaller hole and be "pinched." You can even get stuck while reaming, so it is a thankless, worrisome task, not loved by drillers. We had done a great deal of reaming on this well because we had done much coring, but had not had problems, as we were experienced and careful. But we wanted to end the well; it had not been a good one to drill. Jack Bailey finished reaming and came out of the hole. Then Evans ran the core barrel with a new diamond core head. The geologists were the custodians of the core heads. They acted as though the British crown jewels were in their care. It delighted me and my drillers. We sure as hell did not want to be responsible for the things, since they cost over $6,000 each, a lot of money in 1954.

Evans went in the hole and began coring. The first 15 feet cored normally at about 3½ feet per hour. Then suddenly, he quit making hole, and in the next six hours made a total of 18 inches! Then the bit quit entirely and he drilled one more hour, but didn't make an inch. He applied the old rule: when a bit acts queer, pull it and start out of the hole. He called me on the radio and said he had a puzzle on his hands and asked me to come out to the job. It was 11:00 P.M. I got up and went to the rig.

The boys were changing tours. Dennis was relieving Evans, and Jack had not gotten entirely out of the hole with the core. He told Dennis and me how hard that last 18 inches had drilled and said that the diamond core head acted as though it was worn out, completely. He went home, Dennis finished pulling out of the hole, and I stood in the tool house and cursed the day S-H-K had signed a contract to drill that well. I hoped we had hit granite and could plug and abandon the thing.

We broke off the core head. It was worn slick, and many diamonds were missing. The core barrel was 50 feet long. We had angled it out the vee door, unscrewed the core catcher, and laid down the core on the catwalk. The top of the recovered core was granite wash, but the bottom 18 inches was dark red, smooth, and very heavy.

We woke up our geologist, who had been asleep in my shack. He came out to the catwalk, yawning and rubbing his eyes. The lights strung out the catwalk were bright enough for good visibility. The roughnecks had washed the core off with fresh water, and it was pretty obvious that the bottom of that core was a vastly different substance from the upper 15 feet. Our sleepy-headed rock hound looked at it, never even touched it, then said, "That's some more of that red shale."

I could have killed him, but refrained from murder. I did ask, "Did you look at your diamond core head?" He replied, "No, is there anything wrong with it?"

"It is worn out; it was brand new, and that stuff you just called red shale is heavy as lead and slick as glass. I know we have hit granite, and that should wind us up." He said, "Oh, let me look at it again. By golly, it IS granite. We had better run a drill-stem test." I said, "Why? We haven't seen a sign of oil." He said, "Because we have orders to run a drill-stem test when we hit igneous rock, and that is red porphyry on the bottom of the core."

I knew then that we had been working for a bunch of idiots. I told Dennis to go back in the hole, but *not* to ream. To condition the mud for a DST and that I would radio him when to start out of the hole. I got in my car, then went to call the testers, who were in Hobbs.

We ran that DST, got salt water, lots of it, and thought we were finished. We sure as hell were not though, because those two idiot geologists got on the phone to Lafayette. I don't know who they talked to, but we got the damndest set of orders I ever got in my life.

We stayed out of the hole while the men called Lafayette. I was sure we would get a P and A order, but I was wrong, again. Our rock hounds came back from phoning with smiles on their faces. They told me that the thinking in their home office was that we had a "dike" of porphyry about 20 or more feet thick, and that beneath that dike we would go back into a zone of granite wash which would bear oil.

I was astounded! I had never heard of anything like that in my thirty years in the oil fields. To me, granite was the end, but I learned later that the dike phenomenon *had* occurred a very few times, mostly in Mississippi and Louisiana, never in the Permian or Plainview basins. I asked those men just how they proposed to drill the dike. They said that we would core it. Evans was on tour. He pointed out to them that he had wiped out a core head drilling less than 2 feet of that stuff. They assured us that that had been taken care of, that they still had two new core heads, and Lafayette was shipping them four more heads, surely enough to drill 25 more feet.

I shrugged my shoulders and told them, "Well, it's your nickel." Evans made up the core barrel and went in the hole.

We used all six of their core heads, cored 22 feet of porphyry, used up nine days' rig time, and never did get through our *dike.*

The nine days dragged by. The work was dull, the drilling very slow, and everyone on the rig thought that it was going to take forever to finish that well. Only the local people had fun at all during that time. We still had many visitors, and most of them were fascinated by the cores that we had laid out on the catwalk. The porphyry we cored was beautiful, dark red, with swirling purplish streaks in it. They begged us for pieces of it and marveled at its weight, texture, and beauty. We gave away many small pieces. The cores were 4^1/$_2$ inches in diameter and broke into sections sometimes 4 or 5 inches long. There was one piece over a foot long, the one Evans had cut at the very first of the coring. One gentleman wanted that large piece, and I asked him what in the world he could use it for, since it weighed about 10 or 12 pounds. He said that he had a friend who had a workshop back of his home and had a power hacksaw; that they would saw that piece of rock into two equal parts and he would have the only bookends in Clovis that came from 8,600 feet deep in the ground. I told him that he couldn't cut that chunk of granite with a power hacksaw, but he was welcome to the rock. He grabbed his prize and took off for town. He told me that he was sure his friend's saw could handle the job. The next day he came back and came up into the tool house. He said, "You were right. He couldn't even begin to cut that thing, but did manage to ruin a $30 saw blade. How in the hell do you cut that stuff?"

I told him that I was sure there was an amateur gemstone hunter in Clovis with a diamond saw and a polishing tumbler who would cut and shine his rocks. Sure enough, he found one and the day we were tearing down the rig, he brought his shiny bookends out to show me. They were really beautiful, and he was surely proud of them. I hope that they are gracing some home today.

One small triumph came to me while I was on that job. One day my farmers who had gotten so excited about the water well possibilities came to the rig. This was about three weeks before we finished the well. They were a subdued bunch, told me that they had a big problem, and wanted me to help them. I opened my big mouth and said I would be glad to help them, but I should have kept it shut. These old boys were as serious as cancer. They had pooled their money, hired a local water-well driller and drilled a 1,200-foot-deep well on a farm that one of them owned. The rig was too small for the job and had never before drilled a well 1,200 feet deep. They had struck water, drilled 20 feet into the water sand, and had gotten stuck, and had been stuck for three days. The contractor was charging them by the day, and their money was being used up with nothing to show for it. They wanted *me* to come over to the well and get them loose. Hello, Mr. Genius! I wanted no part of that deal and tried to weasel out of it, but I had promised and they were desperate, so I went, reluctantly. The well they were drilling was 5 miles west of our location. I followed those farmers to their well. The water-well contractor was not glad to see me. He resented me and told me so, but had consented to listen to me, since he was a local man with no desire to have the area farmers down on him, and *they* wanted me.

His main pump was a 4-by-6-inch centrifugal which would only put up 60 pounds pressure. He was still circulating, but just barely. He had mixed some mud and had been drilling with water when he got stuck. The mud had not helped clean the hole. He was at his wits' end, and everybody was mad at him. Everyone was looking at me; I wished that I was elsewhere, wanted to leave, but stood there since I had made a promise. Then I reached back twenty-two years and pulled one out of my hat from my roughnecking days in East Texas. We had drilled some wells just east of Gladewater, Texas, that had a 50-foot-thick section of water sand at 500 feet. This was a loose, unconsolidated sand, and occasionally, when you made a connection while drilling through that zone, you got stuck. Pumping did no good, so strictly by chance, some driller shut the pump down for half an hour, then picked up on the pipe and, lo! he was loose. From that day on that shutdown-pump procedure worked just fine. I had been firing boilers for Leon Farmer when we used that trick, and had never forgotten it.

I suggested to the water-well contractor that he shut his pump down, wait a while for the hydrostatic pressure of the drilling fluid to push the sand away from his bit, then try to pull it loose. He looked at me as though I had lost my mind and flatly refused. I persisted, and my farmer friends got into the act. After all, it was their money going down the drain.

The contractor asked me, "Do you want to plant that bit?" I answered, "It looks to me like you have already planted it. If you haven't, go pull it loose."

"I can't, and haven't been able to move it for three days," he replied.

"It looks like you can't make it any worse, so why not try my method?"

He then said, "I'm afraid that if I shut the pump down, I may not be able to get circulation back, but go ahead if these guys want to try it. It won't work, but maybe it won't make things worse."

My farmers consulted together, then told me it was mine to do with as I pleased. I walked over and told the driller to shut his pump down. His boss nodded, he did, and things got very quiet. I was nervous, but went back to my car, lit a cigarette, and tried to look unconcerned. That was a long, long thirty minutes. My farmers were arguing, the contractor was glaring at me, and I felt lonesome.

I waited it out, alone, then walked over and said to the driller, "Stud, put your little rig in low gear and pick up on your pipe." He did; it came loose, he picked it up, laid down a joint of pipe, and I became a bona fide Genius. It was a heady experience. Everyone should be a genius once in their life, as long as they don't take themselves too seriously. Incidentally, those old boys made a fine well. It did not flow, but the water level stood at 300 feet from the surface, which made pumping feasible. We left soon afterward, so we never heard all the details, but they did get to do some irrigating, so our efforts paid off, finally, for them. I was glad; they were nice people.

We left Clovis with no regrets—glad to get away from our oddball company people, glad to be through with a bad job, glad! Clovis is a nice town. I have never been back, but I remember that well vividly, and all my memories are bad ones. Amy had bought a lot in a new addition, and two years later she sold it for a 50 percent profit. It was the only pleasant thing that happened to us in Clovis.

Chapter Seventeen

Wildcat at Grandfalls, Then on to Lovington, Sweetwater, and Lovington Again

We left Clovis with no regrets. I told my company people an emphatic "goodbye," and didn't bother to even smile, for I was thoroughly tired of them.

Our next location was south of Grandfalls, Texas. We all moved to Monahans, 18 miles north of Grandfalls, because Monahans was large enough to accommodate all of us. Sixteen men, with their wives and kids, made up a sizable bunch of people, and Grandfalls was just a small village.

I found a place in the side yard of a private home, a one-trailer-space deal. It had all utilities except a telephone. I went to the phone office to see about getting one installed and promptly ran into a hassle. It was an old story to me, one I had heard many times. Tool pushers move around a great deal. A phone is vital to their operation, and local phone offices can have some very odd rules. Monahans was no exception.

I went to the phone company office, told the girl at the customer service desk my name, that I was employed by S-H-K Drilling Company, that I had moved my trailer to a certain address, put up a 10-foot-high pole, and would like to get a phone installed as quickly as possible, to list it under S-H-K Drilling, and that the company paid my phone bill.

She then told me that before they would install a phone in a trailer house, they would require a $50 deposit. I had been a customer of Bell Telephone for years, had had phones installed in a number of towns in West Texas and Southeastern New Mexico, with no problems, paid the bills out of my expense account, and did not owe them a penny, so my temper came to a boil. Then our conversation went like this:

"Young lady, I'm not going to put up a deposit. My company will stand good for my bill. Call them and they will verify this."

"Sir, I am not authorized to waive that rule."

"Then I don't want to talk to you. I want to talk to someone who *can* waive that rule."

"That would be our district manager and he is out of the office at this time."

"Who takes his place when he is away?"

"The district engineer."

"Then I'll talk to him."

She called the engineer. He came out and said, "What is the problem?"

I told him the story. He said that they had made the rule themselves as they had been having some trouble with trailer people leaving bills unpaid. Then I told him that S-H-K would stand good for me, and he said, "I'm sorry, Mr. Lynch. I can't change the rule."

"Where is your district office?"

"In Abilene."

I pulled some coins out of my pocket and said, "Call the district manager in Abilene. I want to talk this problem over with him. I've had phones in Odessa, Andrews, Kermit, and Hobbs, New Mexico. I have never had to put up a deposit, and don't intend to do so this time. I want to ask him about your rule."

"That won't be necessary."

"It sure as hell is necessary if you don't put me in a phone. If you think you've heard the end of this, you are wrong. I'm going over your head either now, or as quickly as I can contact my office."

He looked pained, then said, "Well, perhaps we can make an exception." I got my phone the next day, and you people in other occupations thought *you* had trouble with Ma Bell.

The well we were going to drill was 8 miles south and 1 mile east of Grandfalls. The Blank-Blank Oil Company was the operator. It was a rank wildcat, barely on the Midland Uplift and very close to where the uplift made the long deep dip into the Delaware Basin. Our contract had a chert and lost-circulation clause in it, and as things turned out, we needed them. The well turned into a booger. Now chert is a quartzite. It is hard, crystalline, beautiful, and a real eater of bits. I have seen bits, new bits, drill 10 feet of chert and come out of the hole with the bearings out of the cones, cones the size of doorknobs with not a single tooth on them. Hughes Tool Company had come out with a new style tri-cone bit featuring tungsten carbide inserts that was supposed to be the answer to cherty formations. Where chert ran in concentrations of 20 to 30 percent of any formation, they did remarkably well. They were extremely expensive compared with the other bits, but had begun to come into general use. For lack of a better name, we called them "nubbies."

We set and cemented 500 feet of 13³/₈-inch casing, then Blank-Blank threw us a looping curve. They told us that we would drill the intermediate hole using 10-pound-per-gallon brine as drilling fluid. Usually this would have been fine, but in that area, at 1,900 feet, there was a known water sand called the Santa Rosa sand. It was a sand with a strong flow of sulphur water. It could be held static with a viscous mud weighing 9.3 pounds per gallon, but would break down under the hydrostatic weight of 10-pound mud or brine, and it would take fluid or, in other words, lose circulation. Then, when the hydrostatic weight lessened, it would flow back. I had talked with other pushers who had drilled shallow wells in that area, and was well aware of the Santa Rosa. The staff engineer who came out and told me of the decision to use brine took the brunt of my objections. He told me that the decision had been made by the district superintendent, who was opinionated and egotistical; not to argue, but to go on and drill. I didn't like it, but my company was protected by the lost-circulation clause in the contract, so I drilled ahead.

Jack Evans was back on his pushing job, and I had Louis Jones drilling in his place. Jones was an old S-H-K hand. I had drilled against him in the past and knew he was a sound, capable driller. Louis made pusher soon after we finished the well.

I was at the rig one morning soon after we drilled out from under the surface pipe. Mr. Bailey was drilling days that month of August. We had all discussed the problems that might arise from the brine and Santa Rosa sand. When I left the rig to go home about 1:00 P.M., Mr. Bailey was drilling below 1,800 feet at about 20 feet per hour. It was 27 miles from the rig to Monahans. I was looking forward to lunch, but just as I drove into the yard, the radio blared out: "Mr. Lynch, I have a solid 8-inch sulphur water flow. I bypassed the steel pits and am putting the water into the reserve pit." I almost had a heart attack! The reserve pit was 300 feet by 300 feet wide and 7 feet deep. The dike around the reserve pit had been built by a bulldozer, by taking dirt out of the inside. It was a damn big pit, but an 8-inch-diameter water flow would fill it quickly.

I said, "Mr. Bailey, what are you thinking about? Pull up and close the pipe rams on your BOP before that reserve pit dike breaks!"

He came back on the air in just a few minutes. "Mr. Lynch, I was too late. The dike broke and we ran sulphur water over about 15 acres of land." I told him to leave his rams closed and that I would call Blank-Blank for orders, but to open the rams every 15 minutes and move his pipe to prevent sticking the pipe.

The call to Blank-Blank was fruitless. I asked permission to mud up and got a cold NO. They told me that they were ordering out a thousand barrels of brine and to kill the water flow with brine and drill ahead. I told them we had broken down the Santa Rosa, and while we could kill the flow temporarily with brine, we would lose circulation again and get the sulphur water flow AGAIN. No matter, they told me to do as I was told, so I did. When the brine arrived, we pumped it down, killed the flow for about 20 minutes, then lost circulation, had a new water flow and were back where we had been before I called. This went on for three days, thousands of dollars, a few frayed tempers, and lots of talk. I even made a trip to Midland to present my views. The company finally consented, reluctantly, grudgingly, to mudding up. We mixed our pits full of 9.3-pound mud, killed our water flow, and finally drilled ahead. I never knew why they clung to the brine as long as they did, but hard heads were not uncommon in the upper echelons of oil companies.

The land around our location was as bare as a bald man's head. It had not rained for six months before we moved in, and there wasn't a blade of grass in sight. Ten acres would not have supported one jackrabbit, but when our reserve pit broke and spread black sulphur water over a large bit of it, about 7 to 10 acres, we learned how valuable, fragile, and dear it was to the rancher.

We had run several thousand barrels of that black water over the place, and some of it was standing in a few low places when the rancher saw it. The funny thing was, that while it was high in sulphur, it was low in chlorides, not salty at all by West Texas standards. The rancher didn't know this, so he came up to the rig very angry, and was going to sue Blank-Blank, S-H-K, me, the drillers, and anybody else who had helped ruin several acres of his lovely ranch. He was mad as hell, ranted at me and Mr. Bailey for half an hour, then left swearing vengeance. We had tried to tell him we had really done him a favor, but he would have none of that story. We had ruined some very valuable ground, and he intended to be paid for the damage.

Native grass responds to water very swiftly in desert country, so imagine our rancher's surprise when he came back with the county agent four days later and found dark green grass two inches high where the water had run. He deflated a lot, noticed that his bony cattle had moved in on the grass, loaded himself and the county agent into his pickup, and left. We heard nary a bad word out of him.

We set and cemented our intermediate casing at 5,500 feet, then drilled ahead without incident until we reached approximately 9,000 feet. Then we began to get traces of quartzite (chert) in our samples. Chisel tooth bits don't last long in chert, only two or three hours when the chert is 20 percent of the formation, but we felt that with the new button-type bits that Hughes Tool Company had come out with, we could drill chert pretty well. As I said before, the button bits featured tungsten-carbide inserts embedded in a firm matrix. You turned them at 46 revolutions per minute instead of the conventional 65 revolutions. Ran 40,000–45,000 pounds of weight instead of 30,000–35,000 pounds. In other words, instead of tearing and chipping the formation, you crushed it. Those bits were a godsend to the drilling industry as they enabled us to drill extremely hard, abrasive formations with considerable success.

We did all right until the chert began to predominate. I left the rig one day, and Mr. Bailey had pulled a worn bit and Louis Jones put on a brand new "chert bit" as we called them, then went in the hole. I went to town, and one hour after he got on bottom, Jonesy called me on the radio and said he was starting out of the hole and thought he might have lost a cone off his bit.

I couldn't believe it, but went back to the rig. When he got out of the hole, he still had all three cones, barely. All the inserts were worn slick, and the cones looked like doorknobs. That bit had made 8 feet—total! Louis and I looked at the last sample of cuttings, and it was 100 percent chert, the first 100 percent quartzite I had ever drilled. We knew then we had a rough row to hoe.

Our contract had a chert clause in it, and any time the chert exceeded 40 percent, we went on day work and the operating company, Blank-Blank in this instance, paid all the bills. It was a good thing that we had the clause. We used thirty bits and ten days drilling 360 feet. Then, to cap it all, we made a dry hole. The Ellenburger had water in it. The well was a freak, since no wells that had ever been drilled anywhere near us had encountered chert in large amounts.

We plugged and abandoned the hole, then got the news that we had to hurry back to Lovington. Phillips had another big lease 10 miles west of Tatum, New Mexico, that was due to expire in four days. The rig builders were on their way to build a derrick, and we had to spud it in four days. Another company flap, with us to take up the slack.

I called the trailer movers when I called the trucks to move the rig. Amy called the Beals in Lovington and, wonder of wonders, our old space next door to them was vacant. In fact, they had bought the lot we had fixed up years ago, and they seemed glad we were coming back to town.

It was another frantic time. I called Abbott Brothers in Hobbs about drilling a water well. They assured me that they would get the permit and start drilling the next day. We all moved except Louis Jones. He went to pushing tools, and young Bill Banks came over from Rig 4 to drill for me. I had known and liked Bill for years. He was a good, sound driller.

We had one last go-round with Ma Bell. We were moving on a Friday. Amy called for a serviceman to disconnect the phone in the trailer house. She was told that we would have to wait until Monday, so she took a screwdriver and disconnected the instrument, used wire cutters on the outside between post and house, then drove down to the phone office, laid the telephone on the startled young lady's desk, and told her, "Here is your phone. The mover will be here in an hour, so I couldn't wait till Monday." She smiled at the girl, then added, "Send the final bill to the office in Odessa, Texas, please. Goodbye." I wish I could have seen that girl's face.

The whole deal was a great big mess. The rig builders were rushing to build the derrick. I was getting the reserve pit and slush pits dug. The rig began to arrive on location, and *everyone* was in *somebody's* way! Not a good situation; however, we persisted. The rig builders topped out the derrick at noon of the third day. We began to rig up just as fast as we could move, but seemed to be fighting a losing battle.

We broke tour that fourth day, and the day and morning tour crews came out early. The morning tour boys went home at 2:00 P.M. as they had to come back at midnight in order to fill the continuous-operation clause in the lease.

Bill Banks was on evening tour. He came out at 3:30 P.M. Mr. Bailey worked two extra hours to finish "stringing up" the blocks. The water-well people didn't get their well finished. I had a hundred barrels of fresh water hauled to the location. We tied the pump truck into the suction of the main pump, and finally, at last, spudded in and drilled 40 feet before we ran out of water. It was 11:30 P.M. We had beat another deadline by half an hour. Dennis and his crew came on tour, and I told him to finish rigging up. I went to Lovington, then fell in bed, dead beat. The Phillips lease superintendent, the ranch owner, and the State of New Mexico representative left at the time I did. I don't know how they felt, but I felt sure that Phillips Petroleum Company felt good about the whole thing. It was the second time I had beaten a deadline for them. However, they never did even say "well done," just took it all in stride. I resented it a bit, but not much. It was just another tough day.

One good thing came out of the move. We—Amy and I, the hands and their families—all were glad to be back in Lovington. The county seat of Lea County, New Mexico, is not a large town. It is a pleasant place to live. The people, the merchants, and the ranchers all made you feel welcome. All of us felt almost as though we were coming home. It was sure as hell a welcome change, as Monahans had left a bad taste in our mouths.

It was also nice to be working again for Phillips Petroleum Company. We had grown used to their ways, felt at home with their methods, and liked and respected their field people. It made a good job. We had not enjoyed our last two jobs.

The new location was on the Jones Ranch, 10 miles west of Tatum. They specialized in a breed of sheep that they called Deboillet, a cross-breed they had standardized. The boss had the nickname "Punch." He was leery of us at first, but soon thawed, and we all got along fine. Punch Jones also raised horses, thoroughbreds. He raced them at Ruidoso and perhaps at other places, though we never knew for certain. The yearlings and colts were in the pasture where we were drilling. Punch asked us if he should move them, but we assured him that they would not be in the way and would certainly not be harmed. It was September of 1955 and the weather was hot. Mr. Bailey fell in love with the young horses. He had his roughnecks rig a mud gun on the reserve pit wall, about 100 feet from the derrick. In the hottest part of the day, he would pump fresh water through the gun, spray it in a half-circle, and those yearlings would come running, then play in the spray like children. They would toss their heads, run through the water, and cavort around like human kids. It was fun to watch them. The men loved the diversion, it cost us nothing, and gave us all lots of pure pleasure. Punch Jones said we were spoiling his race horses, but he left them in the pasture, so we didn't take his grumbling seriously.

Our well was a wildcat. The nearest well was 7 miles northwest of us. We were slated to the Devonian at 13,500 feet, but were committed to test all "shows" that we drilled through. The show was largely run by the exploration department of Phillips. We had a mud-logger trailer on location. The "loggers" caught and evaluated samples. Their instruments registered any gas that we encountered. They contacted the company geologists, which took a real load off *my* shoulders. Our lease foreman, Leonard Hutsell, was an old friend, so we had an exceptionally fine job.

We had fun. The well drilled easily; no problems. We circulated up samples many times and took a number of drill stem tests, but they were all negative until we hit the Pennsylvania lime at 12,200 feet. There we had a fine show, ran a DST and got a good flowing test, knew that we had a well, then drilled ahead to the Devonian.

The footage between the Penn and Devonian drilled tough—no trouble, just slow drilling. We were confident of some sort of well in the Penn, so everyone was pleased with our little "wildcat" for different reasons. *Our* reasons, of course, were continued work in a good, trouble-free area, and a familiar, pleasant town to live in. Phillips had their reason to be pleased, too—MONEY!

Mr. Bailey had a young man working for him that he had hired in Kermit. Oley was a good, willing, steady man. He was married, had two children, and caused no trouble, on or off the job. Mr. Bailey liked him and had been grooming him for a drilling job. Oley was ambitious, and he wanted to be a driller, but he was a slow thinker, not innovative, stubborn, and, on occasion, argumentative. I did not rate him as a prospective driller at all and told Mr. Bailey that he would never make the grade. It disappointed Mr. Bailey, and for a time I felt that he thought I was against Oley for personal reasons. I learned differently one day on the job.

I drove up to the rig one morning, got out of the car, and went up the steps and into the tool house. Mr. Bailey was explaining to Oley, in great detail, something that he wanted done. Oley kept asking questions and arguing a bit. Finally, Mr. Bailey said, "Just go on and do it my way, Oley." The boy shook his head, but went to do the job. Bailey saw me standing there listening and said, "Mr. Lynch, you were right about that boy. He will *never* make a driller. I'll swear that he gets one day older and two days dumber every day he lives."

He got no argument from me. Some guys can, but many cannot, and there are lots more "cannots" than "cans." We lost Oley on the next well. He evidently thought he would win promotion elsewhere, and it was clear that he had gone as far as he would ever go with me.

We drilled into and tested the Devonian, and it was dry. So we plugged back to the Penn, ran and cemented casing, then received word that we would be off for a few days while Phillips completed the well and evaluated it. The time was mid-December 1955. We had not had a day off in ninety days so everyone welcomed a small vacation.

Roughnecks are a funny breed, funny-odd. They bitch about ever having time off; then let them work for ninety days and they are the most abused people on earth. Then a layoff comes along, the rig is stacked for two weeks or a little longer, and panic sets in. Rumors fly: the company is going broke, the tool pusher is keeping secrets from them, they are going to move 500 miles, and too many other fears to even mention. If the tool pusher stays in town, they besiege his home wanting reassurance, wanting to know when, if ever, they are going back to work. The rig gets a new location, they go to work, and the next thing you hear is that they could have used a few more days off.

Amy and I left town. My family was preparing to all be home at Mother's for Christmas that year, so we went to Corsicana. We spent Christmas and stayed on a few days. We got back to Lovington on the 2nd of January, 1956, found out that Phillips had staked an offset location north of the discovery well, that Rig 6 was slated to drill it, and that we would spud as soon as we could skid the derrick and rig up. I told the drillers, they told the nervous hands that famine had been staved off for a few more days, and we all went back to work.

We had lots of rain in February and March that year. We had been getting to work by driving south off the Tatum-Roswell highway on a county road for 2 miles, then turning east to the rig. The heavy rains flooded the county road and it became almost impassable. Our company man, Leonard Hutsell, and I went to see Punch Jones and his wife. They had a private caliche road, straight south from the highway to ranch headquarters. This road was higher than the county road but needed caliche in some low places, and badly needed grading. We propositioned them to let us dump caliche where it was needed and grade the road with a maintainer, in return for permission to use their private road. They were nice and consented to the deal. So we gained an all-weather road, and they gained a *good* road. We felt lucky, since two more rigs had moved into the area. They were not drilling for Phillips, but did increase traffic on the county road, making a bad matter worse. We certainly took care not to inconvenience the Jones family, and always remembered that it was their road.

Our second well gave no problems. We drilled it in good average time, set pipe the last week in March, then skidded the rig half a mile northeast, and spudded our third well in the new field. The field had been named Ranger Lake. The Ranger Lake field was still producing in 1983, after twenty-seven years. It has been a good field and is now under water flood, a secondary recovery method.

We finished that third well with no problems, then were told to "stack" the rig. We left it on location, locked up as best we could, and waited to see where our next job was.

There had been persistent rumors for some months that Phillips Petroleum were cutting their domestic drilling budget. Much money was being allocated to overseas exploration, and domestic work was being curtailed. It turned out to be true.

Besides, Phillips were still operating five drilling rigs of their own, so it was an odds-on bet that company-owned rigs would be favored over contract rigs for what drilling there would be in the Permian Basin.

S-H-K Drilling Company had tied themselves so closely to Phillips down through the years that any slowdown by Phillips was bound to affect them. Besides, they had grown complacent and, to a degree, lazy. They had lost a great deal of their competitive edge, all of their desire, and had no liking for the hustle and bustle of keeping work for all of their rigs. Some of the men began to worry about their future with the company. I was not one who did, as I still got occasional offers of jobs and figured I could hold my own with any company.

We were off work about two weeks. I told the hands the truth as I knew it, that work was slow, I didn't have any idea when we would go back to

work, that if they could find another job to take it, and if we started up
they could come back to Rig 6 if they so desired. Most of them drifted
away, but I was helpless, since I had nothing to offer them.

The company finally called. They had a location, for Phillips, of
course, about 12 miles south of Roscoe, Texas, in Nolan County. The
well was a shallow one, slated for 6,900 feet. The rig they were sending
was a National "75," and to add to my troubles, I would not be able to
have my own drillers. The company had only two rigs running, and I
would have three tool pushers as drillers. My drillers would have to
roughneck, but would still draw drillers' wages, if they chose to go with
me on the job.

Dennis refused the offer. He had three girls in school, had recently
bought a home in Lovington, and did not intend to move. I certainly
couldn't blame him, though I hated like hell to lose him. He was a fine
driller.

Mr. Bailey went with me. He had a trailer house, was in his mid-
fifties, and didn't want to lose his seniority with the company. It was a
comedown, and his pride was sorely wounded, but it beat the hell out
of starting over with a strange drilling company.

Those three tool pushers weren't too happy to be back drilling either. They all felt abused. It made a sad job; that I found out all too
soon. Still, it wasn't Russia; they could quit if they wanted to do so.
Nobody made them take the drilling jobs, so I did not feel that *I* was
imposing on them. They were free men.

We moved to Sweetwater, Texas. It was a nice, slow-paced farm/
ranch town. It had a population of around 7,500 people, and had some
experience with oil-field trash. It even had a couple of supply houses
and a machine shop. Really a better town to live in than many we had
lived in in the past.

Amy and I moved our trailer. She had found a good parking place for
it. She had a knack for finding a good neighborhood to live in. We
moved in, set up our yard fence for Fritz, and settled down. We knew
that we had at least three wells to drill, perhaps more, so we prepared
to at least spend the summer.

Our location was 12 miles west and 12 miles south of Sweetwater. It
was on the Spires Ranch on the side of a rocky hill. You had to ford two
creeks to reach the location. The first creek, called Plum Creek, was
small, normally just a stream, but the second, Big Silver Creek, was 40
feet wide, usually ran 6 inches deep, had a rocky bottom, and its water
was clear. It was a pretty sizable stream, one to be aware of, as we
found out later.

My three drillers, Leslie Kutin, Jack Gordon, and Louis Jones, were
all tool pushers. They each thought they knew at least as much as I did.

They felt they were victims of circumstance and really would have liked to show me up as incompetent. We had known each other for years, had worked together many times, and off the job, we were friends. On the job there was rivalry. I accepted the fact that they were all a bit jealous, but did not intend to be outdone by any one of them. I was also aware that there would be friction on the job between *them.* They each jockeyed for advantage all of the time.

Fortunately, things came to a head early. When we moved the rig onto location, I had to drive to Odessa to pick up some supplies. It was a 250-mile drive, but I felt free to go, as all three drillers were familiar with the rig. Two of them had pushed tools on it, and all three had drilled on it down through the years. There certainly should have been no problem in a rig-up. Still, when I got back to the job late in the afternoon, I saw that the jackknife derrick had been raised and that the rig was unlevel. I knew the worst. Nobody knew who had leveled the matting boards, but the rig was 6 inches low on the pit side, and the traveling block hung 4 feet off the centerline of the hole.

I was furious. It was an unbelievable act of carelessness, and it had to be corrected. Our rig jacks could not handle the job, and I would have to call the rig builders with their big hydraulic jacks to level the derrick. We simply could not drill until this was done, and no one except myself seemed to care that it was a dumb, costly, stupid bit of work. My hold on my temper was slipping fast, but I managed to hold my tongue, just barely. I told the men to quit and I would have the rig builders out the next morning to level the derrick. I jumped in my car, slammed the door, and took off in a hurry. As it was not my usual way of leaving, I felt sure that they would get the message.

I thought long and hard that night on just how I would handle the situation. If I did not establish my authority immediately, the job would eat me alive, but I couldn't be absolutely sure that Skinny Hunter would back me if I fired one of those hard-headed bastards. On the other hand, they were a lot afraid of Skinny and a little bit afraid of me. I decided to run a big, bold, challenging bluff on my three reluctant drillers.

The next morning while the rig builders were leveling the rig, I called all three men into my shack, told them that we were going to have a meeting of minds, and made one of the longest speeches of my life. It went like this: "Fellows, I am sure that you all know how mad I am about this foul-up, so to keep things clear, I'm telling you all that I am NOT going to put up with this kind of screw-up. I know that we are all tool pushers, but on *this* job, I am THE tool pusher, and I will listen to your words; however, *I* will have the *last* word." Then I ran my bluff. "I talked to Skinny last night, told him that while I was in his office yesterday, *somebody* failed to do his job, that we had to get the rig builders to fix things and I didn't intend to put up with that kind of work. He told me that I didn't have to put up with *anything* I didn't like, so if you guys are going to work for me, you will have to shape up, or I will send you to the office, and *you* can explain to Mr. Hunter why you are there.

They looked at me, then at each other and finally, Jack Gordon said, "I'm speaking for myself only, but I intend to stay."

Louis and Les both nodded their heads, and we went to work. I had not talked to Skinny but knew damned well that none of them would dare call him to find out. We had re-established the pecking order and had another well to drill.

Traffic into the Spires Ranch had always been very sketchy until drilling began in that area. People had always forded Plum and Big Silver creeks during dry weather and avoided them in wet weather. We couldn't do that, as we had to travel, rain or shine. Max Milam, our Phillips company man, had set four 18-inch-diameter corrugated pipes known throughout the oil fields as "tin horns" to carry the waters of Plum Creek. He had dumped dirt over them and raised the road over the tin horns to about 4 feet in height. I inspected our roadway over the creek and pronounced it perfect. We—Max and I—thought we were ready for any kind of weather. We left Big Silver just as it had been. It was wide, shallow, rocky, and clear, not to be really feared, but we were poorly prepared for the weather that we endured that summer.

We moved into the Spires in June, and usually our wet weather was largely gone by then. This year was an exception. On the 9th of June, it rained 8 inches in Sweetwater, and while I didn't ever know for sure, it probably rained more on the Spires Ranch. Anyhow, we had a flood on our hands.

As I drove to the rig the next morning, the roadside ditches were flooded and the lone dry wash south of Roscoe was out of its banks. Water was pouring out of flooded fields into the ditches, and the ditches had nothing to empty themselves in. I felt sure that I couldn't reach the rig.

When I entered the Spires Ranch road and got to Plum Creek, the creek was 40 feet wide, at least 5 feet deep, and there was no sign of our tin horns and raised roadway. They were gone. We never saw them again, but one of the ranch hands said one of the tin horns lodged in a brush pile about 2 miles down Big Silver Creek. Plum was a tributary of Silver, merging with it about half a mile from our crossing. It was obvious that Plum Creek was impassable, so I called the rig on my car radio. Jack Gordon was on morning tour, and when he answered, he told me that one of his men had driven down to Big Silver and it, too, was swift, high, and impassable. So he and his men were stranded at the rig. I told Jack where the key to my shack was, that I had eggs, bacon, ham, and bread in the refrigerator, and for them to cook and eat breakfast while I went back to Sweetwater. I told them that there was another road into the ranch from the south. That I would try to rent a high-wheeled Jeep, bring out the daylight crew, and relieve them, if I could get directions for the other road. That it might take awhile to do all that, likely several hours. He said okay, that breakfast would cheer up the hands and they would keep things going until we arrived.

By great good luck, I did manage to rent a Jeep with 30-inch wheels. The thing looked like a bug on stilts, but certainly ran well, and would go where you wouldn't think of driving a car. The people that I rented it from told me to go to the little town of Maryneal and "anybody" there could tell me how to get into the ranch. Louis Jones, his crew, and I started out, went to Maryneal and stopped at the Maryneal Cafe to ask directions.

The cafe was full; the rain had halted all farm work, and the farmers and ranchers had congregated in the cafe to talk about the weather. The farmers were bellyaching about "too much rain," while the ranchers laughed, patted their feet on the floor, and hollered, "Let it rain!" The West is the only place in America that really "enjoys" rain, anytime, in any amount.

The guys were nice; they gave us more directions than we could use. Everyone had to get into the act, but we finally sorted out a route and started out with a hand-drawn map on a tablet back. It was a darn good map, too. We drove up on location at 11:00 A.M. Jonesy took over while I took Gordon and crew to town. It was 25 miles farther, but a hell of a lot drier and no creeks to ford. We crossed Big Silver up in the hills on a bridge. And that is the way we worked for the next few days. We gave that Jeep a real workout, and it rained for three days, washed out fields, roads, and terraces, did a lot of folks harm, but the ranchers loved it. Those fellows never got enough rain. However, the rain finally did stop, the sun shone, and things dried up rapidly. Max Milam found and bought three 30-inch tin horns. We rebuilt our creek crossing, and the big tin horns did the job. We had two more big rains later, but our crossing never washed out again. One of my friendly rival tool pushers who was working for Great Western Drilling Company had a bit of trouble with Big Silver, but that came later.

We had managed to keep drilling through all the bad weather and had reached a depth in the well that had been giving people who were drilling in that area a very bad time. There was a shale section just below 6,000 feet that had been eating people's lunch. You had to mud up to drill it because if you tried to clear-water it, the stuff would slough on you. Then, when you drilled it, more trouble; the cuttings were lighter than normal shale cuttings and would stay in suspension in your mud. Since they were slow to settle out, you would recirculate them, and they would build up in your mud system, finally reaching the point that the bit would just stop rotating. It would slow down, stop, and you would be stuck on bottom, a real no-no. This would bring on an expensive stuck-point-indicator job, a back-off job, and a long washover job. This kind of thing had happened several times before we moved into the area, so we were warned and Phillips was warned. The people who were still drilling near us, four rigs in all, were nice to tell us about their problems, so we were prepared to cope with the shale.

This was before de-sanding devices had been invented. At least I had never seen one. In order to keep solids from building up in the mud system, you periodically cleaned the pits. To do this you jetted away solids-laden mud, and mixed new clean mud. While doing this, you kept right on drilling. Mud costs even in those days were high. Jetting away mud was costly, and Phillips was greatly concerned, since they bought the mud.

I had operated a guinea pig rig for Phillips several times in the past and was elected to do so again on this job. The steel pits on Rig 2 were good ones, equipped with all the gadgets available in those days. We knew that we were not going to stick our pipe as we drilled, but in order to keep our mud weight below 9.4 pounds per gallon, which was the "sticking point," we had to do much jetting and pit cleaning.

Leroy Pope, whom we all knew and liked, was our mud engineer. He was one of Phillips Petroleum Company's very best mud men. He lived in Odessa, 135 miles from the well, but made it to the well every day and stayed for hours on each visit. I was always on the lookout for improvement in mud properties, and Leroy and I experimented with different types of drilling mud in an effort to find one that would hold back the sloughing and still drop the cuttings, but nothing worked. We almost despaired, but we were both stubborn and felt that if anyone could find a way to beat the problem, we could. Cocky maybe, but we had been lucky in the past.

Mr. Bailey was back on his drilling job. Les Kutin's rig had started up and he had returned to Odessa. Bailey felt sure we would work something out. He, too, had a real interest in drilling mud, so Leroy and I had the best kind of cooperation on the job.

One day while Bailey, Leroy, and I were discussing the problem, Mr. Bailey said, "Well, you all have done about everything you can do to mud, so we are going to have to think of some other way to handle this mess." It was true, but we had a vibrating screen shale shaker, and the solids that were causing all the trouble were the ones that would fall through a 20/20 mesh screen; the mud engineers called them "fines." This was before the days of the double screen shakers, so mechanically, we had the most modern equipment made at that time.

Mr. Bailey's remark triggered Leroy's memory, and he said, "You know, when I visited the mud lab in Bartlesville last summer, one of the chemists was talking about a gizmo he had sketched out that he thought would remove fines from mud. It was just a sketch, but I'll bet we could make one at least similar to it, if my memory hasn't left me."

I jumped on the idea and asked, "Just how much do you remember? Not about the sketch, but the method?"

"We were discussing gravity pull, as I remember, and its relation to mass. That chemist thought that fluid pumped into a vessel in a swirling motion would tend to separate fluid and solids if the vessel had a fairly large opening at its top and a much smaller orifice at the bottom."

"Why the swirling entry of the fluid?" Leroy frowned, then slowly said, "As I remember, he said something about flattening the pipe the fluid entered the vessel through in order to flatten the cross-section area of the fluid. Then as it swirled around a round vessel, the lighter fluids would go out the top and gravity would pull the solids down, and with slight fluid loss, they would pass through the small hole in the bottom of the vessel."

It made sense in a weird sort of way and was at the very least a brand new approach. So I told Leroy, "I like it; let's go out to my shack and try to figure out a way to build one of the damn things."

He grinned and said, "You know good and well Phillips isn't going to let me have the money to build anything. I'm not that high up on the totem pole. Besides, that chemist was talking about trying to patent his idea, so we could be infringing."

"Hell, don't worry about it. I'll build the thing on S-H-K's money. You don't even remember that chemist's name, much less the particulars on how his tool was made, so what's to worry about?"

"Okay, let's get started. Between us, we should come up with something that just might work."

I said, "Come with us, Mr. Bailey. You started this train of thought, so you might as well help end it. Put a roughneck on the brake and let him get a little practice."

Mr. Bailey was delighted and flattered. He got up, put one of his hands to drilling, and we went out to the shack.

We finally came up with a consensus and it did look like a very "homemade" gadget. What we decided on was two 6-inch bull plugs screwed into a 6-inch coupling with a 2-inch line pipe coupling welded into the top of one bull plug and a machined collar in the bottom that would accept a jet nozzle out of a rock bit, the nozzle held in place by a snap ring, exactly as it was held in place in the bit. Then down from the top bull plug, the one with the 2-inch opening, we cut an opening in one side, and inserted a slightly flattened nipple of extra heavy 1½-inch pipe. This nipple was curved to fit the inside of the plug slightly flattened and firmly welded in place; it would be the input pipe.

I drew it up on a piece of foolscap paper. It wasn't pretty, but we really thought that it just might work. We spent a few minutes congratulating each other on being Minor League Geniuses, then split up, Pope to Odessa, Mr. Bailey back to drilling, and me to Sweetwater to start finding the stuff that we needed to build our "thing."

There was a National Supply Company store in Sweetwater. It was fairly small, but had teletype connections nationwide. Six-inch-diameter pipe line bull plugs were certainly not a stock item, but I felt very confident that somewhere in the National empire some store or factory had two of them. Sure enough, they found two standard 6-inch bull plugs in a store in Pennsylvania, ordered them and a coupling, or in oil-field lingo, a "collar," and shipped them to Sweetwater.

Sweetwater had a good small machine shop. I took my sketch to them and told them what I planned to make. I feel sure they thought I was crazy, but were too polite to say so. I took a jet nozzle and snap ring to them, and they built me a collar to contain them. Then we waited for the arrival of the plugs and collar.

Bull plugs are cylindrical in shape, with the closed end rounded off and the threaded end cut off square. The inside is hollow, but in the small high-pressure plugs, the upper end is quite thick. The ones we got from Pennsylvania were low-pressure plugs, 6 inches in diameter and about 14 inches long.

Our plugs arrived in about ten days from the time that I ordered them. Leroy and I took them to the machine shop and proceeded to build our "thing." We assembled our gadget, and it looked pretty good. We attached a bracket to it that would fit the side of the slush pit and hold the tool upright. The whole thing was less than 3 feet long and looked something like an oversized metal sausage.

We took it to the rig, hung it on the side of the No. 1 steel pit so that the orifice at the bottom of the thing was outside the pit on the side away from the derrick, and the 2-inch discharge line emptied back into the slush pit. We connected the 1½-inch input line to one of the mud gun outlets on the pit, started up the "standby" pump and watched to see if it would work at all, and it DID work. A stream of solids and a good deal of mud came out of the bottom and fell to the ground, while the fluid that was returned to the pits was almost completely free of solids. However, the first jet nozzle, a 5/16-inch one, wasted entirely too much mud. Leroy and I changed nozzles until we got one that wasted very little, but still removed lots of solids. It was $1/8$ inch and did a dandy job. We were amazed at the thing's ability to separate solids from mud. Of course, we were only treating a small percentage of our mud, about 15 percent, but we had cut our pit cleaning and jetting time down to less than one-fourth of what it had been, and we were delighted and proud. We had built a workable tool, a useful tool, and a prototype. As far as I know, it was the first de-sander ever used in the West Texas area. It did the job that we wanted, and that is exactly what a tool is supposed to do.

We were very nearly to the end of our first well on the Spires Ranch, so we did not have time to really gloat over our de-shaler. Moving a rig on the Spires was not a simple skid job. The ranch was hilly and wooded. Lots of blackjack and live oaks, some cedar elm trees, a few hackberries, and a few junipers. So, we had to tear down, lay the derrick down, and stay on the roads in order to move the rig.

We started our second well in mid-July. We were beginning to become accustomed to the country, the difference in terrain, and the different kinds of problems in drilling in that area. Amy and Fritz loved the woods. They thought it fine that we were drilling in an interesting part of Texas. Amy loved to hunt artifacts, so they made many trips to the job with me. The area in olden times had been inhabited by the Lipan Apache tribe. Artifacts were not plentiful, but Amy found quite a few. Fritz found ground squirrels, possums, raccoons, squirrels, and lizards. He never caught anything except an occasional lizard, which he promptly ate, to Amy's horror, but he never lost hope. He was sure that he would make a big killing someday.

We all liked Sweetwater. It was then and is now a fine place to live. Amy and the other wives found shopping to be a pleasure. The tradespeople were courteous, easygoing, and polite. They were vastly different from the rude, impatient, "buy it and get out" types we had grown accustomed to dealing with in the boom towns. It was surely different to adjust to a more leisurely pace.

There was a near-tragic, seriocomic thing that happened that summer. One afternoon of a stormy day in late July, I started to the rig. There was a large thunderstorm to the south, and it appeared to be centered over the ranch. I slowed my pace because I did not want to drive into a possible hailstorm. We had been lucky so far; it had hailed all around us, but had not hit us, and I wasn't anxious to break the spell.

The storm was moving west to east toward Maryneal. It was raining, but not very hard. Plum Creek was up a bit, but Maxie's tin horns were handling the rise well, so I had no trouble crossing the creek.

The Silver Creek ford was about three-quarters of a mile from Plum Creek, and when I got to Silver, the water was still clear but was definitely much higher than normal. I stopped, looked across the creek, and saw the tool pusher for Great Western sitting on a rock on the other side of the creek. He yelled at me, "For God's sake, don't drive off in there!" I asked, "Cowboy, what are you doing over there afoot?"

He said, "I drove off into the creek like an idiot without really noticing it was up. The car drowned out, the creek kept rising, the car began to drift downstream, and I got out, fought the car away from me, waded out, then watched that damned brand new Ford wash down the creek. Somehow, I hurt my ankle and I'm over 2 miles from my rig. So I was just waiting. I knew that sooner or later someone would come by."

I called our rig on the radio. Jack Gordon sent a car down to pick up Cowboy and take him to his rig. Jack said that everything was okay at our rig, and that he could get along very well without the pump parts that I was bringing in. I went back to town. Incidentally, they found Cowboy's new Ford $1^1/2$ miles down the creek. It had been pretty well banged around on the rocks and trees. They told me that when they led the insurance adjuster to it, he pronounced it a total loss and made no effort to recover the car. You can see that pushing tools is a real "snap" job. Just ask anyone . . . not connected with the oil fields.

Big Silver Creek was back to normal when the men changed tours at 11:00 P.M. Water drained off those rocky hills swiftly, but after that episode, everyone treated old Silver with respect, knowing that it was capable of drowning you. Before then, we had been pretty casual in our crossing.

Our little de-shaler worked well for us. We managed to hold our mud weight at 9.1 to 9.2 pounds per gallon with a bare minimum of jetting. It was a ninety-day wonder. The drillers and roughnecks popped off about it in town. Cowboy and three other pushers came to the rig, went out to the pits, examined the tool and saw what it would do, then demanded to know, "What's inside the damn thing that separates that shale out?" I very truthfully answered, "Nothing," but was met with "Oh yeah—I'll bet" and "I knew you would lie about it." Not a single one of those suspicious bastards believed me. I tried to explain the principle that we had built the thing by, and was met with extreme skepticism. They went off, irritably, talking about "greedy sons of bitches" who would not share secrets. Since I *had* told the truth, I felt no compunction to convince 'em. Let 'em build their own tools, and put as much gadgetry as they wanted in them. Actually, the tool was just too simple to believe. I would sometimes go out to the catwalk around the pits, gaze at the thing, and be amazed all over again. But it was a good feeling; it's great to build something new that really works. Mr. Bailey, Leroy Pope, and I were as proud as young fathers with a baby son. Even Skinny Hunter liked it; he was a devout believer in learning all that could be learned about handling drilling mud. I drew Skinny a construction blueprint, and he had a tool made for each rig.

We finished our fourth well on the Spires Ranch in mid-December, then had a shutdown. Phillips had probably used up their budget for the year. Anyway, we were on the grass and did not know when the rig would start up again. The hands scattered like quail. Amy and I went to Corsicana for Christmas. Mother and two of my sisters lived there and we had a combined Christmas and family reunion. Jo and her husband, Neil, and their three boys were in Japan, but all the rest of us were at home. It was a good holiday.

Amy and I got back to Sweetwater on the 29th of December. I drove back and forth to Odessa to supervise a motor overhaul on three motors off Rig 2. They didn't need me, but S-H-K did not like to see even a senior tool pusher idle. They tried to keep you occupied. We finally got a location released on the 9th day of January, 1957. Mr. Bailey, Jack Gordon, and a young driller whom I did not know named Walt were to be my drillers. The story that was being told in the patch was that Phillips had earmarked the major portion of their 1957–1958 budget for overseas operations; that it would be a lean year for drilling in the United States. I knew it to be true, for I knew men in Phillips who were high enough up the tree to know, and they told me that the story was correct. But I didn't tell the hands, as they got very edgy when shutdown speculation started. I had been on salary for many years, but still remembered vividly the hopes and fears of the hourly men. It is a bad thing when your job falls out from under you, through no fault of your own. S-H-K's ties to Phillips were so close that anything that affected Phillips certainly affected them, and I feared the future. We had been able to keep good men down through the years because we kept the rigs working steadily. This was changing, and some of our old, steady hands were drifting away, one by one. You couldn't blame them and couldn't help them, so you endured the new men as best you could, knowing that pride in the rig and in the company was slipping away. It was truly a sad thing to see.

After the layoff, I drilled two more wells on the ranch. I'll amend that to almost two more wells. In late April, I got word that Phillips wanted to drill another well in the Ranger Lake field. Rig 6 was still stacked on the last location we had drilled there, so the company wanted me to move back to Lovington, round up as many of my old hands as I could find, and fire Rig 6 up again. We were nearly down on the second well, but I turned his rig back to Jack Gordon, who was delighted to be pushing tools again, and called the trailer mover.

Amy called the Beals in Lovington and was happy to learn that the trailer space next door to them was vacant. We had designed that space to fit our trailer years ago, so it would be like going home. The Beals had bought the space two years before, and were glad to have us return. They were old friends. It was a good feeling.

We had just finished buying a new four-door Chevrolet. It had factory air conditioning, the first year Chevrolet came out with factory-installed equipment. The month was May, the weather was hot, and the air conditioning was a big hit.

The day that we moved the trailer house to Lovington was a hot, muggy thunderstormy day. I drove the company Ford and led the trailer mover. Amy stayed in Sweetwater to get the new car serviced out, and left about three hours behind the mover and me. She had Fritz with her, and he fell in love with the air conditioning. It spoiled him so much that he didn't want to ride with me in the Ford. It was not air conditioned.

We had the trailer set up and functioning by the time Amy got to Lovington. The Beals invited us to dinner, and we felt at home again. It was nice and made for a happy reunion, even though it was stormy.

I was lucky. Mr. Bailey came back with me, I rehired John Wayne Dennis, and my third driller was Bill Banks, a good solid trio of men. We rigged up No. 6 and went to drilling. It was old, familiar territory and things went well. The location was just a quarter-mile north of the Jones Ranch house. It was no problem well, and we bottomed out in early July, skidded the rig one location east, and spudded in what proved to be our last well in the Ranger Lake field.

I had to go to Odessa one day as we were drilling that first well. Some routine thing about company policy. It was a hot day. S-H-K had never allowed us to air condition the company cars. Nearly every other drilling company had put air conditioners in their tool pushers' vehicles, but we had not been able to persuade S-H-K that we needed a cooler car to drive, even though we spent many hours driving. I got to strike a telling blow for us on this trip. When I got into the edge of Odessa, I rolled up the windows on the Ford, and by the time I arrived at the office on East 2nd Street, I was wringing wet with sweat. There literally was not a dry thread on me.

When I walked into the office, Bill Barron, the office manager, said, "My God, man, how did you get so hot?"

Skinny came out of his office, and he, too, said, "Mate, why are you so hot?"

I said, "Well, I've just driven clear across Odessa with all the windows on my car rolled up, and it got pretty hot before I got here."

Skinny asked, "Why in hell did you have your windows rolled up?"

"Because I didn't want people to know that the company I worked for was too damned tight to air condition their tool pushers' cars."

Bill Barron laughed; Skinny gave me a hard look, and then said, "Go put an under-the-dash air conditioner in that Ford. Put it on your expense account, I'll approve it, and shut up about it."

I did, that very day. The other pushers followed suit later, and that is how we got air conditioning in our cars. It certainly made a huge difference in comfort during our "windshield time." I was always sorry that I hadn't done it a year earlier. Sometimes it is hard to get management's attention. *They* were not uncomfortable.

We had a bad experience on our last well. While drilling the surface hole, we got a man killed on the job. I had never had a fatality on Rig 6 before, and it shook me badly. Bill Banks was on tour. He was the daylight driller that month. He was making a mouse-hole connection. As he spun the kelly up in the rotary table, one of the inserts in the drive bushing fell out, dropped 30 feet, and hit the backup man on the back of his neck. The insert weighed about 80 pounds, was a foot wide, 16 inches long, and 3 inches thick, and it broke his spinal column. I was at the rig. In fact, I was in the tool house when it happened. When the commotion started, I ran out on the rig floor. Everyone was in a state of shock. I told Bill not to let anyone move the injured boy, then ran, completely forgetting the car, to ranch headquarters about a quarter-mile away. Mrs. Jones called Tatum for me, as I was out of breath. She got the only doctor in the village and the Tatum ambulance. They hurried out, got there in 20 minutes. We managed to get the injured boy on a stretcher and loaded him in the ambulance. The doctor and I rode with him, and we headed for Roswell, 60 miles away. The man died on the way to Roswell. The doctor told us to turn around and head back to Lovington. We did, but it was a dreadful ride. Death is not a pleasant traveling companion.

The accident was an equipment failure. The bolt holding the screwed-down ring broke. The ring held the four inserts in place, and when it popped off the drive bushing, the bushing fell. The insert that struck the boy was the only one that came out of the bushing. The other three stayed put. It was a freak failure, but drilling rigs do have strange accidents.

The man who got killed was a new hand. He was making his second day when the accident occurred. None of us really knew him. He was married; his wife was a waitress in a local cafe; and I had to tell her of

her husband's death. It was a mean job; words are inadequate and you
are left with a feeling of utter failure. Fortunately, they had no children, and the woman took the news well. I told her that we would keep
in touch, help if we could, and meant it. The insurance company took
over and I went back to the job, but both Bill Banks and I were haunted
by the event for a long, long time.

Bill and his wife, Ruth Ann, were just coming out of an exceedingly
bad time. They had two handsome, healthy kids, a boy and a girl. Their
third baby, a girl, was born early that year. She was a very fragile, ill
baby. They almost lost her, spent most of their savings trying to save
her, did save her, only to find out that she was hopelessly retarded, a
very low blow. Ruth Ann began to beg Bill to get out of drilling, stop
moving around so much, settle down in one place, and stay there.
Smith Bit Company had offered Bill a job. It did not pay as much as a
drilling job, but did offer more stability. He was tempted but had
decided not to quit. The accident finished making up his mind. He
took the job with Smith and moved to Snyder, Texas. I still see him
occasionally. He is one of my old friends who did well. Smith promoted him, and he was happy in Snyder. Ruth Ann has devoted her life
to her retarded daughter, and other retarded kids. She and Bill are fine
people. They are among the cream of oil-field trash. Bill is still with
Smith Bit Company, still in Snyder. A good man to know. He earned
his knowledge.

We were nearing the end of our well. Phillips staked three locations
in the Ranger Lake field, but S-H-K did not get one of them. Phillips
did the same thing that they had done to us for years. We would drill a
wildcat; if it made a well, we would drill four or five offsets; then
Phillips would move their company rigs into the area and move us out.
Company-owned rigs, whatever the company, always had trouble making money. In the first place, they just did not have the incentive that
contract rigs had, since contractors drilled by and were paid by the
foot of hole drilled. Company rigs never were innovative, and so they
would move in and take over the field. Phillips had done it to me in the
Andector, the Maguetex, the Tulk, and now, Ranger Lake. They
phased the company rigs out of existence about five years later, but too
late to help us. We really got hurt by this last move. I began to think
about quitting the drilling business, since it looked more and more like
a no-win deal. Also, the information I had gotten from my friends in
Phillips was being borne out. They *were* curtailing their domestic
drilling programs.

We finished our well, ran and cemented casing, were released by
Phillips, and stacked No. 6 again. I was told to leave my trailer in
Lovington and to come to Odessa and take over supervision of a

National "75" that was running 6 miles south of Odessa. Amy and I moved into a motel near the football stadium. It had a bedroom, bath, kitchen, and a small dining room. The company picked up the tab because they honestly believed that the slump was temporary, that I would be returning to New Mexico soon.

Mr. Bailey came with me; he moved his trailer house to Andrews. His daughter, Nancy, had married and was living in Andrews. He said that he preferred to live in Andrews and did not mind the longer drive.

Dennis stayed in Lovington. He never worked for S-H-K again. I hated to lose him, but since I wasn't sure how long I would stay, I could not promise him any kind of a job. Bill Banks went to work for Smith Bit and moved to Snyder, so the company lost two experienced drillers. It was actually the beginning of the end.

Chapter Eighteen

Winding Up

I t was mid-September 1957 when we went to Odessa. I drilled two 9,000-foot wells south of Odessa with two drillers who had never worked for me before and, of course, Mr. Bailey. Mr. Bailey had been with me for many years, and I insisted on working him. Skinny didn't protest; he didn't like Bailey, but knew he was a good driller, and since so many young men were taking jobs overseas, good drillers were slowly getting in short supply, and nobody had ever accused Skinny Hunter of being dumb. If a thing was good for the company he was much in favor of it and had pretty well followed that policy down through the years.

When we finished the second well south of Odessa, it was early December 1957. We moved the rig to a location in the sand dunes north of Goldsmith. These dunes, described in Chapter 13, are real "walking dunes," and locations and roads built through them have to be heavily caliched, else they will blow out from under you.

The company that we got this location from was the same one that we had drilled the well south of Grandfalls for, some three years before. They were a wholly owned subsidiary of one of the big major companies and were just as opinionated and prone to *not* listen to *anything* you might suggest. So we got off to a nervous start. However, the well went pretty well and I began to think we might be lucky, but the weather turned very bad and the bad weather plagued us on to the end of the well.

We had other problems as well. The string of $5^1/_2$-inch OD casing that the operator bought for the production string had "buttress" threads. Buttress is a rather exotic thread, one not in common use. It is a broad, shallow thread that makes up to a given torque and "shoulders." It must be handled carefully, and you must be very careful to refrain from too tight "make-up torque." If made up too much, or "over-torqued," it will creep inward from the shoulder and cause all kinds of problems. I discussed this with the casing tong operator. He and I agreed to be very careful when running casing and set the torque limits on his tongs in the low range of recommended make-up, then got promptly overruled by our company drilling engineer, who said that we were over-cautious, scared, and he wanted that pipe tonged tightly. I argued with him, heatedly. He pooh-poohed me, so I finally balked and refused to do his bidding unless he put it in writing and signed it. It angered him, but he did it, and it got me off the hook. And a good thing, too, because I heard later that when they pressure-tested that pipe prior to completing the well, they had multiple leaks, but S-H-K and I were in the clear, so the company could not blame us. Their little engineer had to take the blame, and I hope that it taught him a little humility and that it sometimes pays to discuss things, rather than "give orders."

It began to snow while we were logging the well, just before we ran and cemented casing. I had ample water storage, and Halliburton was on location, so we felt secure. Still, it took sixteen hours to log that well, and it snowed steadily all the time. When Schlumberger finished and moved their truck off location, snow was a foot deep on the level and beginning to drift on the road. We ran and cemented casing and finished at 2:00 P.M. Everyone was tired and wanted to go home. The company engineer and lease foreman started, while I was telling my driller what to do, and as I prepared to leave, those two guys came wading back to the rig. The engineer, who was in front, had plowed into a 3-foot-high drift about a quarter-mile down the road and stalled. He smothered his motor, the car died, and they walked back to the rig. I was driving a new Ford coupe. I had an old black rubber slicker in the trunk. Two roughnecks and I tied that thing over the radiator grill to keep the fan from pulling snow in and killing the motor. We lashed it down solidly. I took the engineer and foreman with me. We got to where they were stalled, dried out the engineer's motor, and got it to running. Then I drove in front and "broke trail" for the two fellows. It worked fine. Most of the big drifts were at road intersections and the drifts would only be 6 or 7 feet across and not packed too solidly. I could plow through them, even though I had to take two hitches at one of them. Anyway, I got them to Goldsmith, and the road to Odessa from there was open. I got home about five o'clock and was awfully glad to be out of the weather for the night.

The house that Amy and I owned on West 13th Street became vacant. We gave up the motel and moved into the house. Amy's sister, Essie, was moving her furnishings to Odessa from East Texas, so we just put it to use and she moved in with us. We had owned that house for seven years, and that was the first time we had ever lived in it.

It was January 1958, and the drilling depression was settling over the Permian Basin. The next ten years were going to be very tough ones for drilling contractors: not much work, cutthroat competition, very poor footage prices, and the operating companies' complete indifference to their problems. Many drilling contractors would go out of business, and the experienced hands would drift into other lines of work. It had always been this way. The oil fields lived and died on the boom-and-bust cycle. When things boomed, they were cocky, brave, and arrogant. When the "bust" came, they cut each other's throats, cannibalized the rigs, and became meek and fearful. This is the history of drilling; when jobs are plentiful and good rigs fairly scarce, the contractors get greedy. They demand, and get, day work for their rigs, a set price per hour of rig use, not tied to footage rates. Then the boom flattens out a bit, rigs are no longer in big demand, and the contractors flipflop, plead for footage contracts, swear by all that's holy that they wouldn't even consider riding day work. The operating companies then proceed to rub their noses and pocketbooks in the dirt. Many of them go out of business, and *all* of them get hurt. Things run along fairly evenly for a few years; then they go through the whole cycle again. I watched it happen many times. The last time was in 1981. I have often thought that there must be a better way, but if there is one, no one has ever found it, so even today, they boom and bust. Nowadays when a big drilling contractor or two goes under, they sometimes take a bank down with them. But the glitter of big profits dazzles them, so the merry chase continues, gamblers to the end.

We finished our well and sent the rig to the yard and stacked it. That brought us down to two active rigs. I took over my old original rig, the little National "50." Scott Harris had a "75," and that was the crop.

The "50" was running for Phillips Petroleum, just 6 miles south and 1 mile east of the well we had just finished. I had three tool pushers drilling and twelve drillers roughnecking. It was the worst job I had ever had for S-H-K. Everybody was nervous and upset. Everybody wanted reassurance; everybody wanted to know what the future held in store for them. Since I didn't have any answers, I became a sort of villain. But it did one thing for me; it made up my mind to get out of the drilling industry. The future of S-H-K was clear. They had stopped bidding competitively, and just took the few locations Phillips gave 'em. They, the partners, were rich, aging, and Bill Schoenfeld's health was failing. So you did not have to be at all smart to see the handwriting on the wall. I made up my mind to quit and look for opportunities. In the meantime, I would work, but when the next shutdown came, I resolved to check it to them. It was obvious that my future lay elsewhere.

We drilled two wells in the University Sandhills lease for Phillips, then shut down, moved the rig to the yard, and then had to lay the men off. It was an awful wrench, with a lot of sad faces. I felt sure that everyone felt it was the end of good, steady, well-paid work. A kind of little death.

I asked for time off to go visit my mother. The company gladly gave me two weeks. Amy and I took off, visited my folks in Corsicana, then visited in East Texas with a few old friends. We left East Texas and started home in February of 1958. On the way to Odessa, I told Amy that I was quitting S-H-K. She had a fit; her anxiety complex told her we would starve to death and I would never find another job as suited to me. I told her my reasons and that my mind was fully made up. She was very upset, but finally accepted the fact, but it was a sad, depressing journey home.

The next day, I stripped the company Ford of all my personal plunder, then drove out to the office which was at the intersection of Farm to Market Road 1936 and West 16th Street. The company had moved out there three years ago, but since I had been in New Mexico at the time, it had not made a big impression on me.

I drove into the yard, parked in front of the office and went in. Bill Barron asked me about my trip, then told me Skinny wanted to talk to me. I said, "Great, I want to talk to him, too."

Bill said, "You may not like what he is going to tell you," and I answered, "Oh, that's okay. He probably isn't going to like what I'm going to tell him either." Bill looked a bit odd, then said, "Go on back. He is expecting you."

I walked back to Skinny's office. We greeted each other; he asked about my trip, and then said, "Mate, we had a meeting while you were gone, the other two partners and I. We decided that since work has gotten so spotty, that we won't have permanent tool pushers any more. Since you and Scotty are the oldest pushers and the only ones on the permanent payroll, it will just affect you two. When we have one rig running, Jack Haberlein will act as tool pusher, and you and Scott will have to drill, but when we have two rigs going, you two will push and Jack will revert to drilling superintendent."

I grinned at him and said, "Skinny, I have worked for this outfit for twenty years. It has been a good job, but it is over. I knew some time ago that this would happen, and by a very odd coincidence, I came out this morning to tell you that I am quitting. I see no future in the drilling business, so I believe it is time to change. Here are the keys to the Ford. I have taken all of my things out of it. If you or Jack Haberlein will take me home, we can wind this business up in a hurry."

He looked at me as though I had lost my mind, then said, "Quitting! What in the hell are you going to do? Right now, tool pushers are a dime a dozen. You will be back looking for your job in a month."

I laughed and said, "That's where you are wrong, Skinny. I don't want a tool pushing job. It's time to change. I don't know exactly what I am going to do, but be sure of one thing: I am not going to *ever* push tools again. I'm tired of the grind."

He called Jack Haberlein into his office and announced, "Gerald says that he is quitting," then got his second shock of the day when Jack said, "Yes, I heard you two talking, and I have something to tell you, too. I am also quitting. I have bought a lodge on the Conejos River in Colorado and am giving you two weeks' notice today."

Skinny looked dumbfounded. I don't know what he expected that day, but he surely did not expect two key men to go. He told Bill Barron later that he just couldn't think it was happening to him.

I thanked him and told him and Barron goodbye. Jack Haberlein took me home. He told Amy that he, too, was quitting, and that I had made a good decision. So, on the 11th day of February, 1958, I got out of drilling forever. I supervised many wells later as a consultant, but that was from the "outside." My days "inside" were ended.

Epilogue

After I quit Schoenfeld-Hunter-Kitch, I took a job as manager of a service tool company. The company was MWL Tool and Supply Company, and I had to move to Hobbs, New Mexico. MWL was a subsurface tool company, dealing in down-hole liners, packers, multiple completion tools, and some specialty rental tools.

It was a new world to me, and I had to learn the hard way, by doing the jobs. But I did learn, was successful, and the Hobbs branch grew quite a lot. We became well known in Southeastern New Mexico as a "can-do" outfit.

I ran that branch store six and one-half years, then quit to exploit a tool that I invented and patented. It was a de-gasser for drilling mud and was a good, successful tool. But I was underfinanced and finally had to liquidate my little company. The big outfits cut prices and put me out of business. It was a hard blow to absorb. In fact, it still hurts.

I became a free lance drilling and completion consultant in 1969, working through established companies. One of them, W & H Company in Midland, was doing well blowout control in the Gomez field near Fort Stockton. I worked with and under Mr. Chester Harden and learned much about down-hole abnormal pressures and how to handle them. I was also fortunate to be on jobs with Drilling Well Control, who were compiling data on the subject and were quite successful in controlling wild wells.

I had moved back to Odessa in 1965 when I left MWL. Amy did not like Hobbs, and her health had gone downhill. She had been treated for allergies for years. She smoked heavily and began to have breathing problems. But she refused to see a doctor, so we really didn't know how serious her problems were; we just drifted.

I had built a small reputation as a blowout specialist and in 1972 was called on a job for the Black River Corporation, on a lease 10 miles south of Carlsbad Caverns. I handled the job and set casing on the well, then was asked to take over their drilling campaign. I took the job; it was the beginning of a long, happy association. The work was easy, and Mr. Tom Phipps and Mr. Forrest Miller were easy to work with.

I stayed at the Stevens Motel in Carlsbad while I worked for Black River. I was gone from home most of the time, separated from Amy, who had a big anxiety complex and was afraid I'd run out of work. I called Amy every night to be sure she was OK. This was the late summer of 1974. I called one night, and when Amy answered she said that she was dreadfully ill. I drove 140 miles in one hour forty-five minutes, ran in the house, called an ambulance, and got Amy to the hospital. She was having a massive heart attack. The doctors saved her and kept her in intensive care six days; then ten more days in the hospital. Needless to say, I stayed home when she came home for forty-five days. I took care of Amy, and she seemed to be much better. Then she began to tell me I could go back to work. I finally took a few three- and four-day jobs. Amy's doctor told her she could begin to drive again, and I began to relax.

It was not to be; Amy died in her sleep, and I was badly torn up. The only thing that saved me was my work; I really tore into that, since my house in Odessa was so empty.

Of course I was in Carlsbad, staying as usual in the Stevens Motel.

June Cozby was the dining room hostess at the Stevens. I had known her several years. We were good friends, and after Amy's death became more than friends. We were married in July of 1976. She was a wonderful wife. She went everywhere with me when I was on jobs. And since I was making lots of money, we traveled for pleasure quite a lot—to Tahiti, New Orleans, up the Mississippi on the *Delta Queen,* and certainly did have a delightful ten years together.

I caught pneumonia on a job when I was seventy-five years old, and when I got out of the hospital I retired—I had emphysema and asthma and could no longer stand the rigors of my work.

It took some getting used to, but June, Tom Phipps, and John Berry got me started on this book. I finally finished it, and June contacted the University of Texas Press. They were interested. Hence this epilogue.

I lost June last summer to acute liver failure. So I'm alone again, and miss her sorely. I have dedicated the book to June, because without her pushing and encouragement it would not have happened.

Gerald Lynch
February 1987

Glossary

boll weevil   A new hand in the oil field. The name reportedly derives from the farming background of most of the new workers.

BOP   Blowout preventer.

bumper sub   A sub with a movable break set in a drill string. You can strike either up or down with it.

catline   A heavy manila line used for general hoisting.

Christmas tree   Made up of several valves and chokes placed on the well head of a gas well so that the gas pressure of the well can be reduced enough to put the gas in a pipeline for transport. The term results from the appearance of all the valves and short pieces of pipe connected to them that resemble a bare tree standing several feet high with limbs projecting outward.

circulating sub   A sub run with a drill-stem test tool, usually placed just above the test tool. A dropped crowbar opens two ports and enables you to pump out through them.

collar   Coupling device.

crown block   Timber or steel pulley support connecting the derrick posts at the top.

crown sheet   The plate that forms the top of the firebox of the boiler.

day work   The practice of paying a drilling contractor a set amount per day for his rig.

dog house   A small shed where tools are kept and the men change from street clothes to work clothes at the drill site.

draw works   The big cable reel and associated clutch and brake mechanisms that provide the hoisting and drilling capabilities on a rotary rig.

drill-stem test (DST)   A test for determining the productivity of an oil or gas well by sampling the flow; explained in Chapter 11.

drill string   All the pipe used at one time in drilling.

elevator   Device used to lift and lower drill pipe; described in Chapter 1.

fish   Something that has been lost in the well and must be fished out.

float collar   A short collar usually positioned on top of the casing shoe. The float keeps cement from coming back into the casing but allows you to pump down through it.

footage contract   An agreement with a drilling contractor to drill a well for a set amount per foot drilled.

fourble   A stand of four joints of pipe, about 80 feet altogether, in the old days. (Drill pipe is now 30 feet long.)

fourble derrick   An old-style 108-foot derrick, tall enough to accommodate pipe in fourbles, with about 28 feet of head room.

grass, on the   Out of work.

Greyhound joint   A joint of pipe with a tooled joint box on one end and a tooled joint pin on the other, or a double joint with a box on one end, a pin on the other, and a collar in the middle. They were known as "Greyhound" joints because they were supposed to speed up connections.

grief joint   The technical name for the "kelly joint."

grip ring   A device no longer in use. It was used to grip and turn round pipe before the kelly was invented.

guide shoe   A shoe made of casing with a rounded bottom. It is run on the bottom of casing string to facilitate going in the hole with casing.

"hot box"   An overheated journal box.

jack posts   Wooden posts, usually oak and bound with iron, on old-time drilling rigs. They held the line and drum shafts. No longer in use.

jars   Specialty tools used to fish. They are preset and strike a heavy blow upward when pulled upon.

journal box   Bearing box that the shafts turn in.

kelly hose A strong high-pressure hose, usually 3 inches inside diameter, connecting the swivel to the stand pipe. Today this is about 50 feet long to enable the kelly joint to move up and down.

kelly joint A very heavy octagon-shaped or square pipe, to fit into the rotary table to turn the drill string. See Chapter 3.

mouse hole A shallow rat hole beside the rotary table, with a joint of pipe standing up in it, for use in making up the kelly in tall derricks with substructures.

OD Outside diameter.

overshot A fishing tool.

P and A Plug and abandon.

production man One engaged in actually producing oil from a well, as opposed to one who drills a well.

production string The pipe put into an oil well through which the oil will be brought to the surface.

PSI Pounds per square inch.

pushing job The job of the tool pusher, who is in charge of a particular rig, whereas a driller is only in charge of one of the three crews operating the rig.

rat hole A hole in which to set the kelly joint when making connections. See Chapter 15.

skid To move a derrick on wooden rollers from one site to another, to avoid having to dismantle and rebuild it.

snowbank drilling Drilling in shale and shell formations.

spud in To start drilling.

sub A connection used as a changeover between two different-sized pipes.

swage nipple A short piece of pipe, big on one end and small on the other.

thribble A stand of three joints of pipe (60 feet long in the old days; 90 feet long today).

thribble derrick A derrick tall enough to accommodate pipe in thribbles, with head room (90 feet old style; 120 feet new style).

tool(ed) joint A drill pipe coupler consisting of a pin and box.

tool pusher   *See* pushing job.

traveling block   The gigantic set of pulleys suspended in the derrick by several windings of a cable that goes around another set of pulleys at the top of the derrick. It is used to hoist the drill pipe and other materials needed in the drilling operation.

trip   Pulling pipe out of the hole or running it into the hole.

vee door   A 28-foot inverted-V opening in the side of the derrick, through which pipe is brought into the derrick.

Index